1998

Though theory has become a common language in the humanities in recent years, the relation between theoretical speculation and its practical application has yet to be fully addressed. In *The practice of theory*, Michael Bernard-Donals examines the connection between theory and pedagogy at the level of practice. He asks how such a practice works not only to change the way we read and speak with one another but also the conditions in which these activities become possible. Bernard-Donals argues that the most sophisticated practice linking pedagogy to theory is rhetoric, but the version of this tradition in such thinkers as Rorty and Fish is never broad enough. The conception of rhetoric he proposes instead is linked to other human and natural sciences. *The practice of theory* investigates the degree to which a materialist rhetoric can reinvigorate the link between theory, teaching and practice, and offers a sustained reflection on the production of knowledge across a broad range of contemporary disciplines.

The practice of theory

Literature, Culture, Theory

General editors
TONY CASCARDI, *University of California, Berkeley*
RICHARD MACKSEY, *The Johns Hopkins University*

The practice of theory

Rhetoric, knowledge, and pedagogy in the academy

❖❖❖

MICHAEL BERNARD-DONALS

University of Missouri-Columbia

CAMBRIDGE
UNIVERSITY PRESS

PUBLISHED BY THE PRESS SYNDICATE OF THE UNIVERSITY OF CAMBRIDGE
The Pitt Building, Trumpington Street, Cambridge CB2 1RP

CAMBRIDGE UNIVERSITY PRESS
The Edinburgh Building, Cambridge CB2 2RU, United Kingdom
40 West 20th Street, New York, NY10011-4211, USA
10 Stamford Road, Oakleigh, Melbourne 3166, Australia

First published 1998

Printed in the United Kingdom at the University Press, Cambridge

Typeset in 10/12.5 Palatino

A catalogue record for this book is available from the British Library

Library of Congress cataloguing in publication data

Bernard-Donals, Michael F.
The practice of theory: rhetoric, knowledge, and pedagogy in
the academy / Michael Bernard-Donals.
p. cm. – (Literature, culture, theory: 26)
Includes bibliographical references and index.
ISBN 0 521 59433 2 hardback – ISBN 0 521 59506 1 (paperback)
1. Rhetoric. 2. Knowledge, Theory of. 3. Language and education.
I. Title. II. Series.
P301.B48 1998
808–dc21 98–8796
CIP

ISBN 0 521 59433 2 hardback
ISBN 0 521 59506 1 paperback

Contents

Acknowledgments

This book is about the productive tension between theory and practice. What was remarkable about the process of writing it was that at every stage I became very much engaged in that tension. I think of myself as a teacher first and foremost, and as I struggled with the very theoretical material here, the question that kept running through my mind was, how can this material be shown to have consequences in the classrooms and in the academic (and non-academic) lives of the people I live and work with? In large measure, the extent to which this book succeeds in answering that question – in making clear the real consequences of the theoretical work involved in the rhetorical enterprise – is due to the colleagues and the students with whom I engaged in the difficult work of teaching theory.

The people who had perhaps the most significant impact on the material that initially formed the core of this project were the participants in a seminar I taught in the Winter term of 1994 at the University of Missouri, Columbia, on the connections between rhetoric, science, and historical materialism. Thanks are due to Victoria Salerno and Pennie Pflueger, and especially to Kevin Allton for his thoroughgoing and always well-targeted questions and his sometimes withering defense of the creative and the aesthetic. In many ways, Kevin is the absent interlocutor for much of what I say here.

I also had a great deal of support from students and colleagues as I rethought much of the material we covered in the seminar. I am especially indebted to Richard Glejzer – who saw this project through from its earliest stages, and whose criticism advanced the project during weekly racquetball games – for his intelligence, his moral support, and his marvellous friendship. Thanks are due also to Timothy Spence, who for the last couple of years has taught me the value of paying attention to what rhetoric cannot say but nevertheless effects. I am very grateful to Bryan Roesslet, who helped assemble and revise the first two chapters of the project, but whose effect was finally upon my way of understanding the connection between rhetoric, pedagogy, and theory as work in the classroom. I am also thankful for the support of many of my colleagues in the English Department at the University of Missouri, and to the Office of Research at the University of Missouri for supporting me financially during the summer of 1994.

Throughout the time I was working on the project and teaching portions of it, I was also afforded the opportunity to present a number of the ideas central to it at conferences and in journals. Parts of chapters 4 and 7 were presented at the Conference on College Composition and Communication in the Spring of 1994, and at a colloquium of the English Department in early 1993. A version of chapter 7 appears under the title, "The Rodney King Verdict, the New York *Times*, and the 'Normalization' of the Los Angeles Riots; or, What Anti-Foundationalism Cannot Do," in *Cultural Critique*. I presented a portion of chapter 6 at the University of California at Irvine; other parts of that chapter appear in the journal *Symploke*. I am grateful to anonymous readers at *Rhetoric Society Quarterly* and *Rhetorica* for their useful comments on early drafts of chapters 1 and 2.

I am especially grateful to the people at Cambridge University Press. Ray Ryan's diligence and support of this project and his enthusiasm for bringing the book to print were especially heartening. Con Coroneos's patience and good humour with the copy editing of the manuscript have made enjoyable what could have been a grind; he has made this a much clearer and more readable book. I owe Michael Sprinker a very large debt. He has provided me with a great deal of support and a shining example, both as a scholar and as a teacher, but most especially as a mentor who someday I hope very much to repay. I strive to provide the rigorous criticism and generous advice to my students and colleagues that he has provided to his own.

Finally, I must thank my family. Over the last few years I have never been more aware of just how impossible it is to divide time intelligently or effectively between family and work. One of the valuable lessons I have learned – in part through writing this book but much more so in trying to understand the relation between what we say and what we do, between our sense of ethics and our knowledge of others and ourselves – is that every aspect of what one does bears upon all other aspects of one's endeavors. I have been fortunate to be a part of a loving and supportive family, and express to Hannah, my wife, and to Shoshana, Miryam and Avi, our children, the gratitude I feel. Thank you for continuing to keep things in proper perspective.

Introduction

In the face of the multifaceted critiques of modernity, no one needs to be reminded of how fragile [local forms of civil community] are, how easily they are coopted and perverted. But at a time when the threat of total annihilation no longer seems to be an abstract possibility but the most imminent and real potentiality, it becomes all the more imperative to try again and again to foster and nurture those forms of communal life in which dialogue, conversation, phronesis, practical discourse, and judgment are concretely embodied in our daily life.

(Richard Bernstein, *Beyond Objectivity and Relativism*, 229)

The 1980s and 1990s have been good decades for rhetoric. Stanley Fish, using Richard Lanham's terms, noted the rise of *homo rhetoricus*, suggesting that it was just such a "species" of intellectual that would point us to the future not just of academic inquiry but of human inquiry as well. Such an intellectual would investigate not the world as it is reflected in our scientific practice, but how those reflections themselves are constructed. "[T]he givens of any field of activity – including the facts it commands, the procedures it trusts in, and the values it expresses and extends – are socially and politically constructed, are fashioned by man rather than delivered by God or Nature" (Fish, *Doing* 485), and two of the fields most directly affected by the upswing in the fortunes of "rhetorical man" are economics and science. Much of Fish's work in the 1980s questioned the wisdom of trying to establish foundations – in science, philosophy or any other macro-field – upon which perspective could be built. Fish put forward the competing claim that it is only by examining the contexts of those founda-

1

tions and the ways in which those contexts called for certain responses that were themselves products of other contexts (and so on), that the human sciences could proceed, and that the best way to proceed – though certainly not to solve the antifoundational "problem" – was to undertake a rhetorical project that provided the tools with which to do that work. Fish's book was published in 1989. Other essays and books that made much the same argument were published earlier in the 1980s. Jane Tompkins's anthology, *Reader-Response Criticism*, published at the beginning of the decade, concluded with a call for a revival of the original "reader response theory," rhetoric, suggesting that if what we were after was a rigorous understanding of how language shaped the cultural paradigms within which all a culture's work is done, then we can look back to Aristotle for the original cultural criticism. Never mind that Aristotle's system-building was used in part as a justification for a rigidly hierarchized society that saw a limited role for women and that reserved power for an all-Athenian, slave-holding elite. Terry Eagleton, in two books (*Walter Benjamin* and *Literary Theory: An Introduction*) that were widely read by a generation of graduate students, made a similar case for the study of rhetoric, though he was perhaps less sanguine about rhetoric's institutional use if it came along with its original trappings of a stratified class society. His theory book ends with a chapter on political criticism, and sees rhetoric as an "*activity* inseparable from the wider social relations between writers and readers . . ." and since "all theory and knowledge . . . is 'interested,' in the sense that you can always ask why one should bother to develop it in the first place," rhetoric could be seen as that field that served to inquire into the situations out of which epistemic claims could be made. What is perhaps most interesting in all of these calls for a revival of rhetoric as a form of knowledge that provides a key to the importance of all other ways of knowing is that nearly all of them made some reference to Plato or Aristotle as the individual theorists who began the whole business.

The last two decades have seen not only the resurgence of rhetoric in literary critical fields and, beyond them, in philosophy; they have also witnessed the most profound growth in a field that, in the United States, has come to be called *rhetoric and composition studies*. During these decades, countless rhetoric or composition programs were founded, others were reinvigorated, thousands of graduate students have found positions in English departments specifically to teach writing. These programs and positions are founded on the idea that the teaching of writing has a lineage that stretches back to Plato's argument with the sophists and Aristotle's attempt to codify the middle ground between them. This is a lineage which has in common the idea that the most useful forms of knowledge for a *polis* will be forms of *rhetorical knowledge*. Different versions of composition studies have different perspectives on the value of rhetoric's epistemological foundations – that it is an art, that it produces knowledge, that it is inevitably bound up with the subject of utterance or writing – but all of them see a critical link between theory and practice: the teacher's work in the classroom and the practitioner's research both require that rhetoric be seen as Aristotle had envisioned it, as an *art* that in part involved the production of discourse and in part involved the analysis required in order to produce it. Much of the work in the 1980s was a carry-over from work done a decade earlier. This work had little if anything to do with the rhetorical foundations of the study of reading and writing – I am thinking in particular of the expressivist pedagogies of Peter Elbow, Donald Murray, and James Bruffee from the 1970s according to which the first aim of composition was to allow students to write from their own experience. On the other hand, many theorists of rhetoric and composition took their cue from Ed Corbett and Andrea Lunsford, who saw links between the epistemological assumptions of the Aristotelian rhetorical tradition and the contemporary "crisis of representation" – a crisis which so many in the field held (erroneously) to be the fault of poststructuralism. This development – marked by books with titles such as *Classical Rhetoric for the Modern Student* and *Essays in Classical Rhetoric and Modern Discourse* – presented the rhetorical turn in composition studies as the pedagogical culmination of a theoretical turn that elevated rhetoric's status to a way of producing knowledge. Rhetoric now bore upon all fields of intellectual inquiry, and took as its "objects of knowledge" not just academic or institutional subjects but those outside the institutional context as well. What we wrote and how we wrote it were indicators of our ideological situatedness in a world of constraints both social and material.

On both fronts – the theoretical and the pedagogical – the rhetorical turn has been marked, to my mind, by some serious philosophical problems. The first significant problem could be called something like a confusion between ontological claims and epistemological claims. One of the classical tradition's greatest strengths was that it situated rhetoric among various different ways of knowing that had fairly clearly demarcated "disciplinary" boundaries. Aristotle, for example, unambiguously divided philosophical and metaphysical problems from rhetorical and political ones, and even in *Rhetoric* (a treatise not marked by ambitious cross-disciplinary theoretical forays) suggested that if an orator proves something so clearly that the principle on which its proof rests becomes evident to the audience and as a result the point becomes proven beyond doubt, then the orator has strayed from the ground of rhetoric. When one does science one does science, and when one does rhetoric one does rhetoric. There are, of course, some problems specific to what science could actually prove by means of demonstration and how those scientific demonstrations therefore differed from rhetorical or dialectical proofs by means of enthymeme or syllogism – problems that have been explored by G. E. R. Lloyd, among others, in masterful ways, and which I explore in a limited way in this book. Nevertheless, the point itself is clear: questions about the nature of being and questions about the nature of knowledge each have a distinct method of inquiry because each has a distinct object of knowledge. Science examines questions about the world in which we live and the nature of its properties, while the practical arts examine the human use of objects in the natural world and the dynamics of that use. Of course, the rub is that in the Aristotelian paradigm – as well as in the Platonic one, though by no means to the same degree – the job of rhetoric is to provide proofs to an audience that is unable to understand the demonstrations or proofs provided by other disciplines, in order to move the audience to action (either political or intellectual) in the *polis*. Rhetoric, in other words, could easily be seen as the point of convergence of the more "objective" ways of knowing – science, metaphysics – and their practical deployment in the drear world. Rhetoric's job is not to move back to the principles of philosophy or the sciences in order to examine the ways in which those principles determine what and how the audience can be moved. However, rhetoric is the only means by which many members of the *polis* would be able to understand and be moved at all, and so rhetoric rests upon the work done by the sciences and philosophy, making the job of the orator – to paraphrase Cicero – the toughest and most honorable job in a culture. It is perhaps no surprise, then, that the rediscovery of rhetoric in the 1980s took very seriously the classical injunction to have as wide a knowledge as possible of all the fields upon which rhetorical skill rests. This injunction led Louise Phelps and others to conclude that rhetoric – or, to Phelps's way of thinking, *composition* – should be seen as a practical art. Composition, then, examines the very assumptions on which rest not just the human sciences but also the natural sciences, whose objects of knowledge are not activity in specific situations but phenomena which do not vary from situation to situation but whose properties remain the same outside of our ability to understand them or give them meaning.

Rhetoric, in short, has – to my mind, erroneously – become a way to "reunite" two intellectual forces (or impulses) that have for a long time been working at odds with one another. In Richard Bernstein's words, it might be seen as a way to negotiate the terrain between objectivism and relativism. It is not so much that human understanding is split between ontology and epistemology. Rather, ontology and epistemology are both thrown over in favor of a practical wisdom (*praxis, phronesis*) that examines the ground on which we live our lives. In recent philosophical debates – debates which have more and more included those working both in literary-critical theory and in rhetoric – Bernstein's search for a way to negotiate between the threat of foundational appeals to an immutable, objective capital-T truth and the equally ugly threat of an antifoundational lawlessness of interpretation (or worse, of human action) has been joined by a pragmatism that sees itself as fulfilling rhetoric's "original" epistemic function by engaging philosophical questions without necessarily tying them to the dead dog of "truth." Pragmatism's most forceful proponent over the last fifteen or twenty years of rhetoric's ascendancy has been Richard Rorty, who claims – in his groundbreaking book, *Philosophy and the Mirror of Nature* as well as in subsequent books, including most recently a two-volume collection entitled *Philosophical Investigations* – that epistemology is a more difficult philosophical project if we understand that any model within which we proceed operates by rules that lead us to believe that we have got any control over the game. When we get to the point in an investigation where the inadequacy of those rules becomes self-evident, we should stop doing epistemology and engage in a different sort of inquiry – in *Philosophy and the Mirror of Nature* Rorty calls it "hermeneutics" – that allows us to see that inadequacy as a fortunate one, since the capacity we have to see it in the first place is the one that also allows us to change the rules of the game so that those who have not been allowed to play are then included. Philosophy's project – together with the analyses of language, rhetoric included, that have tied themselves to it – has for too long been that of trying to find a meta-philosophical system that unites the various languages with which we play ontological and epistemological games. This project has kept us from understanding the human suffering that goes on all the while the game proceeds. Having thrown our game of the meta, the liberal ironist is in a position to alleviate human suffering. Instead of following the rules of a game from which some are excluded and that change depending upon who is in a position to change them, she interviews in local situations and manipulates the discursive or ideological situation in which suffering occurs. The liberal ironist, in other words, is the rhetor *par excellence*: she is not interested in understanding the relation between the knowledges of science and philosophy and their deployment on the ground; she is interested instead in finding ways, in specific situations, to alleviate the suffering of groups of individuals by moving them to change their understanding of that situation. In rhetoric and composition studies, this sort of pragmatic practice has been incarnated by a social constructivism that understands pedagogy as enabling members of various ideological or discursive communities to describe their surroundings and in so doing to see how they are circumscribed by utterances – and the practical results of such utterances – that are not of their own choosing. The agency that allows subjects to redescribe their discursive situations is also able to transform their own positions relative to those situations, in effect "changing their lives."

This is an extremely attractive project for rhetoric: it avoids the epistemological and ontological impasses that have confronted language philosophy for millennia, and it finds a way to alleviate human suffering that reclaims rhetoric's role in an ethical project linking human understanding to human goodness. Moreover, it enlarges the human community by providing its various components – micro-communities – a means to communicate its analyses of injustice for use in other smaller communities. But this is the second significant philosophical problem for the return of rhetoric, as I will argue in the chapters that follow: this solution raises many questions of a practical and political nature. One of them is a question of just how plausible the redescriptive project of pragmatic rhetoric actually is if it glosses over the distinctions between what we might call "language" and what we might call language's "exigence." I am not interested in what a rhetor's intent is, what motivates certain people to say the things they say. But part of the problem with pragmatism is that while its intentions are good, it ignores some very difficult issues of power and the ways power can be used to get around intelligent, even hermeneutic, negotiation of a community's orientation and the relations among its members. A pragmatic rhetoric may very well allow us to investigate how the cobbling together of conservative platitudes about family, obligation, and free enterprise into something called the "Contract with America" appeals to the fears of many white Americans who are not happy with their lack of job security, and it may allow us to see how the language of the "Contract" is founded on assumptions about class, about race, and about gender that bear very little resemblance to the social reality of United States culture in the years before the turn of the twenty-first century. But it is hard to see how such a rhetoric allows us to do anything more than construct an alternative rhetoric – a rhetoric of inclusion, one that takes account of the complexities of a society that does not look like Newt Gingrich thinks it does – that may let us argue with the "Contract's" agenda but does not necessarily provide us with an analysis of the social, economic, or other material forces that may in fact *prevent* a discursive analysis from having much effect upon the "Contract's" ultimate effects. Pragmatism tends to ignore the point that discursive analysis – rhetoric – rests upon the investigative work of the sciences (and here I include not just the social sciences but also the natural sciences, which have something to tell us about the limitations of natural resources and the spread of disease under certain conditions). Moreover, it glosses over the methodological connections between rhetorical demonstration of contingent truths and scientific demonstration of the properties of natural and social phenomena. Because of these two factors, it will not be able to do much more than "nurture those forms of communal life in which dialogue, conversation, *phronesis*, practical discourse, and judgment are concretely embodied in our everyday practices," when all the while the practices of domination and the squashing of communal life by means of hunger – to adapt a telling phrase from Rorty – and the secret police continue apace.

This book is an attempt to assess the contemporary rhetorical turn – called for by such people as Tompkins and Eagleton in critical theory, by Rorty and Bernstein in philosophy, and by Phelps and Corbett in rhetoric and composition studies over the last twenty years – in view of these problems. What happens when ontological and epistemological questions about the nature of rhetoric and its seminal texts – such as *Rhetoric, Gorgias* and *Phaedrus* – are not distinguished in the recent call for a "return to rhetoric"? What are the pedagogical implications (in the last four chapters of the book) of this failure? The book begins with an investigation of just such epistemological/ontological questions as they are addressed by these three seminal texts. It concludes with the pedagogical and practical results for critical, materialist rhetorical projects that have been introduced as ways to proceed given the contemporary critical juncture. My aim is to look closely at some of the contemporary assumptions about the overarching epistemological "uses" for rhetoric (as a "way in" to social and natural scientific investigations) at three important points in the contemporary discussions about the field: discussions of rhetoric's classical "roots," discussions of rhetoric's role in the human and natural sciences, and discussions of rhetoric's connection to pedagogy.

First, it is by means of recuperating Platonic and Aristotelian texts on rhetoric that much of both critical theory and rhetoric/composition studies have been able to pose some of the questions they have been asking, questions about the intimacy of the relation between knowledge, truth, and the means of achieving them; questions about the relation between the human and the natural sciences; questions about the possibilty of formulating a systematic pedagogical theory that accounts for the practical and the transcendent. Both Plato and Aristotle had answers of their own for these broad questions, but my contention is that we have rushed so enthusiasticaly into the rhetorical fray that we have not taken the time to look closely at just what these texts have to tell

8

us. Can rhetorical investigations of the practical world serve as a model for other kinds of inquiries? Can science proceed only after we have understood how the paradigmatic ground upon which the sciences rest is thoroughly rhetorical and discursive? These hypotheses have been put forward on the authority of Platonic and Aristotelian rhetoric. To consider these hypotheses, I wanted to go back to those texts and see just what they could offer the contemporary debate. The distinctions between Plato and Aristotle on rhetoric have become almost too commonplace to dispute. Plato insisted that we proceed by means of dialectic rather than rhetoric, implying that rhetoric is an inferior "art" if it is really anything more than mere knack. Aristotle, by contrast, saw a role for rhetoric in conducting an ethical life. Plato found a need to "resort to" rhetoric though he railed violently against its appeals to base emotion, whereas Aristotle embraced the logical components of rhetoric even while he spent a great deal of time justifying its emotional component. While Plato saw rhetoric's failure as a failure to disentangle the natural law and the law of convention, Aristotle saw such distinctions as preceding rhetoric. Yet these distinctions mask some very interesting complexities in the works themselves. The "inconsistency" between the earlier *Gorgias* and the later *Phaedrus*, marked by the former's violent dismissal of rhetoric and by Socrates' almost bitter denunciation of the equation between "might" and "right" and the latter's grudging embrace of rhetoric's figural dimension is not, I would argue, an inconsistency but rather a sign that rhetoric itself is a much more complicated art that it appears. At one point in *Gorgias*, Socrates reaches the stunning conclusion that the four foremost leaders of Athens should be seen as failures because they led the *polis* by appealing to its members' baser concern (such as security from imminent danger and a desire for prosperity) rather than by appealing to an understanding of the general good, no matter that the two appeals could only have been seen as commensurate by any reckoning, philosophical or practical. Socrates, however, sees that there are often only two choices one can make when deciding what action to take in the polis, either to do or to suffer harm, and that neither of these choices may be palatable. Socrates' petulant analysis of Athenian leadership on the one hand and his timid acceptance of the fact that any expression of choice may lead to an unacceptable outcome, on the other, suggest the limitations of rhetoric's ability to proceed logically in a world that often does not operate according to logical principles. The embrace of figure in *Phaedrus*, a means of persuading that operates precisely by means of extra-logical associations, can be seen as an acceptance of the irony that insisting on rhetoric's appeal to logic does not necessarily mean that rhetoric's most successful appeal will be the logical one.

There is an equally interesting methodological question in Aristotle's *Rhetoric*. Plato tries to distinguish between dialectic and rhetoric by clearly articulating their domains but ultimately blurs the line between them. Aristotle, however, tries to distinguish between the principles of science and the contingent proofs of rhetoric. The foundations for such a distinction lie in *Nichomachean Ethics* as well as in the first section of book 1 of *Rhetoric* (1358a3–30). But these lines of demarcation become fuzzy when one puts some critical pressure on them. Consider the language Aristotle uses in *Rhetoric* and *Politics* especially in the light of his injunctions that the rhetor must understand how to instruct the audience even if it is not capable of being instructed. There is evidence to suggest that though the rhetor is not required to be a scientist, he should nevertheless be prepared to understand where rhetoric and science intersect. What I want to suggest is that reading Aristotle's texts on rhetoric does not – as Grimaldi and others have suggested and as a majority in the field of rhetoric / composition has understood – provide the key to understanding the human and the natural sciences. What it does suggest is that in order to understand rhetoric, one must also understand how rhetoric rests upon the sciences, and not the other way around. These two chapters separate what is living and dead in Plato and Aristotle – I am not trying to resurrect an Aristotelian or Platonic epistemology but suggesting what we can learn from what is still relevant in it – and in so doing indicate that the advocates of the present rhetorical turn may have overestimated just what rhetoric can do. If, as Aristotle suggests, rhetoric does in fact rest upon other ways of producing knowledge; if the demonstrative proof in rhetoric is based upon the demonstrative proof employed by philosophy and the natural and exact sciences; and if the upshot of Plato's "inconsistencies" is that rhetoric's use of figure marks its limit; then contemporary rhetoric needs to reexamine the claims it has recently made for *rhetoric*'s ability to supplement *science's* limitations.

This is especially true if we are serious about understanding the human (or social) sciences as more than just a means by which to comprehend the way an individual's world is encumbered by discursive material. The question is not how my desire *to neither do harm nor to suffer harm* is encumbered by the impossibility of making that choice, an encumbrance that may have less to do with the choices available for redescribing the world and more to do with whether my material circumstances even put me in a position to understand that I *have* a choice. Rather, it is a question of how the sciences might be seen as a way to change those circumstances. The popularity of Rorty's pragmatic philosophy and the more general move to localize the possibility of social change by means of human scientific investigation rest in part on the call of the "new rhetoric" to communitarian values and communicative action, but they also rest partly on the beginning assumptions of the human sciences themselves. If the human sciences are distinguished from the natural sciences by the former's explicit attempt to render *self-understanding* rather than an objective knowledge about objects and phenomena outside of the self's capacity to understand them in the first place, it would seem to favor explanations of the social world that do not resort to the cold distance of overarching models or to the teleology of essentialism, both of which assume that completedness is the goal of any explanatory theory. Because completedness is such a problematic term and because it is such a difficult (or impossible) object to achieve, the human sciences' focus on self-understanding and the primacy of reflection would seem to give the lie to grand systems and bold-faced agendas. My inclination, however, as I began this project was seriously to doubt whether the distinctions between the human sciences and the objective sciences could be maintained in such a way as to justify pragmatism's suspicion of a telos, because it seemed to me that such justifications got things the wrong way round in the same way that contemporary readings of Aristotle and Plato have done. That is, it is not so much that scientific or objective ways of knowing (and their attendant methodologies) needed to be recast because of the human sciences' insistence upon the complexities of human cognition and understanding. Rather, the human sciences are to some extent modeled upon the natural sciences, in that they *both* take the object of knowledge to be the regularities of objects and phenomena, the behavior of which under certain circumstances is a reflection of *either* the "laws of nature" or the tendencies of reason and desire. The upshot of a reexamination of the human sciences in relation to the natural sciences that does *not* yield the priority of the first to the second is a significant blow to those who read Kuhn, Rorty and others as advocating a blurring of the line between the objective and the human sciences and a pursuit of that "blur" as a middle way between them. I say this because I think we need to do more than simply argue for our positions in a way that is both rational and forceful: the natural sciences do not give us access to the laws of nature, but they do give us good reason to believe that the natural world behaves in certain regular ways that both affect human participation in the natural world and can be affected by human participation. Whether we explain such behavior in paradigm *a* or paradigm *b* does not change that behavior, and it does not change the fact that it affects, and is affected by, human interaction. Human behavior works in the same way: self-understanding's insistence on incompleteness does not render insignificant the regularities by which human societies operate; it only suggests the difficulty of systematizing that knowledge across broad areas of human behavior. But self-understanding's complexities do *not* translate into its ability to do without trajectories; in fact, self-understanding's emphasis on incompleteness could be read as just such a trajectory, an insistence that human capacity for understanding and discovery is limitless. But the irony is that, if we look closely at what regularities the human sciences do provide for us, human social relations seem to be marked less by communion and communication than they are by coercion, violence and fear. Far from rendering the human sciences superior to the natural sciences insofar as they can provide knowledge for the *polis*, a closer analysis of the human sciences themselves suggests that, like the relation between rhetoric and other more objective or philosophical ways of knowing, the human sciences can work to provide humans a view toward *progress and freedom* if they are brought into a relation with the natural sciences that is not *weakened* by the human sciences's skepticism. To reiterate, the attractiveness of Rorty and Fish (among others) is that their pragmatic approach is skeptical of "agendas" altogether. The ethical dimension of this project becomes clear toward the latter half of the book, but as the book

proceeds from the seminal texts on rhetoric through the human/
natural science split it takes on just this notion of skepticism and
suggests that pragmatism overlooks the possibility that though
the languages with which we describe portions of our worlds
may be incommensurable, they well may be describing the same,
not necessarily different, portions of it, and that an investigation
of just these incommensurabilities may yield further knowledge.
The book's first half concludes with an analysis of Rorty and Fish
that inquires into just this skepticism and how it derives from an
overreading of rhetoric (or, perhaps more precisely, from a reading of rhetoric that does not understand its potential relation with
other ways of knowing).

Where the first half of the book is devoted to epistemological
and ontological questions about the relationship between rhetoric
and other forms of knowledge, the second half is devoted to
pedagogical questions: what are the political and ethical implications of the rhetorical (or anti-foundational) turn that sees *redis-
cription* as the primary goal for the intellectual laborer? Here I
focus, in the fifth and sixth chapters, on two theoretical perspectives that are both thoroughly rhetorical and thoroughly transformative. The first is the work of Louise Phelps, whose book
Composition as a Human Science is more discussed than read as a
way to negotiate a "third way" between the objectivity of theory
and the relativism of practice. It is Phelps's understanding of
composition as a practical means of investigating one's place in
the world that interests me, because while she insists that the
practice of composition must be disciplined by theory, and that
the abstractions of theory are always grounded in practice, it is
never quite clear whether the negotiated undertanding of the
life-world that she has as her goal is ever truly achieved. Moreover, it is also unclear that, given her beginnings with Gadamer,
Dewey and Freire among others, it ever *could* be achieved: all
three of those named are skeptical of the claims of science and its
demands for objectivity, and yet all three also succumb to the
shortcoming to which Rorty also succumbs: the skepticism of
agendas or objectivity leads Phelps (by way of Freire, Dewey and
Gadamer) away from acknowledging that there are dynamics that
the "objective" sciences can in fact explain, dynamics that wreak
havoc with the rational deliberation that is assumed by a certain
view of rhetoric. Gadamer's insistence on an intersubjectivity that

proceeds out of view of political turmoil, Dewey's turning away from the entrenched institutional realities of the scientific and philosophical community, and Freire's apparent idealism: all those ignore the political / material reality that knowledge-making can be coopted by forces that rhetorical investigation sometimes overlooks but that scientific methodology can provide us access to but which, without rhetoric's intervention, it is also powerless to do anything about. While Phelps's pedagogical version of a practical rhetoric suffers from underestimating science, a certain emancipatory pedagogy – and, as its converse, a certain radical pedagogy – suffer by overemphasizing its capacity to regulate the social / material aspect of human life. What emancipatory pedagogue Mas'ud Zavarzadeh ignores in his reading of science's relation with ideology (in Althusser) is the degree to which student resistance does not necessarily accord with a scientific understanding of it *unless* it is reformulated with the help of a rhetorical analysis of how it is refracted by institutional assumptions. In *Philosophy and the Spontaneous Philosophy of the Scientist*, Althusser recognizes that scientific "objectivity" is always compromised by the institutional assumptions within which scientists necessarily work. But Althusser also recognizes that while such assmptions are inevitable (scientific work must always be articulated in terms of the prevailing ideological-material milieu), they need to be assessed *scientifically* inasmuch as the results of scientific work must be assessed *rhetorically/ideologically*. What emancipatory pedagogies of a certain sort ignore is that even the telos toward which scientific practice leads us must be reexamined constantly, and this is particularly true in the classroom. It may be that on examining the language of the "Contract with America," members of a writing class may well be able to understand how the assumptions evident in its rhetorical strategies may be contradicted by the social and political material out of which such strategies are produced. But these results may be mitigated: the students who read the "Contract" successfully may be doing so not because of any scientific or rhetorical analysis they may have learned but *in spite of* such analysis. That is, these students may be providing this "reading" as the successful understanding of the institutional constraints of the classroom or the post-secondary institution, *not* as the successful understanding of materialist analysis. Emancipatory pedagogy needs to recognize that though science is not rendered redundant by the human sciences, neither are the human sciences rendered redundant by the objective sciences; each requires the other.

The book concludes with a chapter that reads the reciprocal relation between rhetorical analysis and the objective sciences in conjunction with Roy Bhaskar's realist philosophy of science. While it may not be true that Bhaskar's transcendental realist project squares completely with the conclusion reached in the first six chapters here, it is true that Bhaskar is aware of two things that *do*. First, in order for the human sciences to be emancipatory, they must not be seen as dealing either with the merely empirical or with the purely contingent, but rather understood as having a place in a two-step method of investigation that first identifies social phenomena to be investigated and then builds a method by which to study them. That is, Bhaskar is aware that the human sciences – like rhetoric – are not simply a means by which we can investigate human inscriptions of their surroundings, but also a means by which we intervene in those surroundings themselves in order to do so. Secondly, Bhaskar requires us to pay attention to the points of convergence between the sciences – insofar as they are able to provide access to the regularities of natural phenomena and the ways these regularities affect human transactions – and interpretation – insofar as it is also based upon phenomena in the social, transitive dimension that are nevertheless regular and which are systematically investigable – so that freedom becomes more than simply being able to be on guard against the fragility of community. Rather, it is marked by our ability to transform our communities and their constraints so they are less susceptible to the "threat of total annihilation." The object of investigation in this concluding chapter is the press's coverage of the 1992 Los Angeles "riots" but also, by implcation, the way in which we can teach – anything – to those interested in the way language works to produce an effect upon a polis.

This project was originally envisioned to address a number of different points in the larger debate over whether rhetoric can be seen as a valuable investigative tool for the human (and perhaps even the natural) sciences. The important locations for the debate are the value of Plato's and Aristotle's rhetorical texts for a critical rhetorical project; the place of rhetoric in the human sciences as distinguished from the exact or natural sciences; and the understanding of rhetoric in the ongoing conversation about anti-foundational philosophy. It is perhaps because the project addresses these points directly that the project might be seen as taking giant leaps between these locations. Given the recent interest in pragmatism and its uses in a more or less broadly conceived rhetorical project, and given the explosion in the fields of both rhetoric / composition and rhetorical theory, I thought it wise to confront these questions as seen by those fields in order to move those fields more closely together and also closer to the ongoing debates in critical theory. Bhaskar's value for such a project seems clear: his work understands the value of science and hermeneutics in the context of a critical project that tries to explain the relation between social forces that are explainable *sui generis* and those that are not, and – *à propos* the latter – it understands the limits and promise of science to "underlabor" for the very practical subsequent work of emancipation. It is my hope that this book can be seen in the spirit of Bhaskar's emancipatory project: as a preliminary investigation of the juncture of rhetoric and other ways of knowing, and as a strong suggestion to examine rhetoric, the human and the natural sciences and their interdependence before we insist upon abandoning any one of them for an emancipatory project.

1

Reconsidering *Gorgias*, *Phaedrus*, and Platonic rhetoric

The two Platonic dialogues that deal most exclusively with rhetoric – the *Gorgias*, written in about 387 BCE, and the *Phaedrus*, written about seventeen years later – are often taken as companion pieces. The more or less traditional reception has it that *Gorgias* is a scathing indictment not necessarily of rhetoric itself but of those who would use discourse to the end of the expedient rather than the good (see Vickers, "Defense"; Kennedy, *Persuasion*; Hunt, "Rhetoric"). *Phaedrus* is then seen as Plato's level-headed reassessment of rhetoric, and is taken by many to "explain" the vituperative tone of *Gorgias*. Whereas in the earlier discourse, Socrates takes his interlocutors to task for blurring the line between knowledge and belief, here Socrates admits that the line is truly hard to make out but that – all things being equal – one should favor knowledge. Whereas *Gorgias* insists upon a reconfiguration of the definitions of "nature" and "convention," *Phaedrus* seems much more willing to concede a role for rhetoric in a conventional world (see Barilli, *Rhetoric*; Cantor, "Rhetoric"; Gosling, *Plato*; Plochman, *Friendly Companion*; Leff, "Modern Sophistic" and "Habituation of Rhetoric"). In short, the two pieces are seen as two sides of the same coin: *Gorgias* condemns a simple (read sophistic) view of rhetoric and upholds a more rigorous, reasonable art, dialectic, as its alternative; and *Phaedrus* is dialectic's consummation, wherein Socrates shows Phaedrus, the lesser rhetorician, the proper use of figure to argue back as far as possible to first causes (see Black, "Plato's View").

This traditional view has given way to a more complicated view

17

of the relation between *Gorgias* and *Phaedrus*. Rather than the consummation of dialectic on the one hand and rhetoric on the other, the dialogues are seen to enact an aporia, the necessary failure of rhetoric that is placed in the service of philosophy. *Gorgias* fails because it begins (as Plato understands it) as a way to build knowledge and truth dialogically but ends with a Socratic monologue, and because it points to a role for rhetoric that is, ironically, necessarily extra-discursive; and *Phaedrus* fails because it upholds speech over writing while it exists only by virtue of writing (see Neel). Both *Gorgias* and *Phaedrus* begin as proofs to guard against the contingency of knowledge that results from a purely discursive world, but go on to fail to understand that because they are also discursive then they also will necessarily fail as philosophy.

Two fairly recent essays – Kasteley's "In Defense of Plato's *Gorgias*" and Vaida's "The Relevance of Plato's *Gorgias*" – suggest that these failures may in fact be purposive. Both Vaida and Kasteley suggest that rather than "say" one thing – that philosophy or dialectic should be seen as an alternative to rhetoric – and do another – call into question philosophy's ability to provide better or less culturally bound knowledge – they actually say and do the same thing. Socrates' failure to end either dialectical proof by way of dialogue is tacit acceptance of the failure of even dialectic to function alone as a way of knowing. It is my contention that Vaida and Kasteley have it right, and in this essay I want to extend their positions. The "performance" we see in *Phaedrus* – a desperate attempt by Socrates to show the proper role for rhetoric in reasoning the properties of the soul proper for love – points, albeit obliquely, to the reasons for *Gorgias'* theoretical impasse: rhetoric can work in the earlier dialogue only if it acknowledges the need for an attendant knowledge (Plato will call it philosophy, Aristotle will call it logic; I will suggest it is something altogether different, a form of objective description or scientific observation) which nevertheless functions highly imperfectly in a complex, political and social world; and *Phaedrus* is only able to consummate such a dialectical interaction between rhetoric and this other form of (extra-discursive) knowledge – ironically and, for my purposes, informatively – by use of figure.

More controversially, I will suggest that Plato's failure of rhetoric in fact opens up a space for a rhetorically derived knowledge that is paradoxically extra-rhetorical: *Gorgias'* problematization of conventional versus "natural" first principles and its acknowledgment of the material constraints that "deflect" rhetorical knowledge and *Phaedrus'* argument to axiomatic first causes by way of an explicitly conventional (and figural) explanation of the soul both call for a way of knowing that mediates the conventional and the "natural," the discursive and the "real." Plato's theory of figuration in *Phaedrus* works to inform the theoretical *Gorgias*: it becomes clear that both dialogues work on the principle that there is common knowledge deployed through human activity and accessible to all men, and that there are various means for deploying this knowledge. Whereas in *Gorgias* this knowledge is deployed through dialectic, in *Phaedrus* it is deployed through figuration. My point will be that, in these dialogues, rhetoric is shown to function alongside other (though unarticulated) ways of knowing – rhetoric being perhaps the practical manifestation of other (perhaps more theoretical or less contingent) forms of knowing – and that the rhetorical aim of both *Phaedrus* and *Gorgias* is to suggest the relation between language and human social activity and those other, less contingent, realms, both of which are accessible.

Gorgias: knowledge and belief

Part of Socrates' complaint against the rhetoric used by sophists such as Gorgias and Polus is that it fails to understand language as able to work toward broad political and moral principles in a polis because of an inadequate understanding of the object of knowledge. Though the "masses may be convinced" (452b), what they will be convinced *of* is unclear. Socrates, arguing with Gorgias near the beginning of the dialogue, suggests that it is not necessarily true that "oratory is productive of conviction, and that this is the be-all and end-all of the whole activity" (453a). As the conversation goes on, it becomes clear that what is at issue is a distinction between belief on the one hand – understanding brought about by the formation of consensus through oratorical skill, but without necessarily exploring the nature of the object or principle at hand – and knowledge on the other.

Polus is convinced that it is possible to adjudicate between right and wrong through the establishment of beliefs but Socrates is not so sure. The distinction Socrates makes between knowledge and belief rests upon the falsifiability of the latter. There can be true and false beliefs, but there cannot be true and false knowledge. The difference – and this follows closely Plato's understanding of mimesis from *Republic*, and contributes to Aristotle's later formulations of it in *Poetics* – is that in order to argue from a position of knowledge, the rhetor must be able to understand at least in part the object of the discussion (in this case not just the craft of building a ship, but also something about wood, about geometry, and about the characteristics and behavior of water). Argument from belief does not require that the rhetor know any such things. Though Gorgias begins his refutation of Socrates with the caveat that "there are of course limits to its proper use, as there are to the use of any other accomplishment," argument based on the establishment of belief through consensus works "on any subject against any opposition in such a way as to prevail on any topic [the speaker] chooses." Though it would be wrong, in this example, to suggest that the superior shipbuilder is in fact inferior by arguing from the belief that he was of bad reputation, or that one of his ships was responsible for the deaths of several people, it is permissible for an orator to do so, because rhetoric's "province" is not limited to the subject matter under investigation. In order to arrive at knowledge, one needs to inquire into the object under consideration by following a logical sequence of steps and to be as certain as possible about the answers to these logically established questions. In order to arrive at belief, it is not necessary to establish the nature of the object of knowledge when deciding in favor of one state of affairs or another. Belief instead works by convincing an audience that the state of affairs – whether or not to hire this shipbuilder – will have a positive or negative result based upon what one knows at a particular, historical time. If one can establish that some shipbuilder was careless during the building of a ship (at some time in the past), and that it is possible that such a thing could happen again, then the juxtaposition of these two historically contingent states of affairs is enough to suggest that the polis should not hire this particular shipbuilder, regardless of that person's expertise.

Now, it is possible to establish belief without knowledge of the object or state of affairs but it is not clear whether one can have knowledge without belief. What is at stake in this distinction, however, is not whether Socrates believes that rhetoric should establish knowledge pure and simple – no one who reads *Gorgias* as a rhetorical or philosophical text has suggested this to be the case – but whether rhetoric can work without an inquiry into what Aristotle calls in another context "first principles." The argument in 464–5 between Gorgias and Socrates about the superiority of the confectioner's understanding of food to the doctor's is essentially an argument about belief versus knowledge: the immediate sense-experience involved in eating sweet-tasting foods involves pleasure, and while it would perhaps be better for the rhetor to point to the knowledge we have of the effect of unwholesome foods on the body, it is not necessary for the establishment of belief. Moreover, it is difficult to argue from knowledge that unwholesome foods are superior to wholesome ones because the facts dictate otherwise. But facts are the province of knowledge, while pleasure is the province of belief. Plato's dialogue is beginning to establish not a definitive critique of rhetoric, as has been suggested by several traditional readers of *Gorgias*, but rather to establish rhetoric's limits, limits formed by the establishment of certain invariant, knowable characteristics of the object under discussion, characteristics that in some ways produce the effect of belief established rhetorically.

Gorgias, the social, and the material

After a preliminary investigation that establishes – somewhat tentatively – the different criteria with which belief and knowledge are established through discourse, *Gorgias* breaks down into roughly three parts. The first two – in which Socrates engages first Polus and then Callicles – involve a discussion, respectively, of the difference between suffering and doing wrong, and of political expediency and power. Both discussions involve the difference between knowledge and belief, in that (1) it is easy to believe that doing wrong is superior to suffering it, but that the criteria for establishing knowledge are so tortuous as to prevent such an argument from easily being made; and (2) that it is necessary – though extremely difficult – to argue from first causes and axiomatic facts to ascertain when power should be used. But more importantly, these discussions confront how rhetoric functions in (and shapes) the polis, and to what extent rhetoric is forced to deal not only with the moral and ethical circumstances of citizens but also their *material* circumstances.

To take up the question of power, Polus had suggested that the orator wields power because he has the capacity to induce others to pursue a course of action and because he can induce them according to what pleases him. For Polus, the orator holds supreme power because he has unlimited agency to act according to impulse, and can induce the polis to act according to these impulses as well. But Socrates makes the point that if it can be shown that to take an action – to advocate, for example, the consumption of unwholesome foods – will lead to an end (sickness or death) not in the best interests of those involved, then such an action is not ultimately pleasing at all. Further, if it can also be shown that the advocacy of such a move might also lead to the punishment and suffering of the person who advocated that course of action, then that action must be unpleasing to the advocate himself. Socrates asks whether it makes sense to suggest that, in believing such a course of action was pleasing, one would therefore *will* the ultimate end that such an action brought about (namely pain and possibly death), and Polus gives the only answer he can: no.

The point Plato is at pains to make here is about the difference between what is pleasing and what is "good," but also – for the study of rhetoric – the difference between a rhetoric that functions epistemically and one that does not. But both points ultimately rest on the same foundation. The difference between belief and knowledge is that belief can be established by the formation of a consensus of individuals in the polis without having to investigate systematically the complex nature of the object or state of affairs under discussion. The difference between doing what one pleases and doing what one wills is that pleasure does not take into account an investigation into the nature of the end that will come of a particular course of action. Agency, on the other hand, requires such an investigation. The difference, in other words, is that Socrates acknowledges a place for the construction of knowledge that does not depend exclusively upon the contingencies of history but nevertheless understands the need to account for the *welfare* of the polis, while Polus eschews the ultimate welfare of the polis in favor of its immediate circumstances. Plato is subtly shifting his discussion of will and the good to include a *social* dimension. Whereas in the argument with Gorgias Socrates criticized rhetoric for its inability to include a systematic investigation into the underlying material dimension of the consensus at which a polis might arrive, here Socrates suggests that such a systematic investigation must itself be guided by political and social concerns. To will the end to be pursued by a particular course of action, one has to understand not only the nature of that end, but also how that end may ultimately be *deferred* by the polis itself.

I use the term "defer" because of an odd passage in the Polus section. Polus asks Socrates, indignantly, if the upshot of his point is that he would rather suffer wrong than to do wrong, and Socrates answers, "I would rather avoid both" (469c). Regardless of whether this statement is Socrates' or Plato's it appears odd: it suggests that Plato's Socrates wants to have it both ways. In fact, this is the central passage of the dialogue, one that pinpoints precisely the aporia Plato, perhaps unconsciously, recognizes: you in fact *must* have it both ways, even if the ways of knowing the ambivalence implied in this position cannot articulate it. Kasteley ("Defense," 101) notes that Socrates is unsuccessful in convincing Polus that any right-thinking Athenian would prefer to suffer wrong than to do it, and adds that common sense would dictate that right-thinking readers would agree. But what we are presented with, says Kasteley, is a dichotomy: either do wrong or suffer wrong; which will it be? Socrates, by providing if only the shadow of a third way – doing neither – points up the human dilemma:

since some consequences of action always escape prediction or control, anyone who acts will occasionally cause suffering. Equally, since no one can create a totally secure environment in which all relevant aspects are under control, everyone is fated to suffer at some time.

(Kasteley, "Defense," 101)

It is possible, according to Plato's earlier discussion of pleasure and will, and necessary, according to the discussion of the object of knowledge for decent rhetoricians, to establish the nature of the object of knowledge, and to use the knowledge one produces in the oration designed to convince members of the polis to pursue a course of action. And it is also necessary to understand, as far as possible and based not upon surmise or the establishment of belief but on the nature of the object itself, the predicted outcomes in any given course of action or situation *beyond* those immediately related to the historical moment. But this passage recognizes the possibility – the inescapability – of a deferral of that prediction. We live in a world, Plato seems to suggest, in which we can try to minimize suffering by using the most reasonable means necessary for dictating policy, but someone, sometime, will inevitably suffer. The best we can do is understand as much as possible the connection between the *welfare* of the polis and its connection to the *nature* of the objects of knowledge under consideration. In effect, Plato's dialogue at this point breaks under the pressure of having to acknowledge the reasonable faculties of the orator and the unreasonable nature of suffering in a world of pain. One will always deflect the other. So, if we can never know for certain what effect our actions will have for certain, we should at least minimize the chance that any human action will result in harm for the polis as a whole. Probability, not certainty, is what we have recourse to, and the best means to test probability is to understand the nature of the object under discussion but also the polis with whom the orator is communicating. There is a need, then, for a discursive knowledge – how does one speak in any given situation? how does one understand the psychologies and the motivations of the members of the polis who confront the rhetor? – and a descriptive, reasonable (perhaps, in the Platonic scheme, philosophical) form of knowledge distinct from but working in connection with the discursive. But as I have also tried to make clear, it has not become evident by this point in the dialogue what such a knowledge looks like.

It does become clear, though, by the time Socrates finishes his disputation with Callicles, the fourth interlocutor in this tag-team match. Socrates has just finished making the point that doing wrong is only the *second* item on the list of evils; the first is failing to denounce ourselves when we have done wrong. Socrates has suggested, contrary to Polus, that doing wrong may very well have been the result of failing to fully understand the implications of an action – that is, failing to work back as far as possible to first causes – but that an orator, if he does not have as his task the reasonable prediction of the outcome of events, at the very least should take as his task the praise or denunciation of those events when the outcome is finally verified. Socrates makes the point (480a) that "a man's duty is to keep himself from doing wrong, because otherwise he will bring great evil upon himself," and further, that if he does evil, he should "most quickly be punished . . . in order that the disease of wickedness may not become chronic and cause his soul to fester till it is incurable," and that oratory's use should be to announce the misdeeds to the polis so that the perpetrator of them should be submitted to the will of law. In effect, this last point backs away from the possibility of a dialectical knowledge based on discursive and extra-discursive reasoning, and relies solely on discourse as a way of submitting to the materiality of the political law. Callicles sees the problem here: by denouncing onesself and one's family in order to submit to the law, the orator will inevitably renounce his position of strength – power being as important to him as it was to Polus – and, again, no right-thinking Athenian would do anything that would make himself weak. What Callicles does next, though, is to attempt to ground his understanding of strength in the immediacy or availability of the natural world. This is an important assertion: Callicles produces in this section of the dialogue what could be called an empiricist argument. He will assert that "strength is in numbers" because that is what he has observed in the natural world. He has deduced this from the observation that there are stronger and weaker men, and that – all things being equal – a group of stronger men will have their way over a group of weaker men, and to conclude that any law established by convention to circumvent the naturally occurring order is inferior to that order and will eventually be superseded again by the force of strength. At this point, Callicles and Socrates (and, by implication perhaps, Plato) are not that far apart: both are attempting to ground a theory of argumentation – and, more broadly, of human understanding – materially. It is not implausible for Socrates to agree with Callicles' assertion that the truth of the matter "can be seen in a variety of examples, drawn both from the animal world and from the complex communities and races of human beings; right consists in the superior ruling over the inferior and having the upper hand" (483d).

What separates these two – and what is important for a discussion of rhetoric and other forms of knowledge necessary to inform a worldview – is an understanding of convention. It is true, perhaps, that the stronger prevail in natural circumstances, suggests Socrates, but does "stronger" always mean "better"? Callicles answers unequivocally that the two terms are synonymous, at which point Socrates imagines another situation (488–9). It is granted – it has been "observed" – that the mass of men are naturally stronger than a single man or a smaller group of men. Such a situation, working in accord with Callicles' rule of the stronger, would dictate that this group is naturally stronger and so by definition better, and any laws they would establish would also by definition be better. But imagine a situation, suggests Socrates, in which such a mass of powerful men would agree among themselves that it was better for all to be equal – even among the heterogeneous group comprised of the stronger *and* the weaker – an agreement that would, in effect, undermine their own position of physical strength. (Such a situation was hardly unimaginable, since it was essentially how Athens was ruled both before and after the war with Sparta.) In such a situation, then, the natural and the conventional are not at odds at all: the naturally occurring stronger group would understand that the situation most beneficial for the welfare of the larger, heterogeneous group would be one of equality, and so would impose laws that would codify (conventionally) the naturally agreed-upon order.

Of course, Callicles will have none of this, and when confronted by the by-now waggish Socrates and asked to clarify what he meant by "better," he answers that he means "more gifted." With this argument, Socrates turns the tables, and also turns his previous example – meant to bring convention and "naturally observed phenomena" into correspondence – on its head.

Then on your theory it must often happen that one wise man is stronger than ten thousand fools, and that he ought to rule over them as subjects and have the lion's share of everything. That is what you seem to mean – there is no verbal trap here, I assure you – if one man is stronger than ten thousand. (490a)

The argument with Callicles goes on to note – importantly, I should say, because it once again points to the need for the production of knowledge beyond simple belief – that the "more gifted" or more intelligent here is stronger by dint of his understanding of the various material and social aspects of his dealings with the other members of the group. For our purposes here, I want to note that the double overturning of the nature / convention pair is symptomatic of Plato's inability quite to articulate the connection between the discursive dimension for rhetoric and the

26

extra-discursive one (the discursive dimension is that which might be connected to the "conventional," the extra-discursive to the natural or, using very different terminology, the "real"). The discussion of strength and power, and its attendant vocabulary (nature versus convention) is also effectively a discussion of the power of persuasion and of discourse more generally. While Socrates may be right about the ethically desirable condition in which the "more gifted" or more knowledgeable – but perhaps physically weaker – individual is granted power by rule of law over the greater number of the less gifted, common sense suggests (and various historians of rhetoric have shown) that this is not always what happens: strength may in fact lie with the larger numbers of the less informed, or in Plato's words, with "ten thousand fools." It would be this group which, by dint of rule by majority, impose the laws and enforce them. In this case "the strong" (the naturally occurring entity) may be equivalent to "the law" (the conventional codification of the empirically present), but it is not equivalent, in Plato's terminology, to the good. Plato's example of rule by minority might itself be logically turned on its head quite easily, and its effect would be to prove just the opposite of Plato's point. In such a case, nature and convention are – as Callicles tried to show – in conflict, in which social structures and objects (the brute materiality of fact, the unprovable, unreasonable, but existent world) do not correspond and actually work against the predicted state of affairs (the ethical "ought") resulting from reasonable deliberation and discourse. What you get in the double reversal, here, is another point in the dialogue in which Plato's rhetorical act points quite clearly to an impasse *produced by* rhetoric and which indirectly points to a need for a knowledge that intervenes between those ways of knowing that should provide us a way of understanding the world outside of its discursive dimension and the rhetorical reflection and interpretation of time- and place-specific conditions.

The result of the impasse is the total isolation of Socrates in the dialogue, reducing the dialogue to monologue and in effect suggesting the failure of a rhetoric (not just sophistic rhetoric but also Platonic rhetoric / dialectic) that does not consciously and precisely formulate a connection between the materiality and extra-discursive properties of the social world and its discursive function, and as a result the failure for rhetoric to effect change in the polis. But both Kasteley and Vaida think differently: they each see, in rather different ways, the possibility of an architectonic rhetoric that functions precisely because of the breakdown of the dialogue into monologue (for Kasteley, pure "refutation"). Their point is that the failure of *Gorgias* points to the possibility of success later on, and that "the 'conclusion' of the inquiry is not made in this dialogue but elsewhere and even with other interlocutors" (Vaida). Elsewhere in *Phaedrus*? With Aristotle? Perhaps, but with implications quite different from those suggested by Vaida, Kasteley, and several others.

Gorgias as monologue, *Phaedrus* as conclusion

It is at this point in *Gorgias* that the dialogics of Plato's work breaks down. By 494, Callicles is reduced to indignation, and by 506, he has had enough: "Go ahead, good sir, and finish on your own." Because it is at precisely this point that Socrates has found himself without recourse to an interlocutor, his attempt to change anyone's mind at all is undermined, and his rhetorical / dialectical method is severely questioned.

Why would the dialogue end this way? One of the conclusions that could be reached from the discussion of nature and convention is that "convention" is always already in place. The natural order is accessible only through the conventional order of discourse which is also well in place beforehand. Perhaps this is pushing the point some, but the reasons why Socrates and Callicles can understand "power" and "intelligence" and "nature" to be synonymous or at odds is because the observations they have made and collected have been categorized by conventional means: "power" and "intelligence" and "nature" are taken as axiomatic because the polis has been organized in a particular way that valorizes those terms. To ensure that a willed course of events is pursued according to "the good," one has to examine the predicted effects that the events will have on the welfare of the polis over the long haul, and in order to do this the orator or politician must examine the already-existing set of conventions – the law – to ensure that it is itself consistent and beneficial. But Plato's Socrates has found himself in an inextricable conundrum: he has come to the conclusion that to assess the good according to which rhetoric should aim, one ultimately needs a position outside the rhetorical (and political) realm; but for the moment, the only tool available for the production of knowledge that can be used for the direction of the polis is rhetoric.

So Plato ends the dialogue monologically in order to (attempt to) resolve this contradiction. The subtitle of the dialogue is "on refutation" or *refutative* – according, respectively, to Irwin and Lamb – and it is by means of refutation that Socrates gains the upper hand on Gorgias, Polus, and Callicles. By standing in isolation, away from the "larger group" that presumably wields power over the polis, Socrates is content to gain the adherence of only one person, his interlocutor, and he will do so by actively engaging that interlocutor by refuting his conventional assumptions about the polis itself and its correspondence to the natural order. Socrates is, in fact, acting to undermine all of the assumptions held by the three sophists – all of them men of good breeding and education – and to force them to reconsider their relations to the polis on terms other than the rhetorical (i.e., conventional). But, as I have suggested, Socrates requires some ground on which to stand, and he is able to find it only by resorting, albeit rhetorically, to knowledge obtained by rhetorically gaining access to extra-rhetorical phenomena.

In fact, Socrates has been looking for this ground from early on in the dialogue. Near the beginning of his argument with Gorgias on the nature of rhetoric, we get the following interruption:

. . . You may wonder why I am saying this. It is because what you are saying now [about rhetoric] does not appear to me quite consistent with what you said at first about oratory, and I am afraid that if I probe the matter further you may suppose that my purpose is not so much to elucidate the subject as to win a verbal victory over you. If you are the same sort of person as myself, I will willingly go on questioning you; otherwise, I will stop. If you ask what I mean, I am one of those people who are glad to have their own mistakes pointed out and glad to point out the mistakes of others, but who would just as soon have the first experience as the second; in fact I consider the first a greater gain, inasmuch as it is better to be relieved of very bad trouble oneself than relieve it in another, and in my opinion no worse trouble can befall a man than to have a false belief about the subjects which we are now discussing.   (457c-8a)

Socrates is well on his way to making his point without the interlude, so it is not clear why it is necessary for him to include it. But it is precisely by way of these interludes that Socrates makes his rhetorical method most plain: it is "the man whom I am arguing with" (474a) who supplies the refutative understanding of the subject at hand. The orator who presses the point and the interlocutor or audience whose favor is being sought each presumably have divergent beliefs (481c), and these beliefs are either founded on an understanding that is formed in part through knowledge or simply by means of discursive formation of a consensus. It is only by means of refutation that each interlocutor will understand the foundations of the other's conventional system of beliefs, by means of judging those systems against the other's, and against "the good." If the orator anticipates his interlocutor's response, he is anticipating that response *from his own perspective*, a response which does not provide him with that (potentially) extra-discursive position from which to judge his own, a response which is synonymous with belief, not knowledge.

Socrates condemns the four Athenian leaders not because they did not provide for the security of the Athenian state – Vickers and others have made the point that the walls and docks they erected were in part what provided Plato with the uninterrupted intellectual time with which to write the condemnation – but because they "pursued in good faith a set of inherited practices" (Kasteley, "Defense," 104). Though Pericles, for example, was the consummate parliamentary politician, working to forge a consensus among the Athenians as to what would immediately secure their good fortune (Havelock, *Liberal Temper*, 9), he was not willing to engage in the kind of discourse – a refutative, dialectical one that engaged not only belief but as far as possible knowledge of the material foundations of those beliefs – that would have allowed Athenians to understand their circumstances as at once conventional and natural / material (501a-c).

But Plato's conclusion of the dialogue, in which Socrates does *not* partake in such a refutative engagement, suggests that rhetoric as it is here conceived will not work to this end. Socrates has not managed to make Callicles change his mind; he has only made him give up. Refutation will work only where the rhetor is able to work to first causes with the rational step-by-step interrogation of belief with an acknowledgment of the very thing Socrates seems at pains to suggest, namely that not everyone is capable of analytic inquiry. The conclusion suggests a need for rhetorical knowledge and, in addition, some other kind (or kinds) of theoretical knowledge simultaneously. Those who try to explain *Phaedrus* as the logical culmination of the kind of rhetoric / dialectic Plato defends in *Gorgias* fail to see that it too is an aporia, one that is explained by – and does not explain – the difficulties of rhetorical and scientific / analytic knowledge implied in *Gorgias*, in particular by its monologic ending.

For me it is less important to square the three different discourses on love in *Phaedrus* – the problem that has perennially concerned those working to reconcile Plato to a theory of rhetoric – than it is to understand how rhetoric functions to construct the dialogue itself. To my mind, Richard Weaver's careful delineation of Plato's theory of figure in "The *Phaedrus* and the Nature of Rhetoric" is useful here because regardless of whether one believes (and I do not) that *Phaedrus* really does what it says it will do (which is Weaver's point) it brings into relief the difficulties Socrates (and Plato) have in defining the a-rhetorical aspects of a proper rhetorical strategy in rhetorical terms. Weaver's essay points dramatically to the figural nature of a dialogue whose aim is to find an explicitly a- (or contra-) rhetorical philosophy that resolves the problems rhetoric itself displays. It is particularly evident that *Phaedrus* is less the culmination of a dialectical rhetoric that "rectifies" the vituperative tone of *Gorgias* than it is a singular example of the impasse that the earlier dialogue cannot come to terms with, thereby suggesting that *Gorgias* explains and completes *Phaedrus* and not the other way around.

The hint of an outline for a proper rhetoric can be seen when Socrates speaks immediately after Phaedrus recites Lysias's speech on the favor that should be granted the non-lover over the lover. "[T]ake the subject of the speech" for example, he says:

[W]ho do you suppose, in arguing that the nonlover ought to be more favored than the lover, could omit praise of the nonlover's calm sense and blame of the lover's unreason, which are inevitable arguments, and then say something else instead? No, such arguments, I think, must be allowed and excused . . .   (235b-6a)

Lamb uses the term "commonplaces" instead of "arguments" in 236: the suggestion seems to be that certain topics, certain subjects – certain objects of knowledge – require or call for certain ways of presenting them. This does three things, all of which are problematic for rhetoric, and all of which pertain to figuration. First, by

31

noting the connection between the "who" in "who could suppose" with the argument of the calmness of the non-lover, Plato
establishes a connection between discursive constructs and natural states of affairs. The problem that becomes immediately apparent – working from the Callicles section of *Gorgias* – is deciding
whether the connection is being established through belief or
through knowledge, and whether the "who" in this passage is
someone who is able systematically to investigate the material
circumstances of the position of the non-lover. Secondly, immediately after the passage just cited, Socrates makes a distinction
between invention and arrangement, and suggests that Lysias'
speech could be praised for its arrangement, but not for its invention, because it fails to account for the connection between a state
of affairs and the necessary investigation (either rhetorically or by
other means) of that state. This makes clear that the process of
"invention" is an altogether different (and unique) part of the
rhetorical art from simple arrangement and consensus-building
(which is consistent with Socrates' earlier complaint about
Pericles), and it elicits the question of just how invention proceeds, and whether there is not a conceptual or metaphysical (or
scientific/technological) aspect to it that goes beyond the rhetorical (a question consistent with the aporias evident in *Gorgias*).
Thirdly, Socrates takes Phaedrus (and, by implication, Lysias) to
task for taking liberties with the argument on love by suggesting
that it has not properly defined its terms (see, immediately after
the passage cited, 237b). But he then does so and immediately
concocts another dialogue that defines love but does so to its
detriment. In the second speech, Socrates' definition is near the
mark, and yet if it is in accord with a naturally occurring state of
affairs (i.e., the irrational, the emotional or unconventional), then
it does not function by way of reason or rhetoric/dialectic, and so
he is forced to correct himself by having, on the spot, to come up
with yet another speech on love. We are faced with a problem
similar to one we encountered in *Gorgias*: if the nature/conven-
tion pair is so tenuous and unstable, how can rhetoric mediate it,
and – if even an epistemic (or philosophical) rhetoric of a Plato/
Socrates fails to mediate the terms – is there another discipline, or
"guide" for rhetoric, that could be used to do so?

All three of these questions hint at the difficulty of establishing a
discursive theory and practice that must also take account of

elements of human life (and its appetites) that operate beyond discursive understanding. They hint, that is, at the need for a rhetoric that at once forges consensus by establishing belief, but is also capable of reaching beyond rhetoric to investigate the material circumstances – insofar as possible – that are implicated in human life and the formation of the polis (and smaller polises) that is itself defined conventionally. After Socrates' second speech, the way to investigate these extra-discursive forces becomes clearer in *Phaedrus* than it had been at any point in the earlier dialogue (269c-70a):

All great arts demand discussion and high speculation about nature. [In Hamilton's translation, "demand" is replaced by *"need to be supplemented by"*; my emphasis.] [In the case of medicine, as in the case of rhetoric], you must analyze a nature, in one that of the body and in the other that of the soul, if you are to proceed in a scientific manner, not merely by practice and routine, to impart health and strength to the body by prescribing medicine and diet, or by proper discourses and training to give to the soul the desired belief and virtue. [In both translations, the term "science" or "scientific" is used for the word *technai*.]

This passage has at least two important implications for the production of knowledge that must be included in (or that must *supplement*) an understanding of rhetoric. First, such a knowledge must be scientific: it should systematically describe the "nature" of the object, in this case either of the body (in medicine) or the soul (in oratory). Of course, it is not explained precisely how such a description should take place *vis-à-vis* the soul (it is my contention that the third speech on love can be seen as a manner of explanation, albeit a highly problematic one), though it is somewhat easier to surmise in the case of the body. Secondly, the production of knowledge has at once both an analytical function – it must describe the state of affairs as it operates currently or generally – and a predictive function: as described rather obliquely in *Gorgias*, medicine, as a science, must have an attendant art which "trains" the body toward some end (in this case, physical well-being), and in order to do so it must be able to predict how various different means – the application of poultices, the consumption of foods, the prescription of various remedies – will move the body toward that end. That is to say, this attendant production of knowledge must systematically engage with questions *beyond* those immediately concerned with the body, and must understand (as in the example of medicine; and much like the earlier example of shipbuilding) the physical and material properties of vegetation, of exercise and so on. At the moment Plato opens the relation of nature to convention (that is, the connection of the extra-rhetorical or extra-political aspect of human life with the conceptual or discursive aspect), he finds the need to invent a supplementary form of knowledge, one that either mediates the human/social and the non-human/social, or one that examines the latter half of the pair only.

It is possible to see Socrates' second speech on love as exemplary of Plato coming to terms with this need, and it is Richard Weaver whose analysis of figuration in *Phaedrus* is the most precise, and the most problematic. After a long description in which Weaver distinguishes between "semantically purified speech," which is characterized by its instrumentality and the "serviceability of objectivity," and "base rhetoric," which is characterized by its embellishment and its ability to inflame the passions at the expense of the will, Weaver notes a third rhetorical strategy, one he thinks Socrates puts to use in his second speech on love, which matches rhetoric with dialectic. This is the language that appeals to belief – because presumably dialectic is only to be used when opinion is divided or when there is no firmly held opinion on the subject in question – and also appeals to brachyological division, classification, observation and prediction. It is particularly those issues that are matters of policy – political questions, but also questions of justice, the good – that Weaver says are peculiarly available through persuasion because the interconnection between "body" and "soul," between human agency (and desire) and the natural world are most at issue. But of course, in order to get anyone to listen to you on questions of policy – particularly on difficult questions having to do with justice and the proper orientation of the "soul" – the rhetor must be able to attract people's attention. Mystically, Weaver suggests that the combination of rhetorical forging of consensus and the analytical evaluation of the situation produces an "excess," namely, figuration, and this, he says, is the method of investigation used in Socrates' second speech on love.

What is important is not which figure is being used to explain the soul in relation to the good, but that figuration is being used at all. Weaver believes that the relationship between "rhetoric" and "dialectic" – or between semantically purified speech (or scientific investigation) on the one hand and rhetoric (or the espousing of one of the contrary positions to be argued on the other) – can be mediated by a discourse that works by way of figuration. Remember that for Weaver at least figuration is the "excess" of signification that results from the rhetor's attempt both to produce knowledge and adherence or consensus on the part of the interlocutor. This excess can be seen – like the process of refutation in *Gorgias* – as a way to mediate the "naturalizing" tendency of discourse to reproduce the worldview that always precedes us and into which we are born and which we have somehow to move beyond if we are to understand the boundaries of this view; and the analytical, perhaps scientific description which, like the system of norms into which we are born, also occupies a middle ground somewhere between the conventional and the extra-discursive – as a way to explain the conundrum of the rhetor. In order to walk a workable middle path between pure dialectic on the one hand and pure (base) rhetoric on the other, the rhetor turns to figuration as a way to accomplish the unaccomplishable. And by the looks of things, by the end of *Phaedrus*, Socrates has done just that. Phaedrus is convinced, Richard Weaver is convinced, and so are we: what has been left undone in *Gorgias* has finally been done, namely, we have been told how a rhetoric works to imbricate the natural and social worlds.

But should we be convinced? I do not think so. The praxis humans undertake based on our "reading" of the excess resulting from figuration – the "prophecy" (*oionoistike*) in which we are able to see, based on our analysis of present states of affairs, what direction we should move in for the future – is an "observation of signs, since they furnish the mind (*nous*) and information (*historia*) to human thought (*oiesis*) from the intellect (*dianoia*)" (244b). That is, figuration itself is a combination of knowledges – conception and individuation, both of which combine to produce thought, and both of which originate in the human mind, suggesting once again a complicated engagement of nature and convention – and cannot be considered all that different from anything else we have seen before in Plato's dialogues. This is consistent with the conclusion of *Phaedrus*, which ends not with the discourse on love, but with a discourse *on* the discourse on love: Socrates and Phaedrus are forced to make sense of what Socrates has just done by providing a taxonomy of the figure. The conclusion with meta-figuration implies that once one has produced a figural excess, it must then be passed back through dialectic, rhetoric and whatever other means are necessary to understand it. Even the rhetoric that Plato presumably offers as a way to negotiate the impasse between nature and convention, science and/or dialectic and "base rhetoric," must itself be supplemented with some other knowledge.

For all his valorization of Platonic rhetoric/dialectic, Weaver too understands this at some level too. Through figuration, he says, the speaker (here Socrates) "sets about moving the listeners toward [a] position, but there is no way to move them except through the operation of an analogy. The analogy proceeds by showing that the position being urged resembles or partakes of something greater or finer" (1061-2). Figuration connects one thing to another, both of which have a particular nature that cannot simply be established through connection of the two, but which natures must also be investigated (if they are to be truly *known* and not simply *cited*). This produces an *incongruity* which must itself be explored and investigated, and there is no guarantee that the audience being persuaded – depending upon their demeanor, their place in the polis, their conventional sense of morality, will and goodness – will not misunderstand the implications of this investigation, and so on.

Noting that Socrates dismisses the historical and scientific explanation of the myth of Boreas at the beginning of *Phaedrus* in favor of its mythical counterpart, Weaver calls scientific criticism of myth "a boorish sort of wisdom" (Weaver's translation), one that does not ever quite get at the truth of the matter. "Socrates is satisfied with the parable, and we infer from numerous other passages that he believed that some things are best told by parable and some perhaps discoverable only by parable. Real investigation goes forward with the help of analogy" (1055). And yet here Weaver suggests that analogy – the use of figure – is the *supplement* to more serious investigation. And this is the point I have been trying to make: while not trying to devalue rhetoric by any means (and it will become clear as this book progresses that I will reverse the claim and suggest, to accompany Weaver's understanding, that analogy [rhetoric, or hermeneutic] goes forward with the help of real [scientific] investigation), it is clear that Plato attempts to distinguish rhetoric from its use by the sophists as a way of producing belief without analyzing belief's constraints, but it is also clear that this distinction casts light on its own complexities. It is complex – if not altogether impossible – because rhetoric is inevitably bound up with other ways of knowing – it borders them, or it includes them, or it mediates them – but can never finally be separated from them, and as much as Plato wishes to carve out a rhetoric that is purely refutative, or that is purely figurative, or that allows the rhetor to occupy a place that is somehow outside or at some remove from the objects of investigation (which will always include the rhetor himself), then that rhetoric will inevitably circle back to reiterate the rhetor. So, while it is true that the *Phaedrus* and the *Gorgias* enact what they claim to enact – they do, in fact, show what the rhetoric defined by Socrates looks like – it is enacted by its very failure to work.

2

✣✣

Why Aristotle's notion of rhetoric and science is important for contemporary critical practice

✣✣

With what has been called the "rhetorical turn" or the antifoundational paradigm, work in the human sciences – by the likes of philosophers such as Rorty and Davidson, of scientists such as Kuhn and Polyani, and of philosophers of science such as Feyerabend – theorists have begun to understand that the search for foundational knowledge either by philosophical or by scientific means is a project bound to fail. In the last ten to fifteen years in particular, people such as Louise Phelps in composition studies and Richard Bernstein – in the name of Hans Georg Gadamer – have looked for a "third way" between (in Bernstein's terms) objectivism and relativism, or between the scylla of foundationalism and the charybdis of knowledge without any foundations. And because this turn has been precisely *rhetorical*, much attention has lately been paid to classical rhetorical texts, like the *Rhetoric*, Plato's dialogues on oratory (*Phaedrus, Gorgias*), and texts on ethics and politics, in order to determine whether that "third way" might not have been hinted at by these earlier thinkers.

This chapter will not join that fray, since the connections between rhetoric and other ways of knowing are already well established. My task here will be instead to suggest that important passages in two of Aristotle's texts on rhetoric – *Nichomachean Ethics* and *Rhetoric* – imply that in order to persuade members of the polis to pursue a particular course of action, the rhetor is bound to use the methodology of the sciences, because it is through observation that you bear out the results of rhetorical knowledge. This is a long way away from claims that there is a third way between the relativism of rhetoric's contingency and the objectivism of science. Instead, it suggests that the commonplace that rhetoric and science overlap is quite true because rhetoric and science, while they are distinct ways of knowing, *share a common methodology*, namely the demonstration that a phenomenon or human activity will proceed in a particular way through more or less rigorous argument from axiomatic starting points. Aristotle suggests that an intimate relation exists between science and rhetoric, that the best rhetoricians must in fact be capable of scientific (not to mention philosophical) observation and categorization, and – quite differently than Bernstein, Phelps and others who have understood praxis as preferable to either theory or common knowledge – that practical wisdom describes nothing other than the dialectical movement between scientific demonstration and what we might call interpretation.

Nichomachean Ethics (1138b15–1145a11)

I take as my point of departure an essay written several years ago now by Eugene Garver, entitled "Aristotle's *Rhetoric* on Unintentionally Hitting the Principles of the Sciences." Garver suggests that in arguing rhetorically, we may be able to "prove" a point by so clearly delineating the nature of the case that we in fact prove it scientifically: we have settled the case. But this does not mean necessarily that we have shown that the case can be extended across all similar cases, since in order to do so, we would have to pass from rhetoric to science, and say "here is the law, and here is why this case conforms with or is at odds with the law." Scientific principles allow us to investigate regularities, and rhetoric allows us to investigate irregularities against the background of regularities. Each must function in relation to the other; to extend Garver's point and make it accord with contemporary philosophy of science, as science produces better and better "explanations" for phenomena, rhetoric keeps pace with it by problematizing the ground of perceptions within which humans operate.

What is most important to recognize in Garver's essay – and Garver makes just this point in his conclusion – is that Aristotle is valuable to contemporary theories of science and their relation to contingency and argument because though he separates science from rhetoric in very specific ways, contemporary epistemologies can see in those distinctions – about observation, about common knowledge, about the relations between the various ways of knowing – the possibility that a "middle way" between science and rhetoric really is not needed at all. Although the two fields are separate, they have in common one very important fact: observation is absolutely necessary in both cases, and the approximation to what may be taken to be a universally applicable law is much like the kind of judgment involved in approximating the probability of certain outcomes of a particular action. What Garver's essay makes clear is that the "exceptional" case of the rhetorical argument hitting on a principle in science in fact sheds light on the contemporary reading of Aristotle that allows us to see these two fields as separate but absolutely compatible. There are hints in both *Rhetoric* and *Nichomachean Ethics* that the nature of that necessary and compatible relationship is a methodological one.

These hints can be seen particularly clearly, I think, in the sixth book of *Ethics*, where Aristotle lays out the different ways of knowing available for humans to investigate the world, the human soul, and the place of human activity in the polis and in the cosmos. One of the reasons I chose *Ethics* as an important text for exploring the methodological relation between rhetoric and science is because Barbara Warnick sees in it a corrective to work that takes rhetoric to subsume or make claims upon the sciences. In an essay that specifically links *Nichomachean Ethics* to *Rhetoric*, entitled "Judgment, Probability, and Aristotle's *Rhetoric*," Warnick complains that William Grimaldi, Christopher Lyle Johnstone and others have erroneously claimed that "rhetoric is general and touches on all areas of human knowledge wherein man attempts to convey understanding, whether it be philosophy, literature, or the physical sciences" (Grimaldi, *Aristotle*, 54; quoted in Warnick, "Judgement," 300). Warnick points to *Nichomachean Ethics* for evidence that rhetoric is a highly particularized art with definite boundaries, and that Aristotle is "more concerned with finding what differentiates one branch of learning from the other and what is particular to each" (Ostwald, "Introduction" to *Nichomachean Ethics* xiii; quoted in Warnick, "Judgement," 302). Aristotle begins the sixth book by noting that the human mind has both an irrational and a rational element: "one by which we contemplate the kind of things whose originative causes are in-

variable, and one by which we contemplate variable things . . . Let
one of these parts be called the scientific and the other the calculative" (1139a6–12). Aristotle goes on to equate the "deliberative" and the calculative principles as one part of the two-part
rational element.

In addition to these two principles of the rational, there are
three elements that, working together or separately, activate the
rational (and the irrational) elements of the soul. The first of these
is sense perception. The two other faculties, intelligence (*nous*)
and desire, in combination with sense perception, work to produce human activity (that is, conduct) or *praxis*. In theoretical
knowledge, sense perception is combined with intelligence without the inclusion of desire. This produces the "attainment of
truth" through "intellectual activity," but it does not concern
itself with praxis. Praxis is the result of "true reasoning" and
"right desire" (1039a23) in combination with sense data. Because
praxis is the production of human activity beyond intellectual
knowledge, it always tends toward some "end." As Aristotle puts
it in *Ethics*,

Choice is the starting point of action: it is the source of motion but not the
end for the sake of which we act. The starting point of choice, however, is
desire and reasoning directed toward some end. That is why there cannot
be choice either without intelligence and thought or without some moral
characteristic.   (1039a)

And it is altogether possible that the activity of desire will *not* tend
toward the good, in which case the production of human activity
will likewise tend away from the good.

It is the second of these three elements of the soul which is
called "intelligence" by Aristotle – the first of the five branches of
knowledge or five different "ways of knowing" – and it in turn
has two components, *nous* and *dianoia*. Intelligence provides the
starting point of all cognition. *Nous*, following J. A. Stewart, is the
intuitive intellect or intuitive reason that directly apprehends
those things that are not directly demonstrable. *Dianoia*, on the
other hand, is the discursive faculty, the connective or associate
part of the intelligence that translates apprehension into conventional symbols or signs that can in turn be put either to theoretical or practical use by other faculties. The combination of the
directly apprehensive faculty of *nous* and the discursive faculty

of *dianoia* "form the bases of scientific knowledge," as Warnick suggests.

The two theoretical knowledges derived from the intelligence are scientific knowledge and theoretical wisdom. The first (*episteme*) refers to knowledge that is grounded in fact or first principles, and its method of inquiry is demonstrative and apodeictic. Its descriptions are assumed to correspond directly to physical reality and they are essential. That is to say, the object and the predicate of the phenomenon or state of affairs under discussion are presumed to be indissolubly linked, as we saw in the earlier example of the predicate "animal's" essential link to the object, "human." The aim of scientific knowledge is to establish the general rules that apply in all instances – humans are in all instances animal – by way of demonstration, instruction and explanation. The use to which such knowledge could be put is outside the purview of scientific knowledge but these uses nevertheless are dependent upon the first principles which theoretical knowledge only can adduce. Theoretical wisdom (*sophia*) has as its province those elements of being that are eternal and changeless, and which are by definition intangible. In effect, *sophia* deals with the qualities of the physical world insofar as they are essential to all being through metaphysics, philosophy and theology, and aims at the "true conception of the eternal and unchanging elements of being" (Warnick, "Judgment," 304).

It is most interesting to note that there is a scientific dimension implicit in the practical arts – the last two of the five knowledges – and that this dimension functions by constantly negotiating the potentially objective and explicitly contingent nature of its object, namely, human action. Both art (*techne*) and practical wisdom (*phronesis*) concern themselves with production of human activity: art is concerned with the production of objects or things, whereas practical wisdom is concerned with the production of a lived life, using the products not only of *techne* but also of *episteme* and *sophia*. Both rhetoric and dialectic fall under the rubric of "art," whose functions are to produce and judge arguments, dialectic in small groups of learned people in interactive, complex discourse, and rhetoric in larger groups of less-well learned people in enthymematic discourse. As I noted earlier, the difference between enthymematic (rhetorical) and syllogistic (dialectic) reasoning does not lie either in the method of argument, or in the inclusion or exclusion of reason. For both scientific / theoretical wisdom as well as for practical wisdom, it is incumbent upon the philosopher or the rhetorician to use the best means at his disposal – given the particular art or science he is using – to understand as many aspects of the object or state of affairs in question. The difference, rather, is in the aims of the intellectual art, but also in which of the three elements that induce human action are in play. All of the intellectual arts or ways of knowing categorize sense experience, and do so on the basis of whether the properties or characteristics of an object or state of affairs are essential or inessential, and whether the deliberation taking place has as its aim either the production of an object or action or simply the production of knowledge.

The editor of a popular edition of *Ethics*, David Ross, notes that deliberation and the principle of choice in Aristotle is something we do

about means [rather than ends], and [Aristotle] indicates the nature of deliberation by comparing it with the process of discovering the solution of a geometrical problem. The problem being to construct a certain kind of figure, we ask what we must first have constructed in order to do this, and so on until we come to a figure which we can construct on the basis of knowledge we already have. (xi)

Here, it seems, is one place where Aristotle acknowledges that deliberation – a function of rhetoric as an art of finding the means of persuasion in every given case, not only those cases that are specific, say, to geometry or politics – proceeds by negotiating between the specifics of an individual case and those things about which we are certain in general cases. We need to know something about ends – the nature of objects reached by successive approximations and observation; the behavior of people reached by prediction based on observation in particular cases – in order to deliberate about the means by which to come to them. But Aristotle also suggests that this is a fairly difficult task – according to Ross, we must consider "what we want to bring about, and ask what we must bring about to bring that about, and what we must bring about to bring that about . . . Until we come to something we can bring about here and now" (xi) – that bears some similarity to the (contemporary) scientific task of building a theory and testing it by finding how the component parts of it function.

Ross also says of science that "Aristotle means the act of drawing correct inferences from premises known to be true . . . By
practical wisdom he means the power of deliberating how a state
of being which will satisfy us is to be brought into existence." If
these definitions hold up, then there is a direct correlation, I think,
between "drawing inferences from premises known to be true"
and "deliberating" how to bring into existence a state of being.
Deliberation is the process by which we determine all of those
things that we need to know, or are in place beforehand, in order
to bring a particular state of being into existence, so there seems to
be an ineradicable connection between the knowledge one needs
to appeal to (that is "in place beforehand") and the particularities
of the situation at hand being examined in practical wisdom. Both
deliberation and scientific wisdom, though different in their "domains," are quite similar in their methods, namely, to determine –
through the observation of evidence ("objective" or rational in the
case of science; specific and situational in the case of deliberation)
– whether a phenomenon or structure will behave the way we
think it will based upon what we already know. Methodologically, not only do these two ways of knowing function similarly in
Aristotle's taxonomy; given our current understanding of science
and the degree to which it functions at least in part in the interpretive (rather than completely in the "objective") dimension, it is
also possible to suggest that Aristotle's taxonomy suggests ways
for the contemporary intellectual world to see ways to distinguish
how rhetoric and science both are and are not alike, how rhetoric
and science cannot function without each other.

Of course, Aristotle's thesis in Book VI of *Nichomachean Ethics* is
that theoretical wisdom is superior to practical wisdom: practical
wisdom "determines which studies are to be pursued in a state,
[but] it is issuing commands not to theoretical wisdom but in its
interests" (vi-vii; see also I.1–I.7). But this thesis is undercut by the
suggestion that all of the faculties converge at a single point,
namely the bringing together of all the faculties to produce virtu-
ous activity in members of the polis. That is, all five of the faculties
function together in order that the individual knows not just
which course of action is most wisely pursued for the individual's
well-being but how a course of action is most wisely pursued that
also is most healthy for the community at large: practical and
scientific (and every other kind of) wisdom are preferably wed-

ded so that a person not only knows how to behave in a particular case but also why one's behavior is better in this case, and this requires that one is able to examine, in Ross's words, "the major premiss [*sic*]". Though rhetoric's participation in the deliberative process and science's ability to suggest what is already known are separate faculties, methodologically they function in the same way – observation of the particular case against the background of what can be said already – and they should preferably function together. In fact, if you go back to Garver's essay, which suggests that when working rhetorically the speaker may hit on a principle which forecloses an argument from disagreement, then one could say not only that they must function together but that though "theoretical wisdom is superior to practical . . . the latter derives some, at least, of its value from its tendency to produce the former." That is, we could say that they *must* function together: we may hit on a principle in rhetoric, but – were humans more perfect – we had hit on them more frequently since the aim of practical reason seems to be a more perfect synthesis between the theoretical / scientific and the practical life, and the more these are brought into accord with one another (knowing full well that, as imperfect beings, this is not possible), the better.

Again, *à propos* of Garver, it is possible (see 1142a10) for people to have philosophical wisdom but not practical wisdom. One can be like Thales, a great thinker, but not know enough to come in out of the rain – in such a case, the thinker is not able to understand the relation between principles, scientific observation, and practical observation of everyday affairs. This passage notes that young men of practical wisdom cannot be found; "the cause is that such wisdom is concerned not only with universals but with particulars." Aristotle's point is that because young men have not had much experience, they are not able to know from observation and experience what the best course of action in a particular case might be, even though they well may be learned in the "exact sciences" (and are able, say, to determine why the shape in front of us is a triangle and not a rectangle). But the phrase in question is "not only." Practical wisdom is not only about universals, but about universals and particulars. Again, one could read this passage to suggest that practical wisdom is bound up with understanding the universals – those aspects of the situation that, if it is possible, one is able to say are unchanging, that we know x or y

will happen – and that the difference is that the situational aspect
of deliberation – what happens in *this* particular case – forces us to
relate the universal and the particular. Again, if we square this
with Garver's reading, this makes perfect sense: if it is possible to
hit on a principle in rhetorical deliberation, then it is possible
because the universals in this particular case may be so well
defined that the particulars of the situation *turn out to be* universals. We should behave this way in this case because we know this
case to be exactly like a previous case, and given this fact, there is
no argument. We have proven that this course of action is simply
and indisputably the one we should follow. This is not to say that
particularities will not arise that are quite similar to this case but
that differ enough from it that we are forced back to the relation
between philosophy and deliberation; and if what Garver says is
true, we are *always* forced back to this, since human activity is
known to be imperfect and exceptional rather than perfect and
constant. And yet the relation seems clear: practical wisdom /
deliberation always exists in connection with science, and yet is
distinct from it.

Rhetoric (1354a1–1359a29)

The earliest section of *Rhetoric* lays out not only that rhetoric and
other ways of knowing – particularly dialectic but also scientific
knowledge – connect with one another (which is the uncontrover-
sial part of this argument) but also how they are related methodologically. This is partly a result of the way Aristotle sets up the
treatise: he is at pains (not just here but also in *Ethics*) to make
distinctions between the contingent and the necessary, those
things that are invariable (which *must* be), and those things which
are variable, contingent, probable. The realm of the necessary is
rendered by the theoretical and scientific ways of knowing, while
the realm of the contingent is rendered by the practical arts, such
as rhetoric and practical wisdom. *Organon* divides these realms
between those sciences that depend upon reasoning based on
absolute premises leading to necessary conclusions, and those
(practical) arts that depend upon reasoning based on probability.
Aristotle's notion of the necessary and the absolute is firmly
established: the nature of the cosmos, the relations between
numbers, geometric relations, and so on, are not questionable. If a

triangle has an angle of 30° and another angle of 60°, we know that the third angle will be of 90°, because the sum of the angles of a triangle is 180°, and we know this because we have done the math. We have, in other words, observed triangles, we have established a way to discuss triangles (i.e., mathematics and geometry), and we have also established a relation between what we observe and the system devised to understand the nature divulged by those observations. But it is also true that induction and deduction function in precisely the same way in the practical arts – i.e., rhetoric – as they do in the scientific and theoretical ways of knowing. The method established for argument based on the observation of human behavior in *Rhetoric* is this:

> When we base the proof of a proposition on a number of similar cases, this is induction in dialectic, example in rhetoric; when it is shown that, certain propositions being true, a further and quite distinct proposition must also be true in consequence, whether invariably or usually, this is called syllogism in dialectic, enthymeme in rhetoric. (I.2: 1356b13–17)

Though it is true that "neither rhetoric nor dialectic is the scientific study of any one separate subject [since] both are faculties for providing arguments," they could both be said to operate on the same principles as scientific study, namely, observation and demonstration. The establishment of the relation between angles in a triangle may be likened to the analysis required to persuade a young man who lives in an oligarchy. This person's character may be established enthymematically – by establishing the proposition that young men "have neither that excess of confidence which amounts to rashness, nor too much timidity, but the right amount of each" (II.13: 1390a30–31), and the proposition that men ruled in an oligarchy are primarily interested in the accumulation of wealth (I.8: 1366a4) – by linking two propositions and then observing whether experience bears out the further proposition that the argument must proceed in a certain way. Or it may be established by accumulating examples of behavior, and establishing a set of rules that approximates the principles of such behavior. In both cases – enthymeme and example – the process by which we discover the means of persuasion in this case runs parallel to the process by which we discover the means of proving that this particular triangle does indeed conform to the general rule.

What is important here is that we see that – whether we are dealing with those matters that exist in the realm of the necessary or with those matters that exist in the realm of the contingent – the means of proof or of argument remain very much the same. It is true that mathematical or scientific reasoning in Aristotle's scheme so far set up is a matter far simpler than arguing rhetorically, since it may not be true that, given the behavior of young men and the behavior of men in an oligarchy, these particular young men will behave the way we think they will. There is a great deal that these enthymemes do not account for (the men may have different qualities from one another; the oligarchy may be quite different from oligarchies we have observed before, etc.). But my argument is that the very same process that led us to understand that triangles have certain characteristics will *better* enable us to approximate, over time and through a closer and closer examination of the complex and particular constraints upon the behavior of this particular group of people. That is, science may be a distinct method of reasoning from rhetoric, but both operate in much the same way: from observation to generalization, and then back to observation.

There is further evidence to support such a claim. In 1355a10–15, Aristotle notes that

he who is best able to see how and from what elements a syllogism is produced will also be best skilled in the enthymeme, when he has further learnt what its subject matter is and in what respects it differs from the syllogism of strict logic. *The true and the approximately true are apprehended by the same faculty*; it may also be noted that men have a sufficient natural instinct for what is true, and usually do arrive at the truth.

One needs to ask here how syllogism, enthymeme and logic are related; and how the truths established in each relate to that which is established scientifically. The passage could be read to imply that enthymematic reason (produced by rhetoric) works somewhere between syllogistic reason – in which it is known with certainty that the objects or states of affairs in question will behave in the way that previous observation has suggested they would (and perhaps scientific reasoning, where the component parts of the object or state of affairs are known beforehand and so investigation is shortened) – and chance statements based on simple experience. Aristotle associates these latter statements with the political oratory of the sophists, where one can effectively define the behavior of the world as one wants at any particular time because the observed regularities of the world are purely constructed and are not derived from any "natural law."

The logic of the natural and exact sciences demands certainty. It depends upon premises that are true, immediate, better known than, prior to, and explanatory of the conclusions. The problem is that Aristotle himself fudged on this point: the sciences deal with what is true "for the most part" as well as with what is true "always" (see, for example, *Physics* 198b34 ff.), suggesting that it is not always possible, when working back to the first principles of scientific wisdom, to say with absolute certainty that those axiomatic points really are axiomatic (see G. E. R. Lloyd's argument in *The Revolutions of Wisdom*, pp. 135–49). It may be true that the ideal towards which the sciences are working might be eventually attained, an ideal which would settle once and for all the principles and axioms on which the natural sciences would rest, but Lloyd notes that it had not in Aristotle's day. If it is true that rhetorical and dialectical reason are tied to a reliance on common opinion, which in turn is based on everyday observation of events in the world (i.e., sense experience), and so the discourse used in the act of persuasion must accord with the regularities observed through that experience; and if it is further true that the experiential work of the natural scientist that would lead him to develop principles that are true "for the most part" does not get him to the ideal of "in every case"; then the lines that we are able to draw between the realm of the certain and the realm of the contingent are difficult to sometimes make out. Now, rhetoric acknowledges that its object – the realm of human activity, in which the lines drawn between the conventional and the natural are already difficult to make out – is one in which the appetitive drive and the reasonable drive are by definition at odds and may deflect the regularities that can be observed. So, enthymematic reason may not simply occupy a space between a purely contingent and a natural world, in which convention and nature operate in accord with one another. It may be the case that it is just not possible to distinguish where these two worlds part company, and that rhetoric has a role in the production of knowledge in both.

Like Plato's world in *Gorgias*, where it is possible to imagine a case in which one might neither do harm nor suffer harm but in which the only options that exist are *either* to do harm *or* to suffer harm based on an investigation into the available and possible outcomes (see *Gorgias*, 469b), the Aristotelian world – and the rhetoric he is building for it – is at once closed and open. It is closed, since certain natural phenomena occur repeatedly and regularly, and in which laws compel certain behaviors and in which the material circumstances of a polis (whether they are ruled by an oligarch or a tyrant, for example [see 1365b-l366a]) will cause certain observable and repeatable effects. It is closed, further, because certain conventionally established logical laws (of non-contradiction, for example) will hold true in all cases. And yet the world is at the same time open: Aristotle acknowledges that individuals will not necessarily behave in ways predicted by observation, that they will not be persuaded by logic but may have to be compelled through other more brutal (extra-discursive) means, and that conventionally established norms (discursive and legal) may be mitigated by extrinsic circumstances. And it is open, further, because the syllogisms used in scientific persuasion themselves do not fulfill the criteria of absolute certainty that reasoning from first principles would seem to require.

In 1355a 34-1355b1 Aristotle suggests that dialectic and rhetoric can each argue opposing conclusions: both can say, neutrally, both that "*x* is the proper course of action" and that "*x* is not the proper course of action." What matters here is that the "proper" conclusion is the one closest to the truth: "the underlying facts do not lend themselves equally well to the contrary views. No; things that are true and things that are better are, by their nature, practically always easier to prove and easier to believe in" (l355a37–40). At their foundation syllogisms and enthymemes both must establish that which is true in order that the rhetor understands whether he must, essentially, work more or less hard at establishing his case. But in order to establish that which is true, one must have recourse to demonstration and observation, or at the very least to some foundational "common sense" that all people have available to them, but we have seen that at least in the case of logical demonstration based on axioms (at least according to Lloyd) such a foundation is hard to come by.

As suggested by Eugene Garver, in such a world rhetoric occupies a space that at once matches "word to world," but also matches "world to word" ("Philosophy," 12–16), and in each case the match that rhetoric accomplishes must be reinvestigated either by way of rhetoric or by some other means (Garver, "Sciences," 384–8). And it is in such a world that the points of conjuncture between "natural law" and "common opinion" on the one hand, and common opinion and objective facticity on the other become most clear. Aristotle makes the point quite clearly that, in spite of the relevance of common opinion and its nearness to truth and to conventional and natural law, it is not true that whatever the majority of the polis says actually goes. Aristotle, in the *Topics* 100a–100b, notes that the *endoxa* do not require that dialectic must always follow common opinion reached by consensus of the majority. Rather, dialectic (and, in connection with it, rhetoric) should be used to grant the validity of common opinions when they tend toward the good; but if those opinions appear questionable – as when the majority endorses the consumption of unhealthful foods and the minority, a single doctor or a number of physicians, takes a dissenting opinion – dialectic and rhetoric are put to use precisely to investigate the relative merits of each opinion and when used effectively and with the long-term health of the polis in mind dialectic will reveal the superiority of the minority opinion in this case.

To go back to the point I tried to make at the outset of this section, rhetoric and other ("scientific") ways of knowing are related methodologically. The passage in 1356a–1357a – "[Rhetoric] is a branch of dialectic and similar to it . . . Neither rhetoric nor dialectic is the scientific study of any one separate object: both are faculties for providing argument"(1356a31–35) – can be read in two ways: one is that rhetoric is separate from scientific inquiry altogether, in that science deals with specific classes of objects, whereas rhetoric has mainly to do with *how* one deals with all classes of objects in specific cases or contexts. But the other way to see it suggests that while rhetoric and science are separate, they are linked, since what one does once one has "hit on a scientific principle" is to determine the specific instances of those principles, and their relevance for daily life. In effect, rhetoric cannot do without science, since science provides rhetoric with the specific classes of objects and their principles; and science cannot do without rhetoric, since the question 'so what' cannot be asked or answered – questions about relevance – without the rhetorical beginning assumption, namely that even scientific observation takes place in "specific cases;" rhetoric and science cannot be equated with one another, but they are related as to method since both deal with the observation and classification of cases and objects.

The reason why it is possible for rhetoric to "hit on a principle" is that argument about a state of affairs or the nature of an object or person is at once connected with the systematic arts / sciences, since there will be points at which they happen upon one another but also disconnected: "rhetoric . . . deals with such matters as we deliberate upon without arts or systems to guide us . . . " (1357a1–4). At the moment of the happenstance connection, according to Garver, once we have proven the specific case by explaining it so thoroughly as to be systematic, that case must then be reinserted into the system, and explained scientifically, or explained first rhetorically in order to know how this specific case allows us to understand its general application to the polis. Though rhetoric is apparently unsystematic, it nevertheless relies upon systems in place beforehand, with which the rhetor must be familiar, or must be understood as having to be inserted into a system after the speech is completed, providing the case with a more general relevance.

The discussion in 1357a, about probabilities and signs, is usually taken to divide rhetoric from science: rhetoric deals with things that are contingent (like human actions), while science deals with things that are necessary. As Garver suggests, though, it is possible to prove the specific case so completely that we do not just shrug and say, well it is possible that such and such will occur, but rather we say that such and such will certainly occur. Rhetoric hits upon principle. In order to be able to move from the contingent to the necessary – in order to say that we have rhetorically proven that such and such will necessarily occur, even though we are not dealing with scientific method – we need to have knowledge beforehand of what constitutes a principle (of a particular class of objects or phenomena). This is important to note, because what it suggests is that here science and rhetoric bear a very particular relation to one another: if the variable bears a relation to the probable as the particular bears a relation to the universal, in both one needs to establish through observation what the probable or the universal *is*. In terms of contemporary epistemology, and given what we today know about scientific observation, a connection may well be established between the contingent case and the reasoning necessary to establish whether it is probable that such a case will recur, and the case of a phenomenon under investigation and the reasoning necessary to establish whether it will behave in a manner consistent with the theory hypothesized.

Conclusions

What I have been talking about are the characteristics of rhetoric and other ways of knowing as they appear in an Aristotelian epistemology. While it may be true that a careful reading of the founding assumptions of the natural and exact sciences and the ethical deployment of rhetoric point to some methodological connections in Aristotle's system, it is not altogether clear why any of this is important for the current conjuncture in the human and the natural sciences. To simply say that the first bears upon the second is problematic: what Aristotle thought of as science is very far removed from contemporary scientific practice and the philosophies that undergird it. Moreover, the divinity that was used to explain the relation beween the natural world and the goodness of the should, and the relation between human political behavior and rationality was also used to justify the keeping of slaves and the second-class status of women. What can an analysis of Aristotelian practical knowledge tell us about our world that does not take account of these difficulties?

The answer is that it is not possible to leave these differences unremarked. But the point I am trying to make is not that Aristotle's formulations of rhetoric and the sciences have something directly to say to rhetoric and science at the turn of the twenty-first century, but that the problems Aristotle was grappling with in fourth-century Greece bear some resemblance to some of the problems that rhetoric, in its contemporary incarnations, has taken upon itself to solve right now. The human and the natural sciences of the last two centuries appear radically different from previous investigations of the human and natural worlds, but both for us and for Aristotle it was important to understand how the faculties of human understanding were adequate to the task of knowing something about the world, and what distinctions could be made, if any, between those faculties.

The practice of theory

To go back to the context with which I began, Louise Phelps for composition and Richard Bernstein in philosophy (and Roy Bhaskar in the philosophy of science) have each tried to understand the degree to which the world, as understood as the natural or material or social dimension of human activity and which proceeds by more or less regular activity, and the word, the cognitive or discursive paradigm within which we make sense of the regularities of that activity and the language we use to describe it, share something in common. And for Bernstein and Phelps, at least, the answer is that they share so much in common, and that the world is only understandable *insofar as we're able to understand it through the language we have at hand to describe it*, that we should pay primary attention to those practical means – phronesis for Phelps, praxis for Bernstein – and the degree to which they may have the capacity to explain what we think of as "the natural world" by non-scientific means. Much of the work that runs parallel to that of Phelps and Bernstein (see two fairly recent books, *The Rhetorical Turn* edited by Simons and *The Interpretive Turn* edited by Hiley et al.) makes direct reference to an Aristotelian rhetorical paradigm and extends it and its preoccupation with the contingent "to matters other than Athenian civic affairs – beyond ethics and politics to philosophy, science, and the academic disciplines in general" (Simons, *The Rhetorical Turn*, 162).

But as I have tried to make clear, rhetoric's concern with contingent affairs does not necessarily provide a warrant for extending it beyond the realm of the contingent as a means of explaining the behavior of the natural world because the separation between rhetoric and science does not do away with the contingencies of the natural world, and the methodological similarities in the two ways of knowing bear this out: we may know with greater certainty that scientific observation and testing of a biological process will yield certain knowledge than that practical observation of human behavior under certain very specific conditions will, but the "paradigm" inside which we examine the first is no less amenable to revision than that with which we examine the second. Maybe more to the point, some recent articulations of rhetoric's primacy of explanatory capacity over other more "objective" ways of knowing have suggested that such a capacity provides for human freedom in a way that scientific explanations of our behavior and surroundings cannot (see, for example, much

54

of Rorty's recent work in *Philosophical Papers 1*). Because rhetoric allows us to match "word to world," we are free to redescribe the situations within which we find ourselves and in so doing we can change those situations themselves. This, however, emphasizes the degree to which the world is describably "open" but forgets that the world is also closed to the degree that there *are* in fact degrees of certainty that we can have about certain aspects of the world, and some of these aspects are those that point to illogical and counterintuitive incidences of poverty, disease, injustice, and war in such an "open" world, the latter two incidences being ones where rhetoric would seem to have a role but the former two being ones where it would not.

Is there a way to see the strange methodological overlap of rhetorical and scientific knowledges as a way to solve the problem that the recent rhetorical turn seems not to have been able to manage? Perhaps the way to see a relation between the material world, describable scientifically and open to investigation, and a rhetorical understanding of it is to see the levels of description to parallel the divisions of knowledge established in *Ethics*. Intelligence provides both scientific and practical reasoning the categorical associations that allow sense-data to remain more than just sensation. The deployment of this faculty allows us to identify the phenomena under observation; at the first level of inquiry, science proceeds by means of observing that phenomenon under controlled conditions. This observation – and experimental testing – do not claim to produce the "laws of nature," but rather produce explanations for why it behaves in the same way in repeated observation. If the scientist is able to say that this explanation is located in the nature of the object or the structure of its system, then it must behave that way all the time, apart from our observation of it. This explanation then needs to be subjected to investigation itself – we need see whether the logical consistency of the "laws" that we have used to describe the tendency of an object or state of affairs withstand scrutiny. What we do next is to deploy the knowledge that we've created in the world of human affairs. The practical wisdom or praxis that people like Bernstein and Phelps describe as the integral human cognitive activity can be seen in an Aristotelian framework as the pivotal moment that connects scientific wisdom to the knowledge of contingent human affairs: to the extent that the knowledge produced by the classification of phenomena and the regulative principles of them is "workable" in the realm of human affairs in their particularities, this in itself produces new knowledge that may let us see that "objective" knowledge as something less than objective. Rhetoric allows us to match world to word, not just word to world.

What I am suggesting is that a more critical analysis of the intersection between scientific and contingent knowledge provides a theory of human agency that allows a connection between the situatedness of human activity and the material constraints (and the characteristics of that material and its role in the situatedness) that deflect and defer it, one that connects human activity like observation and work, to the possibility of real social change. In order to understand this connection we need to do several things. First, we should recognize that the knowledge of social forms generated rhetorically is knowledge of real entities, and that they do play a role in causing "events" that are part of the natural world. Because scientific activity is social work, that activity implicitly obeys the social conventions that have evolved normatively. This does not mean, however, that because of its obedience to social conventions it is unable to do the work it has set out to do. But the converse is also true: because science *is* able to tell us, with some success, how "the world" operates, its social conventions affect our view of that world. Scientists should see their place in such structures objectively and as the "starting points" for scientific projects, from which to ask the questions that will lead them to observe, experiment, and test. Testing new strains of tuberculosis in the center of a city leads researchers to ask rather different questions from those generated by the same kind of research at the Centers for Disease Control in Atlanta. As scientists do the work of observing and experimenting with the regularities of the world, authors similarly observe and redescribe their interpretations of it, and in each case, description guides interpretation, and those interpretations are later tested and observed, and so on. Both kinds of description – scientific and rhetorical – are reformulated, retested, redescribed in connection, and both kinds of description must take into account the real (and objectively verifiable) social effect that the location of the test has upon it.

We also need to grant the existence and the *objectivity* of social structures and behavioral patterns, which are not created by human beings, but which do preexist us. Inasmuch as we are born into families, or classes, and inasmuch as we are born male or female, we are already inside such structures. Any redescription of our selves must include the understanding – and systematic exploration – of this material circumscription *as preexistent*. The observation and description of the "behavior" of new strains of tuberculosis should come with a caveat: scientists are testing the disease under controlled conditions; they are not testing some entity called "tuberculosis," but rather are producing a constant conjunction with which to test the material reality of the disease in a particular time and place, realities that preexist the experimentation and will continue despite that testing. The corollary to this point is that the scientific testing of the disease (testing as social work) will have an effect on how the knowledge of it will be used to vaccinate the homeless. This is another way of saying that social life has a material dimension, and leaves some physical trace. We should recognize that the rhetorical / descriptive dimension must be rigorous and must be understood as yielding valuable knowledge, at the same time that we also recognize the conventions of that knowledge, and so test those conventions and their material traces.

Thirdly, the notion prevalent in much of the thinking involving the "rhetorical turn" that social interaction consists of "coping" with others (see, for example, Rorty) is limited, since we cope not only with people but also with the social structures and the physical world in which they reside. We need to find and disentangle the webs of relations in social life, and engage in explanatory critiques of the practices that sustain them: practically and pedagogically, this means that our students should see themselves as authoring social practices that can be in turn examined scientifically as well as rhetorically. Sad to say, but many male students in my own classes offer up the refrain "feminist theory is so shrill," and any number of other students, male and female, are hard pressed to say why this assessment may not be particularly felicitous or accurate, particularly given my problematizations, in the same class, of normative or institutional codes of behavior. It is necessary to have a way to convince such students that this assessment, and the language with which they offer it, produces materially and socially real effects that have measurable impact. When we say that two views of a polis conflict, we must suppose that there is something – a domain of real objects or relations existing and acting independently of their (conflicting) descriptions – *over* which they clash. Our task at least in part must be to say something about that world which does, after all, have an effect on our rhetorical assessments of it.

All of this leads to a concluding guideline, which suggests that rhetorical analysis does not render the sciences (social or physical) redundant: we may be able to "rewrite" our circumstances that change with a student's utterance of "feminist theory is so shrill," for example, but there are other material circumstances that change as a result that we cannot be aware of hermeneutically; and though we cannot understand them in a rhetorical analysis, we may observe and test those circumstances scientifically.

In short, in order to recognize that there are strategies that can be derived both from rhetoric as well as from science to understand human behavior in the world, we need to reclaim science as a method of investigation that parallels rhetoric in its method though it is distinct in its domain. If we are going to have real effects upon our worlds – rhetoric's aim – then we have to understand that there are material constraints to account for and allow these considerations and analyses to guide rhetoric as well as science. To deny this material dimension is tantamount to simply saying that any argument looks as good as any other, and leaves people saying "I know how to argue, but I'll be damned if I know how this changes anything."

To go back to rhetoric: Lois Self has argued in an essay which articulates rhetoric and *phronesis* that practical wisdom is oriented both toward the good, which requires rigorously reasoned, theoretical inquiry into the nature of the human soul in general terms, and toward the expedient, which requires an understanding of the particularities of a polis. In contrast to those who have taken issue with the likes of Grimaldi, Perelman, and others who have advocated a broadening of rhetoric to include other ways of knowing (including, in extreme cases, science [see Gross, *Rhetoric*]), her thesis suggests that Aristotle's narrow classification of the art of persuasion in *Rhetoric* actually calls for a rhetoric that is guided – both by recognizing the facticity contained in "common opinion," and by recognizing the material aspect of the polis – by theoretical and scientific knowledge. This is not to say that *Rhetoric* grants discourse theorists license to see everything as rhetorical, which is what some have accused Grimaldi and Perelman of doing. But I am suggesting that the upshot of the unacknowledged (but unimpeachable) connection between rhetoric and science is that no rhetor – Aristotle included – can do one without the other.

3

A (rhetorical) reading of the human sciences: toward antifoundationalism

In 1883, with the publication of the first and second volumes of *Introduction to the Human Sciences*, Wilhelm Dilthey endeavored to establish the human sciences within the same conceptual framework as the natural sciences – "a complex of propositions (1) whose elements are concepts that are completely defined . . . (2) whose connections are well grounded, and (3) in which finally the parts are connected into a whole for the purpose of communication" (Dilthey, *Introduction*, 57). The *Geisteswissenschaften*, because they studied human understanding first, saw the natural law as a guide for human practice, and saw the life of man incommensurable with the world without human interaction with it (*Introduction*, 56–9). That is to say, Dilthey once and for all distinguished between the natural world as behaving exterior to (or perhaps behind the back of) human cognition on the one hand, and human cognition and resultant social practice on the other. Natural science established the conceptual systems by which nature could presumably be studied and mapped; the human sciences used similar methodologies to study the possibility that such a mapping could be accomplished at all.

Much has changed in the 100 or so years since the *Introduction*'s publication. Most significantly, the natural sciences have been problematized to such an extent that the division imposed by Dilthey between the human and the natural sciences has been blurred, if not (according to some) completely effaced. In an essay on Thomas Kuhn and Charles Taylor, Joseph Rouse has gone so far as to suggest that the division between the human and natural

sciences need not be upheld at all, because the necessarily ideological study of human cognition that Thomas Kuhn has finally
shown to exist in the natural sciences as much as in the human
sciences renders the division redundant. Dilthey's division, initially intended to suggest a relation between the *Geisteswissenschaften*'s concern with praxis and the guiding conceptual principles of the natural sciences, has in fact led to the subsumption –
for some, at least (see Gross, *Rhetoric*; Shotter, *Cultural Politics*) – of
the natural to the human sciences. The establishment of the division has led to its own collapse in terms very unlike those Dilthey
might have anticipated. And it has been this collapse that has led
to what in contemporary terms has been called the antifoundational paradigm, which suggests that no more than the human
sciences are the natural sciences able to provide us undisputed
knowledge of a world (or a truth) "out there" because human
understanding, and thus conceptual knowledge, is itself a product of human construction and is thus contingent, rendering the
"foundations" upon which science once rested – even in Dilthey's
configuration – flimsy at best and nonexistent at worst.

What I want to explore in this chapter is the extent to which the
dissolution of the natural / human science division actually holds
up under closer scrutiny. In examining the relationship between
the natural and the human sciences – in contemporary terms as
well as in Dilthey's – I want to suggest that there is a connection
between the contemporary understanding of the human sciences,
based on "hermeneutics" or interpretation, and scientific, conceptual knowledge precisely by way of rhetoric. The field of rhetoric
marks the point of overlap between a study of the materiality of
extra-discursive phenomena on the one hand and human understanding of those phenomena and their role (and that role's materiality) in such a study. I want to investigate the four traditional
nodes in the contemporary debate in the human sciences: to what
extent the human sciences bear any resemblance to the natural
sciences; what degree of certainty knowledge generates through
the human sciences; if we grant that there is a hermeneutic component to the natural sciences, what degree of certainty can be
generated through these sciences; and whether an analysis of the
"rhetorics" of the human and natural sciences can provide us
with any new information about how the world works.

For my purposes in this chapter, the primary question is this:

can we go back to Aristotle's link between the epistemic function of rhetoric and the knowledge generated by other kinds of knowledge to provide a model that allows us to understand "hermeneutics" and science as distinct and yet integrally linked? If the answer to this question is "yes' – and I think that it is – then can we say that inasmuch as there is an interpretive component to the natural sciences (that is, that there is a need to build discursive constraints in such a way that we can reach agreement from within certain vocabularies), there is also a material component to interpretation (that is, constraints that exist as objects of knowledge *about which* we find the need to construct discursive constraints)?

In this, my intention is four-fold: (1) to trace the rhetorical turn in the human and natural sciences; (2) to make a preliminary definition of the human sciences through a discussion of Dilthey and in so doing, begin to draw the links between the *geisteswissenschaften* and rhetorical analysis; (3) to examine the "weak" version of science, in which the interpretive dimension is paramount and the "strong" version, in which science proceeds in spite of interpretation; and (4) to suggest one possible scenario in which scientific investigation and hermeneutic interpretation function in tandem. My hypothesis is that we can reformulate the human sciences in such a way as to maintain the significance of hermeneutics to the scientific enterprise *without* having to suggest that hermeneutics makes science somehow "suspect"; and that rhetoric, inasmuch as it functions to account for "things which might be other," also accounts for things "in relation to other, more systematic" forms of knowledge. My aim is to reconfigure the antifoundational paradigm in such a way as to suggest that the human sciences do not render the natural sciences redundant, and that rhetorical knowledge and the human action that follows from it are at one and the same time scientific and contingent, and that – following Dilthey – science requires hermeneutics as a guide as much as hermeneutics requires science.

The human sciences and a role for rhetoric

In an essay that examines the particularly problematic place of rhetoric in the contemporary world, D. P. Gaonkar suggests that throughout its history "rhetoric" has felt the need to attach itself to other disciplines. That is, since Aristotle suggested in the *Rhetoric* that oratory is the art of persuasion in "any given case," rhetoricians have been at pains to describe the outlines of the specific cases in which rhetoric can be used, and in doing so have grasped at Aristotle's sometimes tenuous connection of rhetoric with dialectic, politics and ethics in the early chapters of *Rhetoric* and his other works. Gaonkar's essay is worth examining in some detail, because in its frank acknowledgement of rhetoric's "insecurity" and its attempt to insert itself into other epistemic disciplines, it also points to significant ways in which rhetoric can be seen as a method well suited to inquiry in the human sciences. The logic of Gaonkar's essay suggests that if we understand rhetoric's assertion of itself as supplementary to other fields of knowledge, we might push that assertion as far as it will go and suggest that it is these fields' *need* for a rhetoric (or a practical deployment of the knowledges they themselves autonomously produce) that brings about rhetoric's (epistemic) eruption. Of course, this is not Gaonkar's point: his claim – that "the fortunes of rhetoric, more than any other discipline, turn on the roll of the cultural dice" and that "rhetoric has good days and bad days, mostly bad days" (though this decade is one of its better "days") – is much more modest, and his pointing to the attractiveness of alternative histories of rhetoric is meant to show their oddness. Still, the fact that he has to do this at all suggests that rhetoric is instrumental to other forms of knowledge, most particularly in the sciences (and, for my purposes here, in the human sciences), to which rhetoric claims allegiance.

Gaonkar argues that the supplementary tradition in rhetoric comes about in part because rhetoric rests on public knowledge or common opinion, but also because it establishes itself as a set of rules through which to persuade the public. That is, it has both a formal and a social function. By foregrounding this dual purpose in rhetoric it becomes apparent that we have to determine whether or not rhetoric has an epistemic function: to what extent does rhetoric work to generate this public knowledge and not simply organize it for dissemination? Gaonkar goes on to say that the tradition of "invention" in rhetoric (from Aristotle through Cicero and Quintilian on to the handbooks of the eighteenth and nineteenth centuries) suggests that there is such an epistemic function, but he uses the "rhetoric" of Burke to problematize it.

While rhetoric may have an epistemic function, the aim of rhetoric is the generation of *local* truths, while it is up to dialectic to generate broader truths and realities: "Although dialectical critique occurs in the scenic order of truth with a view toward transcending the conflict intrinsic to opinion, the rhetorical critique occurs in the moral order of action with a view toward managing and transforming conflicting opinions in accordance with the exigencies of a given situation" (Gaonkar, "Rhetoric," 345). But this is not clearly the case. It is true that rhetoric is a separate art from dialectic, its everyday counterpart inasmuch as dialectic is reasoned inquiry through discourse into things which can be other than what they currently admit. But it is also true that rhetoric should also be reasonable, and should proceed by way of demonstration and definition insofar as possible. So while in general it may be the case that the place of rhetoric is the forum while the place of dialectic may be the symposium, and that the aim of the former may be related to a dispute in a particular place and time while the latter may be related to dispute in general and extra-temporal terms, both admit of the same duality, namely, of an epistemic and a formal function.

This duality is characterized as the "escape from 'mere' rhetoric" through the "philosophical move in restoring the sophistic tradition" (347). The duality of the epistemological and the formal function of rhetoric has been noted by Todorov and de Man as the two distinct but related concepts of rhetoric: "They are rhetoric as persuasion and rhetoric as trope," which are derived from two related but distinct human characteristics, humans as symbol-using animals (Burke) and humans as living under conditions of plurality (Arendt). The human condition is such that immediate experience is by necessity mediated by cognition, and so that experience – the intransitive dimension of physical objects and phenomena – is not directly available. Humans are creatures of cognition and of language, and as such humans are in need of a way to negotiate the divergent possibilities that emerge from this mediated and polyglot world. It is persuasion that provides humans with the tools necessary to immediately deal with their world, and as such it provides the most immediate access to a set of phenomena and states of affairs that are not directly accessible at all. But as de Man and Todorov point out, because we have provided language with a set of rules in order that it will be comprehensible to as many interlocutors as possible in any single situation (or across any number of disparate situations), we also need to allow that language will operate relatively autonomously to the intransitive as well as the social dimension of human affairs.

The upshot of this for rhetoric and the "rhetorical turn" in the human sciences is that it may not be the case that "it seems unreasonable to invoke Aristotle to claim that rhetoric has an epistemic function" (Gaonkar, "Rhetoric," 346). It is true that dialectic operates at a farther remove than rhetoric from the immediate situations in which humans find themselves and out of which they sometimes must extricate theselves with some urgency. But rhetoric operates at the juncture of tropological and epistemic knowledge in the same way that dialectic does. Further, rhetoric acknowledges its dual nature in a way that dialectic does not, and it also acknowledges – not in *Rhetoric* explicitly, though certainly in *Nichomachean Ethics*, *Topics* and other works – its relation to other forms of knowledge that dialectic does not. As we shall see, Dilthey also acknowledges the mutually guiding relationship between the local realm of being (the sense-experience that is worked upon by human cognition and which is studied by the human sciences) and the broader, more universalizing realm of the natural sciences. It may be true, in other words, that rhetoric by itself may not have an epistemic function. But the corollary to the point may be that the knowledge generated by the universal disciplines – those operating in the "scenic realms" – may not even be recognizable as knowledge without the ability of rhetoric to place that knowledge locally.

Gaonkar also claims that Aristotle might not be the best authority to invoke in order to suggest an epistemic function for rhetoric "unless one is prepared to collapse the distinction between knowledge and belief" ("Rhetoric," 346). It is not clear, however, that Gaonkar has the distinction right to begin with, or that the texts Gaonkar glosses make a necessary connection between knowledge and belief.

Now, the distinction between knowledge and belief is made by Aristotle in *Rhetoric* (I.1–2), as well as in *Nichomachean Ethics* (VI), *Topics* (164a-b), and elsewhere (*Prior Analytics* 46, 64; *Posterior Analytics* 71–2, 75, 76–7). But Gaonkar's reliance on the one text (i.e., *Rhetoric*) leads him to ignore the connection between public opinion (the *endoxa*) and the *koina archai*, princples related to those from which the sciences also work. Both the *koina* and the *endoxa* originate in immediate sense-experience; and while the latter organize that experience in terms of how it may be put to immediate use in the polis, the former organize it in terms of its general characteristics outside the immediate situation. Rhetoric, then, is the discursive organization of sense-experience in accordance with the natural state of affairs at a given time and place, and in accordance with the conventional laws and practices in play at the time. Dialectic (as well as, to a greater degree, the theoretical and scientific disciplines – *sophia* and *episteme*) is the discursive (or, in the case of the other disciplines, extra-discursive) organization of sense experience in accordance with known first principles and indisputable truths. For Gaonkar, the second of these is associated with "knowledge," the first with "belief": he cites Bitzer to suggest that rhetoric "is a general art consisting not of knowledge about substantive fields but a flexible system of formal and prudential devices – topics, tropes and figures, inferential schemes, probabilities, prudential rules, and so on" ("Rhetoric," 344). But what he fails to recognize is that the discursive, prudential arrangement of sense-experience must be done at the very least against a background of knowledge (given that the *archai* and *endoxa* are pre-scientific and pre-rhetorical knowledges *derived* from sense-experience, not the experience itself) or, perhaps more significantly, such an argument must at some point recognize that the common opinion that it works to generate has a basis in (extra-discursive) knowledge (albeit perhaps dialectical if not immediately scientific or theoretical knowledge). Gaonkar notes that this property of rhetoric marks its psychology (as glossed by Aristotle in the second book of *Rhetoric*) as different from "reductive" psychology "that would try to see what is *behind* what people say and attempt to reduce anger, for instance, to *something else*, something hidden" ("Rhetoric," 346; emphasis in original); whereas rhetorical psychology is immediate and based on "public opinion [which] is the first and last datum" (ibid.).

The failure to distinguish rhetoric's situation between knowledge and opinion bears directly on any discussion of the human sciences. It would be tempting to suggest that what divides the human from the natural sciences is the following. The natural sciences treat sense experience as properties of a natural world. Methodologically, they attempt to generalize those properties to the extent that the natural world becomes known by its behavior not as it bears directly on the human senses but rather as it replicates a pattern of characteristics. The human sciences, by contrast, are more concerned with the sense experiences themselves and how these bear on the human capacity to organize them. But to reiterate, this throws up a problem for both rhetoric and the human sciences. While both are mainly concerned with the human capacity to cognitively (and, in the case of rhetoric, discursively) organize sense-experience for its deployment in contemporary conjunctures rather than on the taxonomies organized by conceptual knowledge itself, both are dependent upon and at the same time necessary for the theoretical sciences. Rhetoric and the theoretical sciences both organize knowledge, though of different kinds; but both require an understanding of the pre-scientific first principles from which sense-data are gathered to begin with. And while rhetoric, by its nature, may not reason all the way back to first principles in its enthymematic arguments, those principles must be available for deliberation either through dialectical reasoning or by scientific and theoretical investigation. But knowledges generated by scientific and theoretical means must be disseminated both to the scientific and sophistic community as well as to the public at large, and so they require a rhetoric with which to do so. Belief does not exist without knowledge: where you have one (*endoxa* or *archai*) you have the other. Rhetoric exists in a symbiotic relationship to the other knowledges as do, I will suggest presently, the human and natural sciences.

Gaonkar notes that there are two versions of rhetoric's history implicit in calls for a "return to rhetoric" or in the constant reminder that the human (and natural) sciences have taken a "rhetorical turn." The first is its manifest history, in which historians of rhetoric begin with Plato's argument against the first sophistic, through Aristotle, Cicero, Quintilian, and then on to Augustine, Boethius, Ramus, Bacon, and culminating with the empiricist tradition of Whately. This is "the history of rhetoric conceived as 'supplement,' a history of obscure places, unfamiliar names, and forgotten texts" ("Rhetoric," 348). The other history is the "hidden" history, which also begins with the argument against the sophists, but in this case the battle is not "won" by Plato's Socrates or by Aristotle, but is called a draw, and it is joined again and again throughout the history of western philosophy, most obviously at "crisis points" or "paradigm shifts" such as, says Gaonkar, the one we are in the midst of now (363). This history becomes submerged after Aristotle conceives of rhetoric as a supplement to various fields (dialectic, politics, ethics) and only resurfaces *as rhetoric* with Kenneth Burke. With rhetoric relegated to the status of supplement to philosophical (read "dialectic") knowledge, its capacity for invention is pared down to nothing, and becomes the province of a few discursive practices and formal devices during times of dispute. Burke "extended" the hidden history at the expense of the manifest history, recovering the rhetorical force of "identification" in such writers as Bentham, Marx, Carlyle, Machiavelli and others. Where Burke recovered the forgotten fathers (and, rarely, mothers) of this other rhetoric, John Nelson and Allan Megill project themselves (and the "rhetoric of inquiry" school at Iowa) forward as the inheritors of the (hidden) rhetorical tradition by noting it is the "Iowa school" that most clearly noted the rhetorical turn in human and scientific inquiry and which has gone farthest in working out the rhetorical nature of the turn itself.

What Gaonkar notes here – in the same way that Pat Bizzell and Bruce Herzberg did when putting together their widely used rhetoric anthology entitled *The Rhetorical Tradition* – is that rhetoric's fortunes (and rhetoric's history) are tied to questions of the status of knowledge and its discursive and material constraints (see Bizzell and Herzberg, *Tradition*, 14 for one example). But these questions are always asked in terms of either / or dichotomies. The manifest history of rhetoric is characterized by rhetoric's gradual banishment from the world of philosophy, begun with Aristotle's placing it at a halfway point between formal system of figures and an epistemic system for invention and ending with the Scots' complete division between form and content, with rhetoric on the side of form, supplementing objective knowledge with beauty. The hidden history of rhetoric functions in much the same way, only this time rhetoric is seen as the only form of knowledge – again, because of Aristotle's initial "supplementary" move – able to mediate the subject / object dichotomies, but repressed because such a messy mediation indicated the shortcomings of other fields. But whether one reads the manifest history or the hidden history, one understands that rhetoric's banishment in the first and its mediation in the second implies a need for rhetoric. As Gaonkar implies, philosophers would not be so determined to marginalize rhetoric if it was not seen as somehow integral (and threatening) to their own pursuits; and he points out (following Derrida and Jasper Neel *vis-à-vis* Plato) that the marginal and problematic status of rhetoric is evidence of its importance. Gaonkar notes that if you "extract [rhetoric] from that to which it is a supplement or from that within which it is embedded . . . it evaporates" ("Rhetoric," 360), though I would suggest that it is equally as difficult (though certainly not impossible) to understand the importance of the theoretical or scientific fields (those to which rhetoric is a supplement) without rhetoric. Those fields would not disappear, but they would find a need to recuperate rhetoric if only to point to it as something alien.

If it is possible to see rhetoric not as a supplement but rather as an integral way of knowing that functions alongside other forms of knowledge, then it can be seen as epistemic, since it (a) it has a material force and (b) it has a "figural" dimension that works against the material dimension in productive but also highly problematic ways. That is, rhetoric works as a way of knowing that because of its connection to the exigencies of immediate time- and space-constraints acknowledges those constraints and examines them insofar as possible in connection with scientific observation, for example, or dialectical reasoning; and – again because of those exigencies – functions relatively autonomously to those material conditions in such a way that it may approximate or closely predict the conduct of human affairs but cannot do so precisely. If rhetoric, on the other hand, is supplementary to other ways of knowing (that is, if it is not autonomous but an "element" of other fields), then its relation to those other fields is two-fold: it operates as a means to convey knowledge, and it operates as a means to study the potential hindrances to that conveyance. If we follow Gaonkar's own (postmodern) tendency to investigate the logic of supplementarity to its farthest point, it becomes clear that this second alternative is unsatisfactory. Still, both ways of conceiving rhetoric and the rhetorical turn provide a way to see rhetoric and the human sciences as linked. Both see a material dimension to human affairs as well as a need to "understand" or "interpret" or "convey" the phenomena and states of affairs at a particular time and place with a relation to their conceptual organization; and both understand human life as contingent (and thus subject to change) and constrained by conventions that work both centrifugally against that change and centripetally (by dint of language's relative autonomy to the materiality of the world) toward it.

On the nature of the human sciences

I want to turn now to Wilhelm Dilthey's initial definition of the human sciences to pinpoint the convergences between a rhetorical understanding of the world, as Gaonkar has (at some points inadvertently) done, and a social scientific one. Though Dilthey excludes rhetoric itself from the realm of the human sciences (along with all of the practicing arts, what Aristotle called *techne*, which involve production), his notion of the object of study for the human sciences is in accord with the object of rhetorical understanding. In the first book of the *Introduction to the Human Sciences*, he notes that

[t]he capacity for understanding operative in the human sciences lies in the whole person; great achievements in the human sciences do not proceed from strength of intellect alone but from a richness and power of personal life. This mental activity is fascinated and satisfied by what is singular and factual in the human world, apart from any further goal of knowing this world as a totality. Here the apprehension [of facts] is connected with a practical interest in evaluating and [in establishing] ideals and rules.

Given these fundamental relationships, the individual has a dual point of departure for reflecting on society. He consciously carries out his activity in this whole, forms rules for that activity, and seeks conditions for it in the system of the human world. On the other hand, however, he assumes the perspective of a contemplative intellect and seeks to grasp this totality cognitively. (89)

In that the rhetor is actively involved in *producing* a discourse that will persuade his audience to take a political position or to take a particular course of action, and in that he uses rhetoric as a tool for the production of such a discourse, then the rhetor and the human scientist engaged in self-understanding are unalike. But rhetoric's endpoint is the production of discourse. The rhetor is able to produce a discourse only after a thoroughgoing analysis of his audience, the situation at hand, and the discourse he has at his disposal. Such analysis involves both the "apprehension of facts" and the "practical interest" in seeking "conditions for it in the system of the human world." There is, in other words, a dual methodology in both rhetorical and human scientific analysis that combines factual / universal (that is, "objective") knowledge on the one hand with subjective and contingent (i.e., discursive) knowledge on the other; or, in Gaonkar's terms, a way to knowledge on the one hand and belief on the other.

In a lecture on Dilthey's categorization of the human sciences, Walter Sokel notes that the human sciences occupied something like a mid-point between the natural and physical sciences and the arts (the productive sciences) "by drawing boundaries for [the human sciences] on both sides. In delimiting [them] from the arts," Dilthey "sought to establish credentials for them as sciences. But within the sciences, he sought to carve out a special subterritory for [them] that would be peculiarly their own"(2). If we go back to Barbara Warnick's delineation of the five ways of knowing established in Aristotle's *Nichomachean Ethics*, it is clear that the rhetorical arts, as *techne*, were closely related to politics, one of the practical arts, as *phronesis*. Both the technical arts and the practical arts are, in that scheme, something like the culmination of human knowledge because they make use of theoretical and scientific knowledge by working back, insofar as possible in a public forum, to principles by way of those sciences (demonstrative reasoning and observation) in order to analyze the audience and the situations of the immediate rhetorical context. But because they were also practical arts, the rhetor understood the exigencies of the moment and acknowledged them by selectively making use of those theoretical and scientific knowledges according to the situation at hand and the composition of the polis to which he was talking. Dilthey's formulation of the human sciences, by placing them midway between the practical arts (*techne*) and the scientific disciplines (*episteme*), makes the human sciences – in their two-fold appeals to truth and objectivity and the exigencies of social life – into what looks like, in the Aristotelian scheme from the sixth book of *Nichomachean Ethics*, a *phronesis*.

What further distinguishes the human from the natural sciences is the subject matter of each. "The practice regarding these disciplines as a unity distinct from the natural sciences is rooted in the depth and totality of human self-consciousness" apart from human consciousness of the natural world. The natural world is characterized by its "mechanical course of natural change which at the outset already contains everything that follows from it," whereas the human world is characterized by "acts of will [which] exert force and involve sacrifices, whose meaning is evident to the individual in his experience and which actually produce something. Acts of will generate a development in the person and in mankind that is more than the empty and tedious recapitulation in consciousness of the course of nature" (*Introduction*, 58–9). Presumably, the natural world will operate whether or not humans apprehend it or actively seek to observe its (ir)regularities. The natural sciences have as their aim the observation of the natural world *as if* those undertaking the analysis (i.e., humans) were not operating upon it. The human sciences are positioned midway between study of the natural world (as if it were uninhabited) and the highly self-conscious study of the products of human activity. They take, as their object of study, the immediate moments of the lived life that are cognitively and intuitively responsible for the possibility of observing the physical world on the one hand and the possibility of producing autonomous, constructed objects on the other. Dilthey calls this the "psychophysical life-unit," which involves understanding the human as an organism, part of the physical / biological world on the one hand, and the social, extra-objective world on the other. The object of study for the human sciences is the materially and cognitively constrained individual acting in response to and actively manipulating those constraints.

Yet inasmuch as the human sciences have a distinct object of study from the natural sciences, their methodology conforms to Dilthey's general idea of that of the natural and physical sciences. The *Wissenschaften* have as their aim the systematic and complete description of some (particular) aspect of the world whose aim is cognitive and conceptual. The "sciences" seek to *understand* that area of the natural (or human) world they set out to investigate rather than to produce some artefact from it, or to morally or politically persuade a polis to one or another view of it. But still, the "aims of the human sciences – namely, to apprehend what is singular and individual in socio-historical reality, to recognize the uniformities operative in its formation, and to establish goals and rules for its further development – can be attained only through the work of the intellect, i.e., by means of analysis and abstraction" (79). In the same way that the *Naturwissenschaften* aim to understand the uniformities in the natural world, and to establish rules for the observation and testing of the phenomena that comprise it, the *Geisteswissenschaften* aim to understand the uniformities that exist in the human interaction with that world, and establish rules for testing those social and individual human realities if only self-reflexively methodological ones. The point to bear in mind is that, like the practice of *phronesis* in the Aristotelian scheme, though the object of knowledge of the human sciences differs from that of the natural sciences (in the same way that the object of *phronesis* – the understanding and practice of lived life in the immediacy of the polis – was different from the object of *episteme* – the systematic observation of the natural and material elements of the world that constrained that lived life), their method of study is the same.

Walter Sokel notes that "[f]ollowing the Cartesian dualistic tradition of Continental thought, Dilthey assumes a substantive difference between material or physical and mental reality" ("Dilthey," 3). While this observation is partly true, it also belies the blurring of the subject matter Dilthey himself recognized. He notes that

[o]n the one hand, nature and its constitution can govern this psychophysical unit in the shaping of purposes themselves; on the other hand, nature qua system of means for attaining these ends codetermines the psychophysical unit . . . [Nevertheless], the purposes of the human world have their repercussions on nature or on the earth, which man in this sense regards as his dwelling and in which he is busily making himself at home. These retroactive influences on nature are also dependent on using the laws of nature.   (*Introduction*, 69)

Dilthey effectively casts doubt – along Kantian lines – on the certainty that can be provided by the physical sciences, because the "retroactive influences" are themselves products of the psychophysical unit and the construction of response. What we recognize as laws are the constructions of those psychophysical units. Of course, these constructed laws are all we have, and until a more persuasive hypothesis can be put forward that better explains the phenomena under observation, we continue our observation based upon the current one. What we are left with, though, is the certainty of *inner* experience, "a special realm of experiences which has its independent origin and its own material in inner experience which is, accordingly, the subject matter of a special science of experience" ("Dilthey," 6l). Like Aristotle's *doxa*, the immediate experience of lived life is the nearest one gets to certainty; and though the physical sciences, like *episteme*, provide us with conceptual knowledge, that knowledge proceeds by way of hypotheses and observation, which brings us immediately back to the realm of sense experience. In order to avoid coming back full circle, we need to investigate the process of observation first. In a direct reversal of the hierarchy set up by Baconian science and Ramist dialectic – which set detached, scientific observation upon the throne of reason, and which subjugated the practical sciences such as rhetoric and ethics to its rule – Dilthey sets up those sciences that are related directly with sense experience and human apprehension upon philosophy's throne, and demotes the physical sciences to the role of attendants. And yet – as I have suggested – there is a certain ambiguity to this reversal, because of Dilthey's placement of the human sciences alongside rather than directly above the natural sciences. Their methodology is presumably the same, and – through the vicious circle of human agency, which at once alters and is constrained by the material reality which the natural sciences presumably provide access to – the one is unavailable without the other. The natural sciences do not so much serve the human sciences as act reciprocally with them; or, if the human sciences are sitting somewhere above the physical sciences, the latter are forever whispering into the ear of the *Geisteswissenschaften* with advice on the best hypothesis available about the constraints within which they must work. Going back to Gaonkar's essay, by correlating the rhetorical-critical function in Aristotle with the understanding offered by Dilthey's human sciences, we might suggest that human science (here substituting for rhetoric) "cannot posit a substantive identity of its own because it has no subject matter of its own; on the other hand, its functional involvement with" immediate experience (here substituting for *doxa*) "threatens its formal identity by . . . an 'overburdening of content'" (Gaonkar, "Rhetoric," 345), making it at once burdened with content and empty of it, provided it does not work alongside the hypotheses offered by the other sciences.

Still, Dilthey's human scientific understanding of "the world" *as scientific* is also partially at odds with his attempt to distinguish his task from the Cartesian or the Kantian project. Descartes's axiomatic realm was the *res cogitans*, intellectual thought. As we have seen, Dilthey's human sciences operate intellectually upon sense experience. But Dilthey's axiomatic realm, the life of the individiual (the psychophysical), the *Erleben*, is closer to what Descartes might call the *res sentiens* or *res experiens*. Dilthey was after a way to intertwine the will of human agency and the feeling that accompanies the interiorization of sense experience with the cognitive understanding of the phenomena under observation. This ran counter to Kant's compartmentalization of human inner life – thinking and knowing, will and morality, feeling and aesthetics (the subject of his critiques) – and united the mental and emotional faculties in such a way that the subject for the human sciences was what Gadamer called a life-world. These faculties formed a "nexus" or "structure" (Neville's translations) in which all the disparate elements of the psyche functioned together interdependently. Both human and non-human nature appear to us in the nexus or structure of the psyche (*Zusammenhang*), but in nonhuman nature (the intransitive realm of objects and phenomena separate from human conceptual knowledge of them) the textures and structures are constructed by us. That is to say, in the interconnection of the inner life of the human mind during the interiorization of sense experience and the sense experience itself, the structuration of that experience of phenomena is entirely of human (cognitive) construction. So the intellectual faculties through which we presumably form sense of the phenomena in question and the non-intellectual *Erlebnis* are always already formulated "by us" (*hinzugedacht*). The rub here is that in such a "structuration" of the experience human science means to explain, even the intellectual "strand" of the *Erlebnis* must operate, by Dilthey's admission, upon "the mechanical course of natural change" upon which human agency does not act. The structure provided by human cognition with which to study the natural component of human affairs must in turn be studied by some other means, and the most likely candidate for such a study would be the natural sciences. This problem is much like the one Plato had in distinguishing the natural and the conventional law in *Gorgias* for the purposes of determining where dialectic and ethics could begin and where scientific demonstration left off, a problem that stemmed at least in part from rhetoric's own ambivalent position between the certain and the contingent. It also connects to Gaonkar's point that even Aristotle's *Rhetoric* distinguishes between knowledge and belief by pointing to their common basis in the *doxa*. That is, Dilthey's structuration of experience in the human sciences is differentiated from the intellectual operations in the objective sciences while that same structuration depends on the overlap of (1) the methodologies both the natural and the human sciences share, and (2) the faculties that are brought to bear upon the constructed component of the *Zusammenhang* and the conceptually given component of it (that is, the immediate object of knowledge). This may be due in part to Dilthey's low regard for the objective sciences' contact (or lack of contact) with the practical world. He claims that the natural sciences lack a pragmatic, experiential element, proceeding entirely by way of theory and hypothesis, while the human sciences are more intimately connected with material, practical life. Of course, the natural sciences do proceed by way of theory and hypothesis, but the experimentation and observation involved in the scientific testing of those hypotheses would seem to contradict Dilthey's understanding of them. It is also true that Dilthey's notion of *Erlebnis* itself could be used to supplement his impoverished understanding of the natural sciences, since all lived life contains strands of both the intellectual as well as the experiential (though it would presumably be the intellectual that would occupy a predominant position in the natural sciences). Still, the point that seems to be missed in Dilthey's scheme is that both the natural and the human sciences – like rhetoric and dialectic as well as phronesis in the classical scheme – proceed by observation and testing (regardless of the conceptual constructedness of the systems used to categorize the experience involved in that testing) as well as by a more immediate concern with the exigencies of the situation itself.

Of course, there is another problem: how do we "test" or "observe" lived life? If experience can only be lived, but lived life is itself accessible only through an articulation of the *Zusammenhang* which is also lived and not produced, then *Erlebnis* would seem to be as inaccessible as the lived life of *phronesis*. But in the same way that Aristotle allowed for the accessibility of *phronesis* through the analysis of rhetorical acts – through the products that were the result of the ethics and conduct of the praxes of the lives of the individual members of the polis – Dilthey allows for the analysis of human lived life as it is expressed and projected in acts, utterances, but more importantly, signs, institutions, works of thought (i.e., non-fiction prose) and works of art. The human sciences take as their object, then, not the direct experiences of individuals, but rather those things that have issued from the life of the mind which have assumed an independent, "objective" life of their own. Of course, the "issues" of mental life are themselves at least in part material – they have been produced out of material that has been gathered from "nature" and transformed by human work – and would as a result seem to require not only "interpretation" but also explanation, which would determine the properties of the object, the natural and produced characteristics of the object, those properties that would allow us to understand the object *as* an object distinguishable from other objects. So, the human sciences would seem to have to proceed in part by interpretation and in part by *semiosis*, for as Sokel suggests in his lecture on Dilthey, "Objective Mind is for him an infinitely complex system of signs," and so "the mental sciences [his term for the human sciences] thus boil down to semiotics and hermeneutics" ("Dilthey," 7). It involves an identification of the elements of the product of human psychophysical life, and an interpretation of the meaning of that product through an intellectual / *erlebnicht* method of analysis.

That analysis proceeds in a three stage process, whose components are, according to Sokel,

(1) Inner Experience [*Erfahrung*], which cannot be grasped immediately; (2) Expression or signification [sometimes referred to by the term *Vorstellung*] by which experience utters and objectifies itself, and which comprises everything we call culture and civilization; (3) Understanding [*Verstehen*], the area of the mental sciences, which results from a successful reading of expressions. ("Dilthey," 7)

Sokel goes on to say that "while the physical sciences rely on hypothesis, verification by experiment, and translation into the language of quantification, the mental sciences have . . . to interpret" (ibid.). If the Kantian "thing-in-itself" is associated with inner experience, which for both Dilthey and for Kant is conceptually ungraspable, expression or signification are so graspable. But these expressions can be analyzed for their materiality and their difference from other objects and phenomena through a process of "hypothesis, verification by experiment, and translation into the language of quantification" (and, perhaps *must* be so analyzed) in the second stage of analysis prior to their availability to the "area of the mental sciences," namely, understanding, at all. In that rhetoric proceeds – in the scheme laid out by Aristotle in *Topics, Nichomachean Ethics, Prior* and *Posterior Analytics* as well as *Rhetoric* – to understand the prudential action to be taken through an oration designed in part to analyze the individual members of the polis who will be undertaking the praxis and in part to analyze the material constraints in place for the members of the polis; so the human sciences proceed by linking explanation of the material (in the rhetorical scheme, the extra-discursive) component of an artefact which can reveal human mental activity to a hermeneutics or an understanding of the extra-material (in the rhetorical scheme, the discursive) component.

There are two final points I want to make about Dilthey and his conception of the human sciences before I move on to more recent characterizations of them by (in this chapter) Joseph Rouse *vis-à-vis* Thomas Kuhn, Richard Harvey Brown, and (in the next chapter) Richard Rorty. These two points have to do with the capacity of the human sciences for shaping future human action, and, in turn, for social change; and it is social change, and the connection between the social sciences (and hermeneutics, phronesis) and social change (and praxis) that will concern me in the central part of this book. For Dilthey, experimental science fails to understand the human mind because it tries to determine the macro-structures of that mind as natural phenomena only. The experimental sciences that render human experience as the collection of biochemical and electrochemical processes and impulses in the human body and brain may be able to gauge accurately the physical workings of that body; but they fail to see the macro-structural components of the human mind as having *meaning*. The decisions humans make are in part the workings of the bio- and electrochemical body in response to sense data, in the same way that Aristotle described the pre-scientific data of the *archai* as interiorized (or potentially interiorizable) sense data. But these decisions are also made in part on the basis of values, ideas, faiths, morality and so on, and these cannot be explained only biologically or chemically (that is, experimentally). It may be possible to predict the behavior of a biological entity under controlled circumstances, just as it is possible to understand the characteristics of certain inert compounds and chemicals under controlled conditions, because these objects (including the non-human, biological object) do not behave according to macro-structures *other* than the chemical / biological. But because human activity is at once chemical / biological (that is, natural) as well as cultural and ethical (that is, discursive and conventional), the possibility of prediction is always deflected, and prediction is never completely possible.

Of course, as I have tried to suggest, the life-processes of humans cannot be studied in themselves to yield the macro-structures that in part determine human activity. We have at our disposal the artefacts that human activity produces. We may not be able to directly explain the actions of a Goethe, for instance, because he is, obviously, unavailable for study, and because even if he were available his mind would not be directly accessible. Yet we do have Goethe's works. In a chapter that was originally intended as part of a multi-volume work on the human sciences (included in the *Introduction* as the first section of Book 4 in the "Berlin" draft, 466–9), Dilthey explains the problem in terms of the difference between descriptive psychology, which he favored, and explanatory psychology. Descriptive psychology does not try to explain human activity in terms of scientific laws (the macro-structural understanding of bio- and electro-chemical patterns characteristic in human life) but rather seeks to describe, with as much precision as possible, the signs and objectifications of particular individuals and groups, such as language, art, recorded actions and so on. From these artefacts – from, for example, the collection of works written by Goethe, along with what we know of him from biographies, letters, published and unpublished accounts, and so on – the descriptive psychologist infers the mind expressed in the available constellation. One can begin to see the connection between Dilthey's methodology of the human sciences (here manifest in descriptive psychology) and a rhetorical analysis. In ways similar to Aristotle's link between the *techne* and *phronesis* – in which rhetoric was seen as an art whose products (orations) were put to political and ethical use in the polis, which in turn had to be materially understood insofar as possible in order for the art to be deployed – the human sciences were seen by Dilthey as ways to treat manifestations of human life as documents (the products of a *techne*) which are to be read and interpreted in order to retrieve from them the intent of the source (the lived or practical life). It is through the human sciences that one is able to piece together, from the various traces available, the coherence or *Zusammenhang* that originated those traces to form a single (or, in the case of a culture, collective) life world. In much the same way Gaonkar does, one can argue the connection between rhetoric and the human sciences as methodologies whose intentions are to outline the various strands, both material and discursive, out of which a particular work – rhetoric – might have been originated. The methodology of the human sciences maintains the distinction, from the Aristotelian scheme, between rhetoric as *techne* and the lived life of the producer or receiver of an oration as phronesis, since it takes as its object of study the oration but also notes the context within which that oration must have taken place. As such, the methodology of the human sciences – in terms different from those which Dilthey might have acknowledged – must be scientific, but must also include data gathered through the natural, not the human, sciences (in the same way that both rhetoric and politics saw themselves as working back to the first causes that were also the province of *sophia* and *episteme*). These data act in part as the constraints and in part as components of the discursive (i.e., conventional) historical micro-structures of the individual action to be described. While it might be too much to equate Gaonkar's "belief" with the human scientific term "understanding," and divide that from "knowledge" in both the natural scientific and the Aristotelian scheme (*episteme*), the point that should not be missed here is that the rhetorical turn in the human sciences – which has to account for rhetorical history as much as it does rhetorical theory – is not particularly new if one understands that the human sciences, as originally conceived, bear a striking resemblance to the practical arts and their connection to the theoretical sciences. It is also clear at this point that the intertwining of the natural and the human sciences, accounted for in both Gaonkar and Aristotle through the *doxa* which form the basis for human understanding, is not necessarily undone by inventing a new, revolutionary science of human lived life.

One of the main contentions raised in favor of the human sciences – at least in their characterization lately as a hermeneutics of lived life that works beyond the cold data of the natural sciences to explain human activity – is that they are revolutionary, both in terms of Kuhn's view that they have a greater explanatory capacity than theories currently in use, and in terms of their ability to change social (and material) reality. This, however, was not originally the case in Dilthey's distinction between the natural and the human sciences. For Dilthey, Western science has as its aim the triumphal conquest of the natural world by human intervention. Science's program is not seen as complete until nature has been completely remade or controlled according to human desire or need. Knowledge is useless unless it has ultimately pratical ends, ends that reside in the conquest of the natural world: knowledge is for the satisfaction of human need or want. Knowledge – as opposed to belief, or understanding – is the only vehicle for the subjugation of nature to human will, and so it is seen – as produced through Baconian scientific inquiry – as transformative, revolutionary, and activist. By contrast, the human sciences are marked by their passive stance. Their goal, for Dilthey, is to receive and lay out the components of the messages left by past and present generations, not to transform the natural, or even the human, world, but to understand it in as comphrehensive a way as possible. Sokel makes the connection between this view of the human sciences' receptivity and Eric Auerbach's valorization of the Hebraic style of the Old Testament, which is marked by "humility and expectant acceptance that lies at the core of man's relation to the noumenal" (Sokel, "Dilthey," 12).

The obvious question is how the knowledge produced by either the natural or the human sciences can be *put* to use at all. How can knowledge – admitted to be conceptual and theoretical and not practical at all, produced by the natural sciences – and understanding – which is the reception and analysis of the material components of cultural artefacts, and which is admittedly passive but which we use in "interhuman" activity – be deployed if there does not exist some mechanism through which to deploy them? Surely the mental sciences must be active to some extent; and surely the natural sciences must be revolutionary not solely by dint of the knowledge they produce but by the transformative

81

power they have in connection with some other human activity. There are two ways to respond to this conundrum. The first is that the passivity of the human sciences is only one part of their methodology. In the second chapter of the *Introduction*, in which Dilthey outlines the relative autonomy of the human sciences, he says that they proceed not by mastery "but primarily [in order] to comprehend. The empirical method requires that we establish the value of the particular procedures necessary for the inquiry on the basis of the subject matter of the human sciences and in a histori-cal-critical manner" (57). The "value" of the methodology must be established, though perhaps not "primarily," by other means. So although there is a sense in which Dilthey understands the passive stance of the human sciences as primarily that of compre-hension and understanding, there is also a more active stance that may well include "mastery" or the practical application of knowl-edge for practical ends. If the human sciences border on the realm of Aristotle's *theoria* or *episteme*, then – consistent with the Aris-totelian scheme – it is possible to suggest such knowledge is most valuable when deployed in the polis for a discernable end and – also consistent with Aristotle – it is possible to suggest the unique-ness of the human sciences lies in their *ability to imbricate the methodologies of the natural (i.e., material) sciences and the discursive (i.e., rhetorical) practical sciences* for their deployment in the polis. The second way of looking at the active / passive problem here is to suggest – again consistent with Aristotle – that the transform-ative capacity of the natural sciences seen by Dilthey (what Polanyi [*Personal Knowledge*, 328–42] and Burke [*A Rhetoric of Motives*, 29–37] in other contexts call "technology") is precisely the province of the human sciences. It is only by analyzing human understanding in the first place that the natural sciences can be deployed. Going back to an earlier example, it may be possible to develop conceptual knowledge of the nature of water, the direc-tion and nature of winds in the tropics, the flotational qualities of various kinds of woods, and the shapes of nautical vessels. Yet without connecting these conceptual knowledges with human desire and need through understanding, one will never pass from natural science to the practical art of shipbuilding. And the practi-cal arts, in Dilthey's terms, are "acts of will [that] exert force and involve sacrifices, whose meaning is evident to the individual in his experience and which actually produce something" (59), acts that themselves need to be understood *in connection with, and by the same methodology as, the natural sciences.*

This is, finally, the point: whether one sees, like Gaonkar, the rhetorical turn in the human sciences as the result of an acknowledgement of a crisis in the (discursive) nature of the life-world and its components or as something originally formulated by the human sciences in the first place, the natural sciences themselves need to be understood not as autonomous but as *relatively autonomous* from the natural sciences. In the same way that Aristotle was able to conceive *techne* and *phronesis* in their relation to the theoretical arts and sciences by grounding their mutual sources in the common opinions held by individual members of the polis, which were in turn grounded in sense-experience, the human and the natural sciences are both grounded in a similar source. And while maintaining a distinction between "knowledge" and "belief," between invention and arrangement, and between object of knowledge and its supplement, maintains a distinction between the human and natural sciences in terms contemporary with current philosophies of science or with Dilthey's nineteenth-century philosophies, those distinctions speak equally to the fact that one discipline cannot function adequately without the other. Again, my point is not to conflate the natural and the human sciences or to claim that rhetoric should be held up as an alternative to science any more than I would suggest the sciences as alternatives to rhetoric. Rather, I go back to Dilthey's distinction between the natural and the human sciences to point out that you cannot have one without the other; and that even the most humanistic of enterprises cannot proceed without science even while the most scientific of enterprises cannot proceed without rhetoric.

Interpretation and the boundaries of the sciences

In his essay entitled "The Natural and the Human Sciences," Thomas Kuhn makes much the same point by restating his thesis from *The Structure of Scientific Revolutions*, namely that the natural sciences proceed by acknowledging phenomena specific to the scientific domain as well as those specific to the ideological or "discursive" domain. Kuhn takes as his point of departure a chapter in Charles Taylor's *Philosophy and the Human Sciences*, and suggests that human actions constitute a text written in behavioral characters. To understand the actions, recover the meaning of the behavior, requires hermeneutic interpretation, and the interpretation appropriate to a particular piece of behavior will . . . differ systematically from culture to culture, sometimes even from individual to individual. It is this characteristic – the intentionality of behavior – that, in Taylor's view, distinguishes the study of human actions from that of natural phenomena. (Kuhn, "Natural and Human Sciences," 18–19)

Kuhn takes issue with Taylor's view that – using Taylor's example – the heavens are the same for all cultures, while the intentionality of those culture's uses or interpretations (i.e., meanings) of "the heavens" differ, and it is these differences which should be the province of the human sciences. For Kuhn, it is not the case, consistent with the points he has been making since 1962, that "though social concepts shape the world to which they are applied, concepts of the natural world do not. For [Taylor] but not for me, the heavens are culture-independent" ("Natural and Human Sciences," 20). So, for Kuhn the conceptual activity that takes place in the realm of the human sciences is virtually the same as that which takes place in the natural sciences: one cannot make out celestial bodies or the "field" within which they can be identified unless one has already provided a conventional definition of the terms "celestial bodies" or "heavens" within which one can identify them. Kuhn is here breaking down the distinction between the human and the natural sciences by suggesting that the natural sciences cannot proceed without deciding on a set of terms with which to identify the phenomena and objects of inquiry. In effect, he is placing natural scientific inquiry *within the realm of* human scientific inquiry and, in a move very different from Dilthey's initial argument about the fundamental methodology common to them while maintaining different objects of study, arguing that there is no access at all to the latter except through the former. In the case of two disparate understandings of "the heavens," "the difference is rooted in conceptual vocabulary. In neither can it be bridged by description in a brute data, behavioral vocabulary" (21). The upshot of Kuhn's argument, then, is that though "the natural sciences . . . may require what I have called a hermeneutic base" through which to investigate the conceptual similarities and differences between views of such things as "the heavens," they "are not in themselves hermeneutic enterprises.

84

The human sciences, on the other hand, often are, and they may have no alternative" (23). The natural sciences, far from Dilthey's workmate of the human sciences, are here subsumed within them: they are based upon the hermeneutic enterprise.

But the language of Kuhn's distinction belies an ambivalence that Joseph Rouse will point out is characteristic of the hermeneutics-science pair. And Kuhn himself seems to take an immediate step or two back away from his claim: "I'm aware of no principle," he notes, "that bars the possibility that one or another part of some human science might find a paradigm capable of supporting normal, puzzle-solving research" characteristic of the physical sciences. "My impression," he goes on, "is that in parts of economics and psychology, the case might already be made" (23). And the case can be made by dint of the "classificatory differences" (19) that such disciplines can surmount, whereby "things like each other in one system were unlike in the other" but which dissimilarities can be identified. If it is true that what was once considered a human science can "become" at least in part a natural science, then it is possible to suggest that the reason for such "progress" is the conceptual clarity the natural sciences can provide but which the human sciences cannot. It is also equally true, Kuhn goes on to say, that the cultural and institutional stability required for the sciences to progress in this manner cannot be assumed because of the exigencies of human agency, and so one cannot suggest that there will be some point in time when the natural sciences will render the human sciences superfluous, because it is the human sciences that account for those exigencies to begin with. Kuhn here takes the hermeneutic realm as supreme because human agency seems to prevent scientific conceptual rigor from being maintained in the face of human ideological differences, in much the same way that Aristotle saw phronesis as the practical culmination of theoretical and scientific knowledge. Unlike Aristotle and to some extent Dilthey, however, Kuhn fails to acknowledge that the intransitive realm operates despite these differences and that an alternative to practical wisdom is needed, if not to anchor those differences in some point of commonality at least to acknowledge that such a realm has an effect upon the polis–an effect which may, in fact, be measurable in both discursive and extra-discursive terms. Transposing into D.P. Gaonkar's terms *apropos* the human sciences, to the extent that rhetoric has an "interpretive" dimension – the capacity to distinguish different kinds of human psychologies and dispositions – it operates in the realm of human action: it is a *techne* that is deployed through phronesis. But Kuhn's rhetoric does not bleed over into the natural world, since we presume other disciplines will be responsible for inquiry into that world. Phronesis is the basis for episteme, but the two do not operate upon a (part) world in common. But for Taylor – as for Aristotle, Dilthey, and (albeit in unacknowledged fashion) Gaonkar – rhetoric and phronesis are a set of distinct social practices that operate alongside theoretical and scientific practices, and yet both sets of practices operate upon a common world distinctly yet simultaneously.

In "Interpretation in Natural and Human Science," Joseph Rouse neatly outlines the disparate positions of Kuhn and Taylor, but to a rather different end. Rouse points out that, in the nearly two decades since *The Structure of Scientific Revolutions* made the rounds, Kuhn has given up the attempt to distinguish the human sciences as hermeneutical, and this is borne out in his statement that *both* the human and the natural sciences are founded upon hermeneutics. But there is still the matter of the distinction between them, and whereas Kuhn comes down on the side of blurring the distinctions substantially by imbricating historical and conceptual data (thereby invoking "human activity" as the object of study for both), Taylor claims that the objects of the human sciences are "*essentially* self-interpreting agents for whom their actions are significant" (Rouse, "Interpretation" 43–4) while the objects of the natural sciences are not. Rouse will come down on Kuhn's side of the argument, in that he also wants to blur the line between the two disciplines (if not erase it altogether); but he disagrees with the primacy Kuhn gives to the human sciences. Far from seeing the natural sciences as able to operate only after the initial establishment of a science of human understanding, he – like Gaonkar, and to some extent like Dilthey – sees the human sciences and the hermeneutic enterprise by which they work as taking their object of knowledge as conventional (i.e., discursive) *material*, and that this material does not require a separate field of inquiry. Rather, because it is material, and because it has certain measurable effects and works within discernable constraints, one must understand the degree to which the "paradigms" and belief systems within which the interlocutors (working in science or any other field) operate are not constituted by "beliefs," but that those beliefs are materially constrained and – because they are "fields of activity" rather than simply "shared beliefs" (46) – have both a practical and a theoretical component. Far from requiring a separate field of activity, the natural sciences should simply be seen as having a practical component (a *phronesis*) without which they could not be constituted at all.

Putting this another way, Rouse suggests that "it would be better to say that language and the real are mutually dependent" than it would to suggest, like Kuhn, that "language is somehow constitutive of the world" (Rouse, "Interpretation," 47, 46). In Kuhn's view, you have language, and you have "the world" – as in Aristotle's dichotomous understanding, in which you have the realm of the contingent on the one hand and the realm of the certain on the other – and in order to study "language" or the cultural / discursive realm one has access through the human sciences, whereas in order to study "the world," one has the natural sciences, but that does not provide access to the world because it is always already discursively constituted. But Rouse is not ready to concede this latter point, and with it the division of natural and human worlds. He goes on to say that,

in the case of scientific inquiry, the relevant practices include ways of encountering, responding to, and being resisted by the things scientists are dealing with. The intertwining of language, social practice, and reality cannot be neatly bounded at the points where we run up against the natural world, for our encounters with the world, and indeed the very boundaries between self and world, belong to our interpretive social practices.

Rather than suggest that scientific practice is *practice* and thus part of the realm of the contingent, thus making scientific knowledge itself contingent, Rouse here effectively suggests – with Kuhn and against Taylor – that we cannot simply restrict the process of understanding in a social scientific mode of inquiry to those points at which we "run up against the natural world" because those points are never clear, and as such we need to continue to do both natural and human science. It is necessary to maintain a dialectical movement between a discursive (human scientific) analysis of those institutions and conventions that allow scientific inquiry to proceed, yielding what Dilthey would call "understanding," and those scientific inquiries into the apparent "natural" tendencies displayed by material objects and their constraints involved in the inquiry, yielding what Dilthey would call "knowledge." Again to translate into Gaonkar's language, the job of the social scientist at the moment of the rhetorical turn is not to distinguish between belief and knowledge, and to understand belief and the discursive product of particular historical moments and exigencies. Rather, her job involves seeing the material and the discursive as mutually constraining, not to see one as a "supplement" to the other, and proceed accordingly. To invert the position of rhetoric (and the human sciences) from that of "supplement" to that of "object" is to risk preventing any method of inquiry from understanding how individuals and groups within the polis *change* as the result of rhetorical or scientific inquiry, a result unimaginable for Aristotle but also for Dilthey, who understood the sciences as capable of providing revolutionary knowledge and as a result social change. If we understand the human sciences and their attendant hermeneutic methodology as the primary method of understanding the human relationship with the world, then one begins down the path cleared by Kuhn and Polanyi and ends – through people such as Charles Taylor and Donald Davidson – with an antifoundational language theory the likes of which has been popularized by Richard Rorty and, in literary studies, Stanley Fish (for responses, see Bernard-Donals, Review; Sprinker, "Knowing"; Norris, "Right"). Such a path "will seriously misunderstand some politically important phenomena when it limits itself to considering only political action identifiable *within* a given configuration of 'intersubjective meanings' and 'common meanings'" (Rouse, "Interpretation," 47). If everything boils down to the conventional configurations of knowledge (i.e., understanding) without being able to say anything meaningful about the world that delimits understanding, then it will be hard to suggest the incommensurable positions *different* polises take that produce conflict. It would be easy enough to go back to Aristotle and Plato and suggest that their understanding of the interconnection between phronesis and episteme was sufficient. That solution, as understood within the context of Dilthey's separation of the human and natural sciences, provided a methodological connection between the sciences and the practical arts, suggesting that praxis was the culmination of episteme's knowledge put to practical use to transform the polis. But there are solutions aplenty in the contemporary social and / or natural sciences, some of which I will discuss below.

To solve the problem of trying to maintain a distinction between ontological questions of a biological entity's relation to the environment and our own (i.e., the biologists') conception of individual agency and our capacity of engaging such questions, for example, Richard Levins and Richard Lewontin, in Part I of *The Dialectical Biologist*, suggest that the distinction is available so that we are forced to see both questions, but that they are ultimately inseparable and perhaps unsustainable. Evelyn Fox Keller, describing how chemical processes are "regulated" or "controlled" by "master molecules," has suggested that gendered conceptions of human agency are inescapable even as scientists engage in the most rigorous of theoretical and experimental activity (see especially her eighth chapter). But the point Rouse (along with Fox Keller and Levins and Lewontin) attempts to make is *not* that scientific theory and practice are so ideological that science jumps to the wrong conclusions, although instances of such ideological misfires do occur. Rather, "the opposite point is apropos: natural science proceeds quite well without needing to try to eliminate aspects of our self-understanding from scientific interpretations of the natural world" (Rouse, "Interpretation," 51). It may be that self-understanding along the lines proposed by Dilthey and the long line of human and social scientists that have followed his work may provide a framework that provides the questions that may be asked and for which answers science may provide. Further, science may – using interpretation again as a guide – begin negotiating the constraints within which inquiry and testing occurs, at which point science may proceed unabated. Once science has provided conceptual knowledge of the phenomena or objects tested, the human sciences are then deployed to suggest the social and cultural polises within which that knowledge may be put to use, and for what end.

But rather than take this path, Rouse backs away to suggest (with Mark Okrent) that it does not follow from the fact that human understanding occurs within a field of intersubjective meanings that that fact is one about human beings *as objects*. Once again holding up the human sciences as something like a macro-discipline whose explanatory capacity subsumes scientific inquiry, he notes that "there is less homogeneity and more room for construal and misconstrual even within a familiar and shared field of activity" such as science than can be easily assumed ("Interpretation," 55), and holds up hermeneutics as a way to imbricate the scientific form of inquiry about objects and the humanistic inquiry about humans as self-interpreting agents. Again, this valorization of hermeneutic / discursive reasoning winds up doing what the "stated" bias in Aristotle and Plato did, and what D. P. Gaonkar suggests through his reevaluation of rhetoric's supplementary status: it lets us forget that humans live in a world of objects, and that humans are in part biological entities, and that part of our self-understanding must border on, if not proceed by, engaging in (albeit tentative) conceptually rigorous scientific inquiry. To state the obvious again, dividing the human from the natural sciences – or stressing the discursive turn in humanistic inquiry – does not obviate the need in the human sciences for science itself.

There is one conception of hermeneutics, provided by Richard Harvey Brown, that comes close to a workable and decidedly rhetorical route out of the impasse between a completely anti-foundational view of the human sciences on the one hand and a need for science on the other, and which paves the way for a discussion of Richard Rorty's understanding of a similar (albeit unarticulated) view of hermeneutics in the next chapter. For now, I simply want to outline it by way of a conclusion, and return to it later. Brown narrates the current debate in the human sciences between a "post-Nietzschean, deconstructive relativism of the romantic tradition" which denies human access to any foundation which might result from natural scientific investigation on the grounds – similar to Kuhn's – that any such investigation is contingent; and the foundationalist positions of absolute positivism and reductivist hermeneutics, which provide for human access through either a hard-headed disavowal of ideology on the one hand or through a total immersion in ideological criticism on the other. Brown wonders whether, if "Derrida is right to point out that absolute objectivity is a chimera, and Searle is right to note that absolute relativity is self-defeating," we should have to choose between them at all (Brown, "Symbolic Realism," 325). He notes that it is "essential to science, law and other domains of discourse that one be able to say *something* without knowing everything," and proposes a "critical rhetoric" to lead the search for "trans-situational" phenomena, or at least characteristics of phenomena that need to be accounted for in an antifoundational "situational" inquiry (326). It is worth noting that he combines the vocabularies of Dilthey, Aristotle and Gaonkar in his assertion that "rhetoric eases us into new conceptual experience by naming the conditions for possible kinds of *knowledge*, advocating certain *procedures* as correct and certain statements as true, and inviting and legitimating *belief* in a certain (version of) the world" (ibid.).

Citing Vico rather than Dilthey as the originator of the human sciences, Brown notes, along the lines traced by Dilthey, that human works, produced by the human mind through contact with the natural world require that the human sciences come up with "a preexistent something from which [works] can be made. And this prior something, which man himself did not make, of this he has no privileged understanding" ("Symbolic Realism," 327). Nevertheless, it does not mean that we do not have any understanding of it at all. In a turn that is reminiscent of Rouse's outline of the Kuhn / Taylor debate over the distinctiveness of the (Diltheyan) human scientific project, Brown notes that human social activity *does* require a hermeneutics on the one hand, which will investigate the relatively autonomous self-interpretive coventional schemes through which humans develop rules, laws and frameworks for knowing; but it also requires that those frameworks are conceptually sound and internally consistent on the other hand (see Sanders). If the human sciences really do take as their object of study human social practice, then we should deploy what could be called a *critical* hermeneutics, which allows us to investigate "society [as] not only praxis, but also [as] practico-inert . . . [as], in part, like nature" (328). It may not be possible to investigate all of the material constraints that have an effect upon the situation-specific occurrences in the socio-historical real, but it may allow for a science that investigates the kinds of constraints that impinge upon human agency and which can speculate, with (one would think) a fair degree of certainty, about how those constraints might further influence future agency. As Aristotle noted in the second book of *Rhetoric*, the discussion of the behavioral regularities that he and others had observed of various different classes and ages of individuals in certain kinds of polises, human interactions have properties that do not vary and that are presuppositions of meaningful discourse, even though the rules that adjudicate those interactions may vary across cultures (see, for example, Garfinkel, *Ethnomethodology*). Even critics of positivism, notes Brown, find that calling rival epistemologies just different language games suggests that those games have different purposes, and that those purposes can be evaluated, by either human or natural scientific means. Of course, it may well be that the purposes that these games reveal, and that the invariant properties that different cultures engage through practice, are available only at the level of what may not be expressible by conventional means: Brown quotes Marx ("Language is real, practical consciousness") to suggest that that consciousness may exist at the level of the *inexpressible*, or at a level in which expression may mask or diverge from the tendencies that are observable in the same instance. "To draw what cannot be articulated into a previously unavailable discourse is to abolish a linguistically encoded false consciousness," and it is the role of hermeneutics to work, alongside a methodology that is capable of observing the tendencies in social or natural "reality" that conflict with or prevent the articulation of them in the discursive (conscious) realm, to make them available.

The critical hermeneutics Brown calls "symbolic realism" foregrounds linguistic material in the same way that Dilthey foregrounded cultural material, and suggests that it does not *reflect* either the world or the mind, but that it reflects both through human practice. Like Aristotle's *Nichomachean Ethics*, it suggests that language is a product of social practice, and should be seen as resulting from "socially coordinated actions," which result from both conventional systems of belief and conceptual systems of knowledge. It works by defending generalized explanations of the natural as well as the human world, but also by refusing to reduce these explanations to material or mechanistic causalities. As Brown puts it, "in such a view, causal, law-like explanation is itself an interpretive procedure, and critical interpretation itself can be a rigorous way of knowing" (332). Science, in other words, must be subjected to discursive analysis; and discourse should be subjected to the conceptual analysis made available by science. "Symbolic realism seeks a warrant for both scientific *and* ethical judgments, and hence for a public discourse that would be adequate both for moral self-understanding of the lifeworld as well as for management of complex systems" (ibid.). It understands the world in both its transitive and intransitive dimensions – as being comprised of both belief and knowledge, the real and the "real" – which includes the necessarily unnoticed realm that is unnamed and which "goes without saying," but which is expressible as those bothersome tendencies of either natural or social reality that deflect discourse, that which can be stated. Critical realism works to show how either purely analytical or purely interpretive accounts of social or natural reality fail adequately to provide for the intransitive dimension because they cannot "bring out the incoherence of a discourse which . . . has the capacity to survive every *reductio ad absurdum*" (Bordieu, *Practice*, 164).

Brown's critical realism is, for him at least, consistent with a rhetorical analysis that seeks to reveal the material and social constraints – provided both by conventional and (often contradictorily) natural "rules" or "laws" – that represent and misrepresent practical social relations, and does so by "decoding disjunctions and mistranslations between different levels and orders of symbolization" (335). If this rhetorical task for a reconfigured human science might seem at odds with the Aristotelian rhetoric set up in his work (i.e., *Rhetoric, Topics, Prior* and *Posterior Analytics* and *Nichomachean Ethics*), in that it might seem to consign the knowledge originally intended for the theoretical and scientific arts to rhetoric and to the practical arts, I wish simply to reiterate Aristotle's claim that while the *phronimos* was not required to be a scientist or a philosopher, he had the even tougher job of deploying scientific and theoretical knowledge in the minefield that was the political world. What the *phronimos* had at his or her disposal were the practical arts – rhetoric, dialectic, and the musical and sculptural arts – but also the *endoxa* of the polis which rested upon everyday practicalities but which corresponded (sometimes more, sometimes less) to the theoretical principles of *dianoia, sophia* and *episteme*. What is most clear from Brown's (perhaps overly hopeful) assessment of a hermeneutics that works alongside the conventional systems of thought that nevertheless provide conceptual knowledge is that only a practical scientific understanding of the social world which sees language as at once material and intentional (and thus capable of orienting human agents in historical as well as in intransitive reality) can work as a useful theory of human activity. Whether such a theory of human agency is consistent with a strong view of the sciences remains the task of the remainder of this book, and will be of immediate concern presently when I turn my attention to the most popular of antifoundational philosophers, Richard Rorty.

4

❖❖

Rorty and the mirror of nature: hermeneutics and the possibility of social change

❖❖

When Richard Rorty published *Philosophy and the Mirror of Nature* in 1979, he codified what had already become apparent – the human and the natural sciences, along with philosophy (the primary subject of Rorty's book) had taken a decided turn away from "objectivity" and "realism," and had questioned the methodologies fundamental to the disciplines themselves. There had been rumblings of such a structural revolution early in the previous decade: Thomas Kuhn (one of Rorty's unsung heroes in *Philosophy* and subsequent books) had done for the sciences in *The Structure of Scientific Revolutions* what Rorty had done for philosophy with his book. Within two decades, normative science and positivist philosophy of science – each of which had a tradition stretching back to the early renaissance – had been overthrown, and what resulted was, depending upon how you look at revolution, either wholesale chaos in which scientists and philosophers had to rethink their centuries-old *modus operandi* without so much as a roadmap; or a fecund multidisciplinary soup, in which the boundaries between traditionally demarcated fields broke down to yield shared methodologies and borrowed metaphysics.

Of course, this revolution did not come overnight. Careful readers of Kuhn had seen it coming for a while. The natural sciences had not been up to the task of explaining the phenomena they took for their job to explain, not because their theories were not complex enough, but because the paradigm within which theoretizing could be done at all had become threatened by

95

methodologies that grew up in the human sciences; and analytic philosophy, far from failing to theorize the epistemological and ontological problems it had set for itself, found instead that the very questions it had been asking were mooted by problems articulated by Foucault and Derrida and raised by others before them. Rorty was not responsible for the revolution; he simply announced for anyone who had not been paying attention that it was here, and that it was time to adjust our philosophies accordingly. The revolution took the form of what D. P. Gaonkar and many, many others have called the "rhetorical turn," in which the epistemological problems of cognition and knowledge and the discourse which could accommodate them seeped all the way down to the fundamental, "objective" sciences and philosophies. If language goes all the way down, Rorty told us, then the foundations we surmised were there were flimsy at best, and the standards to which we adhered to adjudicate incommensurable accounts and truth claims about the world had to be reevaluated. If language goes all the way down, said some like Stanley Fish, then the way human subjects wield power and acquire knowledge is by *persuasive force*. Of course, I have so far argued that this rhetorical (re)turn had been slowly moving since Dilthey discerned the human sciences as a separate discipline from the natural sciences, and that the "discovery" of the human sciences has led to the same kind of crisis, in which the objective sciences became subsumed as a province of the human science of understanding, since we cannot know objects unless we understand how we know. Further, the specifically rhetorical character of this (re)turn was a reformulation of the divisions of knowledge established, in different terms, by Aristotle. Nevertheless, it is worth asking: what exactly does Rorty's characterization of the rhetorical or hermeneutic turn in philosophy look like? There are two reason for asking this question of Rorty specifically. First, as I have intimated, his book appeared during a time when many others in the sciences and in philosophy were reaching the same conclusions, and so his book might be taken as representative. But more important, perhaps, is Rorty's influence over a generation of philosophers and thinkers in other fields. While it may not be safe to say that Rorty's influence in America is equivalent to the influence of a Foucault or a Derrida, it could be said that American philosophy and scientific thinking has been forced to confront Rorty (and Kuhn) at every turn at the very least because of the accessibility of a text such as *Philosophy and the Mirror of Nature*. Rorty is something of a "philosopher for everyman," whose prose is as readable as his ideas are persuasive, and as a result, molecular biologists and literary theorists and everyone in between seem to have read Rorty's seminal work.

My task in this chapter is to confront Rorty's text on its own ground, but also on the ground of rhetoric. That is, I want to investigate Rorty's division of epistemological and hermeneutic philosophy and science and the methodologies implied by each, to see if the line drawn between them is as sharp as Rorty makes it out to be. My hypothesis is that, similar to the division between the human and the natural sciences scouted by Dilthey 100 years earlier in response to what he also saw as a crisis in the production of knowledge, Rorty's ways of knowing overlap to the extent that a distinction between them becomes nearly useless. More to the point, their area of overlap is precisely the same as it was for Dilthey, namely practical knowledge, and the reason they overlap is also similar, namely because normal and revolutionary production of knowledge have both a discursive *and* an "objective" component. But I also want to confront Rorty on rhetoric's ground. If it is true that revolutionary or hermeneutic ways of knowing proceed by "negotiating versions of reality" by engaging with disputants through dialogue, and if it is also true that these versions of reality do have a material component, then the hermeneutic / rhetorical knowledge proposed by Rorty must also have a material dimension to it. And it is worth investigating whether hermeneutics is, alone, up to the task of understanding the material dimension (and the material constraints to discursive "negotiation") or whether scientific investigation of some kind is not also necessary.

In order to do so, I want to closely examine the sections in *Philosophy and the Mirror of Nature* where Rorty most closely imbricates science and rhetoric (that is, material investigations of the natural world and the schemes within which such investigations take place), and to push the conclusions he reaches as far as they will go to point out their fault lines. If we really do live in an antifoundational world (and I do not think there is any escaping this fact), what can we do and how does doing it get us anywhere better than where we are now?

Pure and impure language games: the meaning of meaning

In his introduction to *Philosophy and the Mirror of Nature*, Rorty writes that, in their early years Heidegger, Dewey and Wittgenstein had each tried to reformulate the philosophical "foundations" that had eluded Decartes and Kant and Hegel, but later on discovered that their foundationalist attempts at making work for philosophers was as doomed to failure as those of their predecessors. "The aim of the book," he goes on, "is to undermine the reader's confidence in 'the mind' as something about which one should have a 'philosophical' view, in 'knowledge' as something about which there ought to be a theory and which has 'foundations,' and in 'philosophy' as it has been conceived since Kant" (*Mirror*, 7). The three post- or anti-Kantian philosophers he notes were significant because they eschewed epistemology for a "therapeutic rather than constructive, edifying rather than systematic" philosophy. Because epistemology had failed to adequately understand the human mind and its ability to know the world, Rorty wishes to recuperate for philosophy some other role. While Descartes, Kant and Hegel were presumably right in seeing something unique in human cognitive ability, and the language with which that ability was made manifest and operative upon a world of material and objects, the positing of that uniqueness itself placed what amounted to a barrier between the human mind and the world it apprehended. That is, by the very establishment of the philosophical project, philosophers created a void between the two entities, mind and world, and philosophy found itself unequal to the task of conjoining them.

That gap might be seen as the same one that was posited by Dilthey between the human and the natural sciences. Dilthey began with the same premise – that capacity for understanding, cognition, is what renders humans unique entities in the natural world – and draws the same conclusions, as much as he tried to avoid doing so, as Kant had before him: despite similar methodologies, the human sciences took as their object the human project of self-understanding and the products by which that project is carried forward (and which result from it); while the natural sciences took as their object the characteristics of naturally occurring phenomena and objects. But, as with Kant and Hegel, it was

difficult for Dilthey to get past the conundrum of forming conceptual knowledge (that is, doing science) while the entire enterprise
of human cognition and the forming of conceptions itself was
open to question. Rorty's task in the middle portion of *Philosophy
and the Mirror of Nature* is to suggest that language philosophy was
seen as one way to reformulate the epistemological impasse (or, to
continue the metaphor, bridge the epistemological gap) that results from having two sets of problems, one concerning the mind,
and the other concerning the world. Such a philosophy understands itself as putting language in a position to mediate between
"the mind" and "the world," since it has a foot in both camps (as a
"mental effect" and a tangible, material and measurable effect in
"the world"). For my purposes, it is particularly interesting that
language philosophy occupies a similar position in contemporary
philosophy as rhetoric and the practical arts did for Aristotle,
namely, as a way to mediate "knowledge" and "belief."

Rorty distinguishes between two kinds of language philosophy,
the "pure" and the "impure." Pure language theory understands
its purview as problems of "how to systematize our notions of
meaning and reference in such a way as to take advantage of logic,
preserve our intuitions about modality, and generally produce a
clear and intuitively satisfying picture of the way in which notions
like 'truth,' 'meaning,' 'necessity,' and 'name' fit together" (257).
It treats language, in other words, as an inherently logical system
which can be understood autonomously from other systems of
knowledge, one that does not have any necessary connections to
problems of mind's relation to the world. Impure language theory
is explicitly epistemological, in which "philosophical points about
the nature and extent of human knowledge . . . could be stated as
remarks about language" (258). The hope was to make impure
language theory a way to understand philosophy as dealing both
with questions of a material substance, a naturally occurring
phenomenon (language) that operated by a testable set of rules
(through the new science of linguistics); and dealing with the
higher processes of "a manifold intuition" that was the province
of the human mind, as a unique entity understandable separately
from the world. That is, impure language philosophy seemed to
offer a link between the relatively autonomous human mind on
the one hand, and the world on which that mind presumably
operated on the other hand through a medium (language) that

gave us access to both because it was shared by human culture and had a foot in both the intellectual and the purely material (i.e., natural) world. "Rephrased by Bertrand Russell and C. I. Lewis, this became the view that every true statement contained our contribution (in the form of the meanings of the component terms) as well as the world's (in the form of the facts of sense-perception)" (258–9). Like Dilthey's conception of the *Geisteswissenschaften*, impure language philosophy saw human understanding as having both a material and a discursive component.

As we have seen with Dilthey, however, the facticity of sense-perception as different from the facticity of language can be problematized if we ask whether the world's contribution (sense-perceptions) could be understood at all *outside of* our own contribution. We understand the world's contribution *as* the world's because we have constructed a (conventional) set of rules by which to make a distinction between us and the world in the first place. Like Dilthey's axiomatic understanding that the intransitive dimension is accessible, in human science, only by means of the transitive (or conventional), impure language theory's attempt to connect the mind to the world through language is hindered by what Rorty calls the "mirror" metaphor: it assumes that there must be a direct, representational, relation that language facilitates. In response to these problems, Rorty cites two solutions, one provided by Donald Davidson and another provided by Hilary Putnam, that privilege discursive theories of knowledge while trying to fend off objections about the "world's contribution."

Davidson's solution is to dissolve the "dualism of scheme and content, of organizing system and something waiting to be organized" in favor of a theory of meaning "as an understanding of the inferential relations between sentences" (Davidson, "On the Very Idea of a Conceptual Scheme," ll; "Truth and Meaning," 316–18). The fact that truth is discussed in connection with questions of both truth and language does not mean that we can discern

A theory of meaning will analyze the meaning of all referring expressions other than those for sensory qualia in terms of those which do refer to sensory qualia

from

Our only evidence for empirical truths is the patterns of qualia in our sensory fields [sic]. (Davidson, "Truth and Meaning," 316–l8; quoted in Rorty, *Mirror*, 260)

Davidson, in other words, wishes to work back to what looks like pure language theory in order to completely disengage problems of language from problems of knowledge. All we understand through an analysis of sentences is the inferential relations among them, and their truth claims. This is relatively simple if all we are dealing with are sentences such as "the cat is on the mat:" it is easy to see that the relation between the truth claim being made has a great deal to do with the truth claims of other sentences ("cats are x," "mats are y," etc.). Once we move to more complex sentences, though, things become more difficult, and the adjudication of truth claims in sentences such as the one I am writing become highly complex logical operations. But that is the point: language in this theory sees itself as having only to do with the logic inherent within its own system. Davidson's reaction to impure language theory is to go back to a pure language theory that says little or nothing about problems of human understanding.

But one of the implications of such a theory – one that Rorty doesn't recognize – is that it has affinities with the relatively autonomous *function* of language noted by Barthes, De Man and others whom D. P. Gaonkar, in "Rhetoric and Its Double," cites with some approval. That is to say, Davidson has tripped over the "tropological dimension" of rhetoric (and language generally) in which the figural possibilities in language and its truth claims vary radically, and (in a point very far from the one Davidson wishes to make, and related to a point Rorty makes only in *Contingency, Irony, and Solidarity*, and then only tentatively) in which they "are testable only by their susceptibility to integration within a theory of truth-conditions of other sentences," truth conditions which themselves are multiply understandable. Whereas Davidson and Rorty might admit to the relative autonomy of the discursive dimension in this view of language, both admit that the " 'ontological' results are bound to be bland" (261). But the results are far from bland. To read sentences the way De Man does most certainly has effects, as he has shown us over and over again, both in and upon the institutions in which such readings take place and are disseminated, and indirectly upon the individuals in any given polis. Moreover, given that Rorty's purpose in this book is to move philosophy away from the traditional problems of truth and logic, and toward a way to guide human action in the everyday world, it seems odd that he would relegate

101

Davidson's "pure" language theory to "the traditional province of the grammarian – the attempt to find ways of describing sentences which help to explain how those sentences are *used*" (261; emphasis added), and to "simply lay out perspicuously the relation between parts of a social practice (the use of certain sentences) and other parts (the use of other sentences)" (262). If it is possible to generate sentences that may be seen to transform both the inherent relations among a larger set of sentences and which also carry with them truth claims, then it could be said that such a "bland" project may function at the practical level to reformulate truth claims themselves. Davidson suggests, and Rorty at this point in his argument does not debate the suggestion, that the testability of truth claims would be the job of some field other than philosophy. In a move similar to Plato's in *Gorgias*, he is attempting to divorce a purely rhetorical theory from any epistemological or ontological status. But by doing so – in fact, by insisting upon it – he opens, again in much the same way Plato does, a space for some other field that is required to go to work alongside rhetoric (or, in the case of Davidson, pure language theory), and in the same way that de Man has implied that a blindness to rhetoric's relatively autonomous status allows for the insight into the radical effects such an autonomous status has at the practical level. Pure language theory, then, is not as bland as it looks; and it is not as pure as it looks either, given that the testability it assumes for some other field (it would be too much at this point to suggest that that field might be scientific or conceptual inquiry) will require it to carry that field around with it. If rhetoric has use-value, in other words, then it needs to carry with it a theory (perhaps a scientific one) of the social. Of course, Rorty will go so far as to admit that the shortcomings of any language theory are intimately tied to those theories' lack of an understanding of social movement and change. But, as we will see soon enough, hermeneutics does not succeed in the task at which pure language theory has failed.

Hilary Putnam and Michael Dummett offer a second alternative to the scheme / content conundrum (see Dummett, "What is a Theory of Meaning?"; Putnam, "The Refutation of Conventionalism"). In an explicit attempt to make philosophy foundational – directly counter to the "pure" language theory of Davidson – without having to be concerned with ideas (epistemology) or things (ontology), Dummett makes a direct equation between philosophy and *meaning*. He takes as a given the point Rorty begins with, that the history of philosophy is a history of failing to understand the human capacity for knowing the world. This began with Aristotle's attempt to formulate a logic that would directly link activity in the polis and phenomena in nature with human understanding, and continued through the seventeenth century with the admission that we may not be able to formulate a logic without understanding *how* such a logic can be formulated by the human capacity for thought. Saner contemporary minds understand that even this enterprise is doomed to failure because it also requires a *self*-understanding that runs into the very same problems the objectivist philosophies did. What we finally have recourse to are meanings – everyone knows, according to their own lights at least, what things *mean* – and so the goal of philosophy should be to understand these meanings, their divergences, and ways in which they can be made to converge. Dummett takes the rhetorical turn since he sees philosophy's task as describing the ways in which humans persuade one another of their understandings of the world constructed through discourse. Because everyone's "take" on the world is granted to be different (having dispensed with the ontological and epistemological tasks of earlier philosophies), it is enough, suggests Dummett, to mediate these claims. Of course, because Dummett's philosophy is *impure*, he has to maintain the distinctions, given up by pure philosophies of language, between "givens" and interpretations of the given, and between the "necessary" and the "contingent," distinctions that are likewise maintained in any rhetoric. And this, suggests Rorty, is precisely where Dummett's notion of a pure language theory as foundational breaks down: meanings are not "foundational," and the philosophy that seeks to delineate them will have to contend with these two realms. Meaning is derived by something outside the linguistic construction – presumably in reaction to some state of affairs which has both a human (i.e., discursive and conventional) and a natural (i.e., extra-discursive) component – and so as much as it appears to be a good solution to see language philosophy as concerned with meaning alone, it is impossible to stop there. Impure language philosophy may be superior to the "pure" language theory set up by Davidson, in that the former is able to say "more interesting things" about the human situation than the latter's claims to sentence relations; but it does not solve the problems it sets out to solve. Rorty puts it this way: philosophy

is a cultural genre, a "voice in the conversation of mankind" (to use Michael Oakeshott's phrase), which centers on one topic rather than another at some given time not by dialectical necessity but as a result of various things happening elsewhere in the conversation (the New Science, the French Revolution, the modern novel), or of individual men of genius who think of something new . . . or perhaps of the resultant of several such forces. (264)

Philosophy and self understanding are not privileged places standing outside culture, but rather are themselves culturally generated.

But if philosophy in the latter part of the twentieth century is about meaning (and thus integrally connected to language), and if both pure and impure language philosophies are not up to the task of philosophy (the first because it cannot tell us about the world, the second because it tells us only so much), then what is left for it to do? Rorty provides a hint of the answer in his appeal to Oakeshott. If it is necessary to understand "the New Science" and "the French Revolution" and "the modern novel," then philosophy has to account for what have traditionally been diverse fields of human inquiry. Going back to Aristotle's scheme in *Nichomachean Ethics*, an adequate philosophy of meaning imbricates (taking Rorty's list in order) *episteme* (science), *phronesis* (politics), and *techne* (art). And if we take Rorty seriously in his appeal to Oakeshott that philosophy is a "voice," that is, an explicitly discursive way of constructing knowledge dependent upon the exploration of how conventional and extra-discursive constraints work together to have an effect on a human subject such that the subject is "interpellated" and can speak in certain ways to an audience which is likewise individually (or collectively) interpellated, then we might understand what Rorty is getting at is a practical art, a phronesis related but not reducible to politics. Quine dissolved the dogmas of empiricism – the first, that every object which could be discussed had an essence to which one could appeal in order to adjudicate meaning; the second, that commensurating divergent meanings could always be done – and with them, suggests Rorty, has dissolved the certainty that there existed some objects "out there" to which we could appeal through science or some other conceptual system of knowledge, and with it dissolved the distinction "between science and non-science" (269). If this is true, we have further evidence that the distinction beteween the natural and the human sciences can also be dissolved (or, if not dissolved, then – taking a cue from Kuhn – resolved in favor of the latter).

In effect, Rorty anticipates the move a number of latter-day human scientists have made, suggesting that because both pure and impure theories of language and meaning (the descendants of philosophy) cannot function in a world where the distinction between "the world" and "the word" has been dissolved, then we need to produce a practical philosophy that understands the human life-world as having both a material and a discursive dimension. It is altogether possible to understand this move as one that parallels the Aristotelian solution to the Platonic problem of language's coercive power in the polis, a solution that laid out quite carefully the divisions of knowledge and understood practical wisdom as the combination of knowledge put to proper use. Here Rorty points to a theory of practical meaning that likewise imbricates politics, conceptual knowledge and artistic creation. But immediately after he takes on and in turn dismisses Davidson and Dummett on meaning, he begins to formulate a "proper philosophy of language" around "meaning-change," one that more completely follows Oakeshott's metaphor of the conversation of mankind, and it is through this metaphor that we can begin to see both the potential for success of Rorty's hermeneutic project and its aporias.

So you say you want change?

With the overthrow of the dogmas, Quine not only overthrew the distinction between science and non-science; according to Rorty he also endangered rationality (*Mirror*, 269). If there is no way to determine what was "out there" once and for all, what in the world have philosophers (and scientists, for that matter) been arguing over for all these years? It seemed obvious that, even though philosophy had not solved any of the problems it had set for itself over the long haul, it had much more adequately system-atized those problems (we had a better understanding of language's function in human social relations and we had a sense of how human thought might be understood); and it also seemed obvious that, in spite of Kuhn's warning that "discovery" might not be the proper metaphor for how science proceeds, we nevertheless are better able to explain phenomena today than were our ancestors (we have a better understanding of lightning now that we understand the characteristics of electricity, and we can say more about geography since we hypothesized plate tectonics). Surely there are not only objects "out there" to which all these theories referred, but there also surely must be a way to understand how these theories came to change (if not evolve) over the long haul. And in practical terms, there must be a way to adjudicate competing claims over everday matters.

Because of the contemporary insistence that "truths" cannot be adjudicated by understanding how meanings "hook onto the world" by seeing which meanings are more accurate representations than others, it was impossible to maintain the scheme-content distinction of meaning. It is possible to suggest that we know more about planetary motion because the "content" of the object or phenomenon in question (the fact that celestial bodies appear to revolve around the earth, and the fact that they do so at regular intervals of time) makes more sense in one explanatory scheme than another (it was hard to explain what looked like oscillation in planetary movement in an earth-centered solar system, and astronomers were in effect forced into the unwieldy theory of parallax; it was much easier to explain in a sun-centered system, in which heliocentric orbits did away with the need for parallax). This would seem to be the case even more clearly if we could say either that sense-experience of a phenomenon or object was independent of cognition or if we could maintain "meaning invariance," in which a phenomenon or object could be invariably understood in a scheme of schemes, knowable *a priori*. Without these two anchors, it is difficult to say why one way of understanding a phenomenon or state of affairs is any better than any other.

But giving up on the scheme-content distinction because of the highly variable nature of schemes does not mean that we have to give up any notion of the ability to commensurate "ways of seeing" objects of knowledge. The most radical claim that results from the overthrow of the scheme-content dualism is that, along the lines established by Davidson, if we change the meaning of a term, then along with it change our beliefs revolving around the use of that term. That is, if all we can do is change the character of an object by changing its meaning, then change would occur at an incredibly rapid pace, but it would not be clear whether that change would have any noticeable effects. Putnam puts it this way, *apropos* of Paul Feyerabend's critique of meaning invariance:

> [T]o say that any change in our empirical beliefs about Xs is a change in the meaning of the term X would be to abandon the distinction between questions of meaning and questions of fact. To say that the semantic rules of English cannot at all be distinguished from the empirical beliefs of English speakers would just be to throw the notion of a semantical rule of English overboard . . . All appearance of sensation would have vanished if Feyerabend had taken this course. For the "sensation" here depends on sliding back and forth between a noncustomary conception of meaning and the customary conception. (Putnam, *Mind*, 124–5).

We need to be able, says Rorty, to "pick out objects without help of definitions, essences, and meanings of terms" (*Mirror*, 274), which requires a theory of reference, but which had to also recognize – along the lines suggested by Kuhn and Feyerabend – that some sort of scheme was necessary, albeit not necessarily an *a priori* or a universally commensurable one.

So what kind of scheme can we use within which to adjudicate competing knowledge claims, and how do we adjudicate them? Rorty points back to Kuhn to suggest that reference to a scheme should be "taken as simply a reference to what we believe now – the collection of views which make up our present day culture" (276). It would be too much to say that such a scheme allows us to suggest that nature is malleable to thought, but it would not be too much to suggest that philosophy should have as its aim a description of the views that comprise the scheme. The problem that immediately faces Rorty, then, is how to provide the understanding (in Dilthey's terms) or to decide what one can say (in Rorty's) or to systematically analyze (in Kuhn's normal scientific terms) that context. More specifically, if nature is not malleable to thought, how does one change one's way of thinking *about* nature if the scheme within which we do that thinking is simply "a collection of views" that, depending upon what segment of the social world you happen to be looking at, comprises the conceptual grid?

Rorty will not have anything to do with Hilary Putnam's realist solution to the problem, but it is Putnam's defense of realism that brings into relief the implicit realism of Rorty's own program, a realist component that it *must* have in order to be more than just a conversation about conversation. There are two lines to Putnam's thinking which are immediately relevant here. The first suggests that, in order to make any sense at all of the "collection of views" that comprises a particular paradigm, the philosopher needs to have access to scientific sociological data, which is only explainable on realist grounds. The second is that it is not possible to suggest that because "old" explanations of the world are no longer valid then the explanations we are using now are likely to be invalid.

Apropos of the first point, Rorty becomes indignant when he wonders just why we need a "reliably standard method of scientific inquiry" for understanding the collection of views that comprises a paradigm. For him, the answer Putnam provides, that it is necessary to explain the reasons why scientists agree that some explanations for certain phenomena are better than others, doesn't wash. Richard Boyd, a one-time collaborator with Putnam, suggests that convergence (or agreement) might be interpreted as "reliability," and that an explanation for a phenomenon is reliable to the extent that the explanation will not fail where other, previous explanations succeeded, and that causal mechanisms already known won't interfere with it. If these two criteria hold true but the scientist is still able to predict, given the scientific framework operating at the time, that the object or phenomenon will not behave according to the explanation, then that theory has been falsified on *realist* grounds. There is something about the phenomenon itself that acts in ways other than the conventional explanation is able to express. This explanation, for Boyd, guards against arbitrarily chosen explanations by ruling out competing theories that might for reasons of expediency, convenience and politics be included for consideration; and by testing new theories empirically. In other words, Boyd is trying to suggest that scientific evaluation, despite the fact that it proceeds at least in part by convention, can nevertheless provide systematic criteria by which to judge the superiority of one theory over another by dint of its explanatory capacity, something against which even Kuhn does not argue (see especially chapter 7 of *The Structure of Scientific Revolutions*). But Rorty does take issue with this explanation because, he says, it is not always the case that new explanations for phenomena or states of affairs will fail where the previous ones say they will. That is, science does not proceed by checking the new theory off against the old one, but it does proceed by "marrying" the old theory's observation language, testing procedures and regulative principles with the explanation the new theory offers of the "anomaly" that suggested the need for it in the first place. Far from suggesting, as Putnam and Boyd do, that convergence takes place because the phenomenon under investigation provides the need for a new explanation, Rorty's convergence takes place by commensurating one convention with another.

But this misses the fundamental importance of acknowledging the mind-independence of the reality under investigation, and the part that such a reality plays in the conventions that guide investigation in the first place. And this goes directly to the problem we have seen in Dilthey's somewhat inaccurate distinction between "what science knows" and "what human science knows." As we saw, it is not necessarily the case that the human sciences can be divided from the natural sciences by distinguishing their objects of knowledge, such that in the latter the objects are naturally occurring phenomena while in the former the object is human self-understanding within the constraints provided by those phenomena, because our knowledge of the phenomena themselves, even under the highly controlled conditions of scientific investigation, are in part also the products of self-understanding. That is to say, there is no such thing as non-instrumental knowledge, because even knowledge produced "purely" by the physical sciences was done so out of a set of instrumentally reasoned questions, and has practical consequences. Rorty's response to Putnam and Boyd – that there are no theory-independent entities that can be identified as being responsible for change in the schemes with which we explain them because anomalies themselves are instrumentally produced – begs the question of reference. Aristotle's conjoining of the several disciplinary knowledges suggested that it is not necessary to say that, since there is no theory-independent method of understanding truth or goodness or "the world," then we need to give up trying to find ways to investigate "objective reality." It may be the case that realism – the notion that there does exist something "out there" that surpasses our ability to talk about or theorize it – in spite of its redundancy, nevertheless provides a certain amount of information about the nature of the physical or "natural" aspect of the acknowledged instrumental process of scientific or theoretical investigation. It is this "objective" information that then may be turned back into an understanding of realism itself, a realism that is nevertheless only possible within a scheme. Like Plato's process of refutation – in which the nature of an object was investigated "as if" it were possible to discover that nature scientifically or theoretically; the object was placed into the contingent world of political exigency, likewise to be investigated for the knowledge it yields; and that knowledge is turned back to scientific or theoretical investigation – realism is not rendered moot because "realism" itself is tied to an instrumental or conventional scheme. Without some way to imagine that the "truths" which must be "married" in Rorty's anti-realist account of change are somehow tied to real states of affairs that have a measurable impact – and without a way to measure that impact (call it sociology, or social science, or anthropology, or even human science) regardless of its conventional aspect – then social change is simply a matter of one story about the world winning out over another by its rhetorical force. As both Aristotle and Plato acknowledged, rhetorical force is no match for the measurable, material force of extra-rhetorical "persuasion" like torture, imprisonment, and other brute forms of coercion, all of which must also be considered part of the instrumentality of change.

To avoid begging that question, Rorty next considers the question of referentiality: he admits that, if we are going to have an impure language theory like Putnam's, then along with language philosophy we also need an epistemology, a way to decide what language refers to. But he dismisses the question of referentiality in much the same way that he dismissed realism, and suggests that though doubtless Aristotle and Descartes and Rorty are all "talking about" the same thing in philosophy – or, using an example Kuhn is fond of, that dephlogisticated air and oxygen are simply different ways of "talking about" the same set of phenomena or objects – it is impossible to say anything about the character of "aboutness" in language that itself is not conventionally arranged or schematic. Once we have decided that a statement is "true," something we do by determining "the existence or nonexistence of various entities that are talked about" in the statement in question, then "we can adopt one of four attitudes toward beliefs in which . . . the person in question is talking about non-existent entities":

1. declare all of them false . . . or truth-valueless . . .
    or
2. divide them into the ones which are false or truth-valueless because they are about nothing and those which are "really about" some real thing and which thus may be true
    or
3. divide them into the ones which are false or truth-valueless because they are about nothing and those which are "really about" fictional entities, and which thus may perhaps be true
    or
4. combine strategies (2) and (3). (*Mirror*, 290–1)

But Rorty suggests that making a decision about which of these cases holds true is impossible, because the possible variations on each one are virtually endless, since each one of the criteria listed itself devolves into having to be "verified" somehow either by a theory of reference or a theory of semantic inherence. The "fictional thing" and the "real thing" which may grant a statement "truth" must also be verified according to a theory of reference, so by boiling down a theory of reference to a theory of what one is "really talking about" only displaces the question of what's "out there" to begin with. "'Reference' only arises when one has made one's decision about the various strategies used to express the error that one finds in the world – the decision among (1) - (4) above – and then wishes to cast the result of one's decision into 'canonical' form, that is, into a language which uses standard quantificational logic as a matrix" (292). Theories of reference, in other words, are simply ways to justify decisions which are already made instrumentally and practically.

Still, there must be some rule of thumb by which these decisions get made that would make us want to justify them in the first place. Sure enough, Rorty gives us a hint at the coming of his hermeneutic project when he says that even decisions that are justified only by theories of reference are not simply intuitive decisions. In such cases when we are trying to decide what someone is really talking about, he says, "we are simply recasting our description of the situation in a way which avoids paradox and maximizes coherence" (*Mirror*, 291). Theories of reference, or theories of "what someone's really talking about," or any theories at all, are actually ways to avoid disagreement between parties involved in a conversation or, ideally, to provide for agreement in such a way as to make "the world" coherent. But consistent with Rorty's lineage as a human scientist in the mold of a Dilthey, he does not find himself ready to suggest that the philosophical project he is carving out for himself can be seen as an alternative to the physical or natural sciences or to a realist philosophy of science. Thomas Kuhn, after outlining the ways paradigm shifts occur in the natural sciences, notes that "the act of judgment that leads scientists to reject a previously accepted theory is always based upon more than a comparison of that theory with the world. The decision to reject one paradigm is always simultaneously the decision to accept another, and the judgment leading to that decision involves the comparison of both paradigms with nature and with each other" (*Structure*, 77). There are instrumental decisions that need to be made – about coherence, about explanatory capacity, about "maximizing coherence" and "avoiding paradox," in Rorty's terms – but there is also the need to measure the physical aspect of "the world" regardless of the conventional nature of the tools with which the measurements can be taken. And Rorty agrees when he suggests that there must be some way to suggest that our criteria of successful inquiry "are not just *our* criteria but also the *right* criteria, nature's criteria" (*Mirror*, 299). Rorty seems to be leaving room for the human scientific project of linking different ways of knowing – in a transdisciplinary or interdisciplinary fashion – in such a way as to understand theoretical knowledge as having a measurable impact upon human activity, and that such an impact will necessarily change human agency (either individually or collectively). He also seems to want to maintain a distinction between "material" investigations, in which the criteria generated by description and observation are held to be axiomatic within a given paradigm, and investigations of self-understanding, in which the paradigms themselves are subject for investigation, and in which both knowledges affect one another. Rorty takes Putnam to task for trying to "be epistemological," and makes a great deal of Putnam's "recantation" in which he admits that theories of reference are only rationalizations for what we have already decided instrumentally about "things in general," but he also seems to recognize the need for understanding human social activity as being at once the result of both scientific and discursive investigations. Story-telling is not enough either: if we boil everything down to "'pure' Davidsonian semantics" then it is difficult "to raise philosophically interesting questions about meaning and reference" (299). In effect, Rorty suggests, changing the terms of the discourse is not the same as changing the conditions of discourse: saying you are changing does not mean you are extricating yourself from one situation and inserting yourself into another.

But it is this last point that poses problems for Rorty's hermeneutics, a hermeneutics that blurs the distinction – difficult to sustain as it was even in Dilthey's case – between material (non- or extra-discursive) investigation on the one hand, and rhetorical or discursive self-understanding on the other. In the final section of the chapter on language philosophy, Rorty stops talking about meaning, and starts talking about the contexts within which the idea of "meaning" makes sense. We may never be able to say once and for all what terms (like, for example, "the good") refer to, but "there is . . . an ordinary sense of 'good,' the sense the word has when used to commend – to remark that something answers to some interest" (*Mirror*, 307). This is the "homely and shopworn" sense that acquires meaning through its repeated use over time to refer to certain situations which we all recognize, and to which – to a greater or lesser extent – we would all assent. Whatever doubts we might have about the particular use of the term "the good" in one situation or another would have to be expressed within "a context of general agreement" (309). It is this context of general agreement that is axiomatic for Rorty's hermeneutics, which he calls "an expression of hope that the cultural space left by the demise of epistemology will not be filled – that our culture should become one in which the demand for constraint and confrontation is no longer felt" (315). Instead of assuming that all conflicting discourses (or versions of reality) are commensurable, hermeneutics suggests that "all residual disagreements will be seen" as "capable of being resolved by doing something further. What matters is that there should be agreement about what would have to be done if a resolution *were* to be achieved. In the meantime, the interlocutors can agree to differ –

being satisfied of each other's rationality the while" (316). By living hermeneutically, we must first assume a condition of rationality, in which all the interlocutors (or co-investigators) taking part in some conversation agree upon the context within which the conversation takes place. The interlocutors may disagree about certain aspects of their world(s) within that context, and it may be that a resolution of such a conflict is impossible to reach, given the terms of the conversation and the current context. But it may be possible to take some future action – readjusting the boundaries of the scheme within which the conversation takes place, for example – after which a resolution (but not necessarily agreement) might be possible. "Hermeneutics sees the relations between various discourses as those of strands in a possible conversation, a conversation which presupposes no disciplinary matrix which unites the speakers, but where the hope of agreement is never lost so long as the conversation lasts." "[T]o be rational is to be willing . . . to pick up the jargon of the interlocutor rather than translating it into one's own" (318).

What we have so far sounds much like a pure philosophy of language without the abstract terminology. When confronted by two mutually exclusive truth claims made within a conceptual scheme or paradigm, we do not have any way to resolve the apparent contradiction by appealing to some situation outside the scheme, because the "demand for constraints" that might be provided by some extra-discursive material reality or "objectivist" state of affairs is impossible. What we are left with is the need for one of the interlocutors to "pick up the jargon" of the other. This will be strange territory – it may be language that has never been used before – but this territory must be traversed in order to keep the conversation going and to provide the possibility that this "strangeness" will lead to some future course of action (apart from the conversation taking place at the hermeneutical moment) that will lead to progress. You can see this as the working of a pure language theory to the extent that at no time does either of the interlocutors attempt to make sense of the conversation by appealing to something outside the conversation itself; and that whatever action is taken will be understood in terms of agreed-upon conventions. "[T]he interlocutors can agree to differ – being satisfied of each other's *rationality* the while" (*Mirror*, 316; emphasis added).

114

But what about this rationality? Is it safe to assume that an agreement to keep the conversation going is a rational act? And can it be assumed that rationality is always discursive, that it is possible to "pick up the other's jargon" at all? Rorty hints that it may not be possible – on a strictly hermeneutical accounting – to do so. We cannot really say what kinds of evidence we can adduce when making an argument in a conversation, or what elements are important, because our foregrounding of them will depend at least in part upon how we understand those elements against a background of a host of other elements and forces. "[W]e shall never be able to avoid the 'hermeneutic circle' – the fact that we cannot understand the parts of a strange culture, practice, theory, language, or whatever, unless we know something about how the whole thing works, whereas we cannot get a grasp on how the whole thing works until we have some understanding of its parts . . .'" (319). There is at least an element, in Rorty's hermeneutic understanding of "becoming acquainted" with objects and phenomena alien to their investigators, of *both* the discursive "playing back and forth between guesses" about how to describe statements or events *and* an extradiscursive investigation of the object itself. This extra-discursive element may have nothing to do with the interlocutor's "rationality" (that is, the assumption that her participation in the conversation implies common cause with the other investigator, or that the instrumentality of the conversation, or the action that may take place as a result of incommensurability, will be shared); it may only have to do with the observation and careful measurement of the individual parts, describable under certain conditions, of a phenomenon or state of affairs. Language may not go all the way down after all: there may be some other method of investigation required, even in hermeneutics.

These different methods of investigation are each relegated to a separate sphere of inquiry: "normal discourse" and "abnormal discourse." Normal discourse

is that which is conducted within an agreed-upon set of conventions about what counts as a relevant contribution, what counts as answering a question, what counts as having a good argument for that answer or a good criticism of it. Abnormal discourse is what happens when someone joins in the discourse who is ignorant of these conventions or who sets them aside . . . The product of abnormal discourse can be anything from nonsense to intellectual revolution, and there is no discipline which describes it, any more than there is a discipline devoted to the study of the unpredictable, or to "creativity."   (*Mirror*, 320)

Rorty goes on to say that the line between epistemology and hermeneutics is not easily drawn between "the sciences of nature" and "the sciences of man" respectively, but between understanding things normally and understanding them abnormally. The significance of this for the human sciences – and for rhetoric in particular, something to which we have not paid much attention so far – is that *both* naturally occurring phenomena (including the natural dimension in human activity) and human self-understanding of the role of human activity upon the natural world (through cognition) can be understood both normally and abnormally; that the natural sciences may proceed either within paradigms or move outside of them into other, different paradigmatic structures, and that the human sciences may proceed likewise. Further, the role of rhetoric (the conventional arrangements of discursive material that has both a material and an ethical element as well as both a purely theoretical as well as a practical range) may lie somewhere in between normal and abnormal investigation of discourse, as an investigation into the ways in which conventional descriptions of "the world" may or may not be adequate expressions of human states of affairs and of the human capacity to change them, and as a way to arbitrate between systematic investigations that proceed scientifically and theoretically and non-systematic, contingent, and contestable deployment of such knowledges. Rorty's introduction of the distinction between hermeneutics and epistemology, far from erasing the distinctions between the scientific and the rhetorical (the necessary and the contingent), seems to suggest that it can be maintained – and in fact, that it may be necessary to maintain it – because hermeneutics can be seen as a way to bridge the gap between the two by saying both that the constraints within which we work are conventionally established, and that they are also nevertheless inescapable and always already there. Like the imperfect world of *Gorgias*, we cannot escape material constraints, nor can we find adequate ways of rendering them objectively understandable, so we do what we can in both systematic, theoretical ways, as well as in highly contingent, highly debatable ways.

116

A broken mirror

So where has Rorty's valorization of hermeneutics left other, non-discursive (i.e., theoretical or scientific) ways of knowing? Rorty does not go so far as to say that hermeneutics covers everything. To say that we must always and everywhere understand "the world" hermeneutically, and "to deny . . . that there is something called 'rational reconstruction' which can *legitimize* current scientific practice, is still not to say that the atoms, wave packages, etc., discovered by the physical scientists are creations of the human spirit" (*Mirror*, 345). But this is also not to say that the sciences are "objective" in any sense "in which politics or poetry may not be. . . . To say, with Sartre, that man makes himself, and that he differs thereby from atoms and inkwells, is quite compatible with repudiating any suggestion that part of his self-creation consists in 'constituting' atoms and inkwells" (346). The hermeneutic dimension in human activity, which involves reconfiguring the discursivity of the world, does not necessarily allow human activity to change the materiality of the world exclusive of discourse. We may be able to call an inkwell something else, but that does not change its materiality, or its facticity. But the converse – as we have seen with Dilthey – is also true: it may be that the materiality and facticity of inkwells is immutable, but that our cognition of it is not, and it also may be true that our cognition of human activity is all the more susceptible to the exigencies of material constraint because of its discursive dimension. But human activity also has a material dimension which is available for inquiry under "normal" circumstances regardless of whether those circumstances may be "rearranged" through the process of hermeneutics. Epistemological ways of knowing (the *Naturwissenschaften:* science, physics, political science) do not compete with hermeneutic ways of knowing (the *Geisteswissenschaften*: "edifying philosophy," poetry), but rather they "help each other out" (346). Rhetoric, because it has place in both dimensions because of its analysis of both conventional and theoretical codifications of discourse, occupies for Rorty (and, as we shall see, for Fish) a pivotal place in such a scheme.

Yet as Kuhn made clear years earlier, there are certain things science simply cannot do, and it is in such instances that hermeneutics (the attempt to understand abnormal discourse) has a special and unique role. But what does one do when one runs across something so foreign, something so outside the realm of current explanatory schemes, that it defies normal scientific or epistemological inquiry? We could act epistemologically, and make an attempt to translate the activity or phenomenon into the language of the current paradigm, "translating" it into understandable codes. To do so would require both a theoretical and a rhetorical inquiry into the "nature" of the phenomenon and into the community of interlocutors and the polis to which such a phenomenon would be relevant. But this act of translation may render the "strange" familiar, and will undoubtedly leave aspects of the phenomenon – those which made it odd or susceptible for translation in the first place – outside of its explanation. The other choice is to operate hermeneutically: we may be required to overthrow the familiar, normalizing language (both the theoretical / scientific as well as the conventional / everyday) in favor of a completely different set of terms and a completely different way of thinking. In the same way that the Los Angeles riots in the wake of the Rodney King verdict in the Spring of l992 defied the easy classifications of the event in terms of "race," in terms of "class," and in terms of "culture," Rorty would suggest that we may have to transpose into a hermeneutical key in order to understand the phenomena of April and May l992 in south-central LA in completely different terms. "We should not assume that the vocabulary used so far will work on everything else that turns up . . . [W]hat interferes with predicting the behavior of inhabitants of the unfamiliar culture [or situation, or phenomenon] is simply the incommensurability of their language" (349–50).

Of course, there are problems with this latter view. Rorty notes that the line between epistemology and hermeneutics is not the line "between the human and the nonhuman but between that portion of the field of inquiry where we feel rather uncertain that we have the right vocabulary at hand and that portion where we feel rather certain that we do," and he goes on to note that it is *this* distinction that roughly coincides with the difference between the *Geistes-* and the *Naturewissenschaften*. Going back to the Los Angeles riots (the "normalization" of which I will take up later in some detail), it may be true that the series of events – so easily describable, during their first hours, in the same terms used to report on the Watts riots nearly twenty years ealier – may have eventually caused doubt as to whether the vocabulary we had at hand was adequate for our understanding of it. But if hermeneutics is the attempt to "keep the conversation going" by reinscribing the event in a vocabulary that does not try to identify it but rather imagines the possibilities for future action, one wonders just what this conversation looks like. Were the utterances of some of those involved in the looting, or those of the then presidential candidates (talking about how the social programs of the 1960s did or did not contribute to the uprising) productive of the continuing conversation Rorty is interested in promulgating? It may be that, even in such a case where the occurrences being observed and the phenomena under investigation yield knowledge entirely foreign to the contemporary paradigm, the paradigm may not be so inadequate as to fail to yield any useful knowledge at all. It may be that conventional social scientific methodologies may be quite useful – especially when used alongside other, hermeneutically generated methodologies (perhaps such as ethnographies) – in generating useful knowledges for deployment in the public sphere, though the normal methods of inquiry being used may eventually be overthrown as a result of that very process of inquiry and knowledge production. It may be that even in the most abnormal of situations there is a use for normal scientific inquiry, though abnormal (hermeneutic) inquiry may have to show a path for it, and may eventually alert the scientist to its obsolescence. It may be necessary, when we are acting hermeneutical and "trying to show how the odd or paradoxical or offensive things [others] say [or do] hang together with the rest of what they want to say, and how what they say looks when put in our own alternative idiom" (365), to use normal, scientific or epistemological ways of knowing to investigate just why those things look so odd in the first place, and whether odd should mean "potentially adaptable for deployment in the public" or "potentially damaging to the polis and something to reject." There may be a need for examining "the scarcity of food and the [dangers of] the secret police" hermeneutically, but if such an abnormal discourse is threatened, as Rorty admits, then perhaps we might best not rule normal inquiry out of court just yet (389).

What we are left with is some uncertainty about just what the role of abnormal discourse (hermeneutics) is in Rorty's scheme, and how it functions alongside rhetoric on the one hand, and scientific and theoretical inquiry on the other. There are at least two ways of looking at the project of *Philosophy and the Mirror of Nature*. The first is to say that Rorty's antifoundational or hermeneutic revision of language and philosophy is misguided at best (or delusional at worst): in bifurcating the procedure investigators pursue in reading cultures or texts or phenomena, one part hermeneutical and one part "normal" or epistemological (one that eschews foundations or "neutral observation language" or "the real," another that works "as if" such foundations existed), Rorty wants to have it both ways. By establishing a hermeneutics of "abnormal" investigation when things sound "aberrant" or strange or when we run into incommensurable discourses or ways of measuring phenomena, we do our best to continue the conversation in such cases. This effectively calls into question when things are normal and when things are abnormal. We reside on a slippery slope on which all discourses (scientific and poetic) and all phenomena can be seen as having some revolutionary or incommensurable aspect – in rhetorical terms, some aspect that does not seem to fall under the purview of the traditional canons of rhetoric, or which does not appear to reside in the world of the certain, or the contingent, but perhaps both – and so one wonders where we draw the line. Why are we unable to see everything as susceptible to hermeneutic investigation? (In rhetorical terms, why not simply go back to Plato and say that disciplinary lines are blurred once and for all, or to Dilthey and say that the human sciences are the realm of the hermeneutic and subsume the natural sciences to human scientific investigation?) On such a view of Rorty's project – and this is Stanley Fish's view when it is pushed farther than perhaps Fish himself would like it to go – antifoundational philosophy or language theory looks rather foundational, with hermeneutics serving as the cornerstone.

There is no such thing as an a-perspectival knowledge because humans do and say the damnedest things, and because these potentially aberrant behaviors (and actions) must be accounted for even in scientific investigation, there must be an alternative to working *as if* a-perspectival knowledge were possible because humans do speak from different positions with different vocabularies signifying all kinds of odd behavior. What these views ignore, however, is that even the most aberrant of descriptions can be internally consistent or inconsistent; and they can exhibit similarities across many different types and classes of interlocutors. Even in the most abnormal of conversations, it is true that there will be descriptions (of objects or phenomena) that are internally inconsistent: a person will at once appear angry and joyous during a riot; members of the moneyed class will loot a grocery store alongside unemployed single parents; light will exhibit the properties of both a wave and a particle. Hermeneutics resists the forming of a foundation by making these conflicting aspects of the "conversation" commensurable, and presumably will work toward taking future action that results from the continued conversation, albeit in abnormal, perhaps mutually incompatible descriptions. But on the accounting of Rorty (and Fish and Bruffee), there is no way to examine, in other than hermeneutic terms, the causes of such internal inconsistencies, because those inconsistencies themselves are a sign that "commensurating" discourses such as the systematic observation language of a physical science or the "objectivity" and quantitative studies of political science should not be put to use.

What we are left with, in Fish's and Rorty's antifoundational hermeneutics, is not social action, but pedagogy: we must "teach situations" (or, in slightly more political terms, we should follow Gerald Graff's injunction to "teach the conflicts"), but this kind of teaching is "ineffectual." "[I]f antifoundationalism is correct and everything we know is always a function of situations, then everything we teach is always situational knowledge, whether we label it so or not. That is to say, even if a student is being presented with a piece of knowledge – of grammar, of propriety, of whatever – as if it were independent, detached, and transferable (i.e., 'cashable' in any and all situations), it is not thereby *rendered* independent, detached, transferable" (*Mirror*, 352). And yet teaching these situations does not render the student capable of changing her place in the social order. If she is caught in situations that are in part (if not, Rorty and Fish would say, for the most part) discursively formulated, and if those discursive formulations are connected to, but not accessible through, material situations and extra-discursive knowledge of them, then by changing her discourse the subject should just give up trying to change her material situation. Again, this is something Fish so much as admits: "if all knowledge is situational and we are always already in a situation, then we can never be at any distance from the knowledge we need" (353). If this sounds positive, you only need to turn the page to see why it is not: though it has been suggested that the above hermeneutical dictum can be read to say "we learn by doing, so just do it," this dictum "belongs properly to the *foundationalist* hero, to someone who has just discovered a truth above the situational and now returns to implement it; it cannot, without contradiction, be the narrative of the antifoundationalist hero who can only enact his heroism by refusing to take either comfort or method from his creed" (354). As Fish goes on to say, the yield of hermeneutics is small, though it has been his point: it offers "nothing but the assurance that what it is able to give you – knowledge, goals, purposes, strategies – is what you already have" (355), which, for those living in South Central Los Angeles, or Rwanda, or Hebron, is small comfort, since what they want is not assurance, but change.

But the other way of looking at Rorty's project is to suggest that he really has not got anything wrong. In fact, Rorty is on absolutely the right path, but he has not followed the full implications of his own theory, and as a result he does not carry it as far forward as he ought. This is Charles Guignon's argument *vis-à-vis* Rorty and Taylor, though I should say that Guignon does take Rorty to task at certain turns, and does rely more on Heidegger where Rorty champions Gadamer. Still, Guignon's view of *Philosophy and the Mirror of Nature*'s hermeneutic task is that it is less an overthrow of epistemology in favor of hermeneutics (and he notes that Rorty has explicitly disavowed such a task, a fact overlooked by some popularizations of Rorty) than it is a supplanting of one kind of epistemology with another, radically different one. For our purposes, it may be that (in Guignon's terms) Rorty's new way of viewing the world is a *rhetorical* one, in the tradition of Plato or an ethics-building Aristotle, in that human cognitive and discursive activity is discernable – and analyzable – only in terms of a lived praxis. If so, then we need a theory of human activity that works alongside or within a theory of discourse, but it does not necessarily follow that there are no "foundational" or systematic ways of theorizing or, in fact, doing the observational and experimental work in order to justify such a hermeneutic theory.

But there is another way of looking at the hermeneutic project begun by Rorty, which is rather different from Fish's attempt to have it both ways (and as a result have neither): Charles Guignon invokes Charles Taylor (and, back farther, Wittgenstein and Heidegger) to suggest that Stanley Fish and others, who demand allegiance to the antifoundational premise which does away with epistemology in favor of hermeneutics and which divides normal and abnormal ways of knowing for different purposes, have presented a false dichotomy and that they themselves have become mired in the resulting morass. The overthrow of epistemology, suggests Guignon, has resulted *not* in the need to adhere to a completely non-epistemological worldview when confronted by "abnormal discourse" (which, as several people have suggested, is a component of all discourse), but rather presents the opportunity for an altogether different mode of human understanding, one that has been around for a while but, in Kuhn's words, was not recognized as a paradigm candidate because the "crisis" that would force its recognition had not occurred (or been itself recognized *as* crisis) by the early twentieth century. Fish and Rorty do not have hermeneutics wrong so much as they have hamstrung it by failing to recognize that it functions alongside other knowledges in what amounts to a dialectical movement between hermeneutic and scientific knowledge, each of which guides the other. On such a view, Rorty's view of hermeneutics could be used in all "conversations," both normal and abnormal, because Heidegger and Wittgenstein take all language as having an abnormal component, and take all human situations as being constrained by discursive and extra-discursive material, each of which can be analyzed systematically and rhetorically.

What Guignon takes from Charles Taylor is an "operational view," which Taylor in turn gets from Wittgenstein and Heidegger. The everyday descriptions that humans make to understand their lives proceed by a kind of "transcendental argument" to reveal the conditions that make our involvement – and our description – of that world possible in the first place. Heidegger called this agency "being-in-the-world," which foregrounds the practical activities of human life, its praxis (or, in Aristotle's terms, phronesis). "What is 'given' at the most basic level in ordinary practical activity, for Heidegger, is not isolated objects with properties (present-at-hand) things, but a holistic web of functional relations organized around our projects (the ready-to-hand)." Agents are defined by the activities in which they are engaged, and by the ethical course those actions take to form a life. In such a world, there is no separation of subjects and objects, and it is equally the case that separating the material (extra-discursive) from the discursive dimension of such a world is difficult. It is an illusion that things are merely present-at-hand, an illusion that is constituted when we "bring close" an object from its temporal / spatial location in historical time. But this bringing close is itself an activity of a being-in-time, and needs to be described as a component of it, rather than to try to divorce the object, as in the *Naturwissenschaften* (see Heidegger, *Being and Time*, 418–23). Of course, this does not rule out the systematic investigations of objects in isolation and a treatment of their individual properties. This kind of scientific investigation provides us with a way of construing a world that has certain advantages, one of which is the ability to predict the patterns of events which material objects participate in without human interaction; and to predict the patterns of events that occur in the material dimension of human life. But, as Guignon suggests, the "regional ontology" provided by science does not provide privileged access to the material dimension, and any formulation and justification of human beliefs (that is, the ethical self-understanding of the components of a lived life) "are made possible by a practically engaged 'know-how' where we are, so to speak, already up to our elbows in the midsts of things" (Guignon, "Pragmatism," 84), and so we are forced to recognize the inextricable interweaving of natural scientific and human scientific (or hermeneutic) under-standings. This interwoven fabric Taylor calls "transcendental," since it shows "the indispensable conditions of there being any-thing like experience or awareness of the world in the first place" ("Overcoming Epistemology," 473). What should be noted, at this point, is that Taylor, via Heidegger, is trying to avoid the antifoundational problem that hamstrung Fish (and the weaker version of Rorty's hermeneutic understanding), namely, the strong assertion that hermeneutics is not a foundation, and that any foundational epistemology should be radically questioned in such a revision. Here all Guignon suggests is that, while science does not provide any privileged understanding of the world, even the "primordiality" of being-in-time can be supplemented or enriched by placing it alongside older epistemological systems, like the physical sciences. And this is perfectly consistent with the model of the knowledges presented by Aristotle – albeit within a

different general worldview – that placed phronesis as a culmination of the theoretical and metaphysical sciences but nevertheless
relied upon the knowledge produced by them, and which had its
source in the sense-data and common opinions of individual
members of the polis, also like the theoretical and metaphysical
sciences. In holding up Heidegger as his model, Guignon is proposing another small change in his understanding of hermeneutics. Whereas Rorty's first touchstone was Gadamer, who
understood the pinnacle of human activity as aesthetic, and in
which the hermeneutic circle was most useful in classically originated, nearly extra-historical texts, Guignon, *apropos* of Taylor,
notes that Wittgenstein and Heidegger pointed to "language [as]
the medium which orients us within the shared life world," a
language that is first and always "public" and which "articulates
the centers of significance of our practical life-world and [which]
makes manifest what counts for us" (Guignon, "Pragmatism,"
84). Though both Gadamer and Heidegger hold as a first premise
that "we are . . . unavoidably caught up in a hermeneutic circle to
the extent that our grasp of things around us is always preshaped
by a general mastery of the meaning of the entire context," the
questions and answers of Gadamer's hermeneutics always have
as their object the aesthetic object and its relation to the observing
subject, whereas for Heidegger, the background is equally as
important as the aesthetic object, because it is the location of the
subject to begin with. Like a rhetorical understanding of situated
knowledges, Heidegger's – and Taylor's – beginning and ending
points are both the practical life of the subject (and groups of
subjects) for whom the investigation, scientific or hermeneutic,
takes place.

This view of lived life involves both a descriptive and a hermeneutic (or interpretive) moment: sounding much like Dilthey,
Guignon notes that "we must always have a privileged access to
our own agency because action (as opposed to inadvertent movement) is *directed* by the self-understanding of the person who
acts." But he goes on to say that "action is identifiable only under
a description," which has two parts:

When my hand goes up at a meeting, for example, it is true of me that I
am flexing my deltoids, displacing air molecules, and voting for the man I
like. But you have correctly identified my action only if you grasp it

125

under the description it bears for me. Of course, you may have a better insight into what I am really doing than I have; you may see, perhaps, that actually I am displaying my sexist attitudes by voting for the man rather than for the woman. But this sort of revisionary description must start out from, and be able to make sense of, the original explanandum, my own self-description.   (Guignon, "Pragmatism," 85)

Of course, Guignon makes the point that self-understanding takes precedence over such physical scientific descriptions of the movement of muscles in my arm, and the social scientific descriptions of the political dynamic of gender and power that are taking place in the micro-polis of the meeting house. But the converse is true, and Taylor says so – to have a grasp of our own action is to have some understanding of the conditions that make the action possible. Like Rorty's and Fish's point that there are always already constraints upon our actions that render them understandable in the first place, Taylor goes on to suggest that it may be necessary to understand not just the political and gender implications of voting – and their physical as well as discursive constraints – but also the physical and biological processes that allow me to raise my hand to make my choice. (Things might be different – and Guignon's relatively easy to understand example might not be so easy – if I were to suggest that the voter has cerebral palsy and the neuro-electrical process that might be described has a very definite effect upon whether the voter is able to raise his or her hand at all, and for what reasons, and why amenities were not offered to equalize the ability of all in the meeting house to vote.) Taylor notes that my version of the voting story and someone else's – perhaps a woman with cerebral palsy – might be different, because "our ordinary self-understanding often is shot through with distortions and deceptions mediated by popular theories and current fads," and so we need to "try to clarify what goes on in the kinds of validation we actually find in everday life" ("Overcoming Epistemology," 86). We do this by "telling stories," but stories that can be seen as foundational because they are grounded in common experience, and can be understood in theoretical as well as in practical terms. A "new outlook supersedes the older one because it can explain the inadequacy of the older view in its own terms," much like a new scientific praradigm can be said to be superior to previous ones because of its greater explanatory capacity. In both cases, redescription involves not just narrative, but a careful examination of the object of narration itself for internal coherence, the match between conventional understanding of the object of narration and the description being used to understand it in other terms, and they originate in "common opinion" and are useful for any number of different knowledges (see Sanders, "Discursive Constraints,").

Of course, Rorty will not have any of this, because he sees the material / ontological dimension as having been thrown over with his "endless repetitive, literary-historical 'deconstruction' of the 'Western metaphysicals of presence'" (Rorty, *Consequences*, xxii). All the recognition that we are self-interpreting animals allows us to do is recognize that, as "a self-changing being, [we are] *capable of remaking [our]selves by remaking [our] own speech*" (Rorty, "Epistemological Behaviorism," 10). But as we have seen, Guignon suggests *apropos* of Taylor, "we can always make our current views look good by cooking up some story about how those views supersede other ones, but this fact shows us more about our skills at storytelling than about the validity of our beliefs" ("Pragmatism," 89). For Rorty, once we see that there is "no way to underwrite or criticize the ongoing, self-modifying know-how of the user of language," then we will "become increasingly ironic, playful, free and inventive in our choice of self-descriptions" (Rorty, "Language Play," 751; *Contingency*, 39). Guignon wonders whether everyone has the choice to be playful in such a hermeneutic world, and what the constraints are if the answer to that question is no.

I conclude this chapter by simultaneously pointing out the biggest weakness in Rorty's hermeneutic (and its biggest potential strength, when tied to other kinds of knowledge) by reiterating Guignon's foregrounding of the material dimension to the ready-to-hand in Heidegger's scheme. Rorty's "private spinner of webs of belief and desire" might be imagined as someone set before a dizzying array of possible descriptions and courses of action, any of which might be chosen. Because of the vastness of the array (and its presumed incommensurability), there exists no stable vocabulary for expressing the superiority of one course of action over another, and so the choice involves something like closing one's eyes, imagining one's desire, and pointing to a choice. Justification for the choice of whatever action is taken comes later, and can be judged successful or not depending upon whether the desire that allowed the subject to choose that course of action was satisfied. But there is another way to look at this. Where for Rorty the incommensurability of the options and the wide-open ability to choose from among them amount to freedom, for Taylor (and Guignon) they amount to nothing short of compulsion. If there is no way to adjudicate between the available choices, and the subject judges based upon his or her ability to tell a justifiable story about the imagined course of action or its completion, then if someone else was able to tell a better story than you, your options would be foreclosed. Choice among competing courses of action – as well as among descriptions and among competing knowledges and beliefs – depends upon your ability to tell a better story.

But how do you get to tell better stories? For Rorty, we either use the normal language of the epistemologically centered observer, "making sociological and historical observations about where we currently stand in our postmodernist culture," or we abnormally engage in a guessing game (between interlocutors) in which other possible choices (or objects, or states of affairs) are offered as alternatives to the incommensurable choices currently available, and hope something sticks. The second of these choices is difficult at best, because there is no guarantee that changing your description will change your social or material position. But the first, in which we use the normal language of description from the outsider's perspective, is precisely what Rorty wishes to get past, the epistemological stance in which knowledge is objective and detached from lived life. Moreover, there is no way to say whether the quality of one person's story – over against another's – is not itself the result of certain materially ascertainable social relations and extra-discursive conditions that one simply cannot leave unexamined. If one does leave these conditions unexamined, then those in better social and material positions will, more often than not, tell the better stories, and those who are not in such conditions will remain unfree. Rorty's hermeneutics is reduced to something he wanted desperately to distance it from: language games.

Guignon would have us attend more closely to the everyday, practical knowledge that ties us to the world. "When we start from a description of our everyday agency before theorizing, we see that our own identity as agents is bound up with concrete situations and a practical life-world that we *find* rather than create" (Guignon, "Pragmatism," 99). What he calls hermeneutic realism, derived from the work of Heidegger via Charles Taylor, insists on the "primordiality" of the ready-to-hand, but also acknowledges that the project of interpreting the world may be an interminable dialectic of describing the material and the discursive elements of the practical life-world, then applying normal scientific analytical tools to those descriptions, and then deploying that knowledge back in the practical world of the common opinion and praxis, and so on. Hermeneutics of this sort recognizes that the constraints that impinge upon subjects are accessible through the discursive / rhetorical realm, but only partially so; and that human activity's extra-discursive component may be made manifest in the discursive dimension, but only partially. It also recognizes that scientific inquiry is one instrument with which the partial manifestation of the extra-discursive may be described. Hermeneutics acknowledges, in other words, that the only complete understanding of the life-world is a complicated one in which the hermeneutical and the scientific are interrelated. It will be my contention in the next section of this book that the combination of historical and dialectical materialism may be one way to reconcile rhetorical constructions of the life world and conceptual knowledge of it, though this contention will have to be modified radically by the work of several pedagogues who have written after Althusser's reformulation of conceptual knowledge.

5

Louise Phelps and Theory: toward a human science disciplined by practical wisdom

Near the beginning of *Composition as a Human Science*, Louise Phelps notes that "the framework on which the positive directions of postmodern culture converge is an essentially rhetorical one, and as such both fits the needs of composition for a global philosophy of knowledge in relation to praxis and also opens the way for composition to help articulate and realize this paradigm" (6). The book goes on to trace the rise of the "postmodern consciousness," characterized by its rejection of positivism and its uncritical acceptance of science as both objective and progressive, and by the adoption of acutely self-reflexive modes of thought that situate both the object of inquiry and the methodology for inquiry in sites of contestation. Because the postmodern situation understands the world as mediated primarily by means of language, then it is natural to assume that any discipline that understands itself as primarily interested in the complexities of language and writing should be at the center of contemporary epistemological debates: what can be known, and what is the nature of that knowledge? Phelps suggests that it is composition which recognizes itself as central to these debates, but that the field is currently in something like a crisis of confidence. This crisis begins with compositionists' questions about the nature of their "field," and its connection to other fields of knowledge, not just in the human but also in the natural sciences. The challenge for compositionists is to recognize that their task forces them in two directions at once – to know the contours of the terrain broadly understood as the "human sciences," and to define the structure of a field that takes on the huge question of how language works.

If Phelps saw herself as challenging composition, as a field of inquiry, to do the work that would place it squarely at the juncture of the human and the natural sciences in a postmodern paradigm, that challenge went largely unmet. *Composition as a Human Science* was read and reviewed immediately after its publication with something like hostility on the one hand and utter incomprehension on the other. In journals mainly devoted to the teaching of writing, some of John Schilb's comments are characteristic: "Phelps's book is highly selective and utterly recondite, insistently echoing the terminology of hermeneutics, phenomenology, cognitive psychology, and physics" and that even specialists in the field of composition "[wi]ll get bogged down at times." More theoretically oriented journals did not seem to want to recognize it at all: *Pre/Text*, *Philosophy and Rhetoric* and *Rhetoric Society Quarterly* not only did not review it, but many of the articles in the years immediately after *Composition*'s publication do not cite it. There are a couple of reasons why the book's reception might have been chilly. First, Phelps's challenge to the field of composition is truly a daunting one, reconfiguring the field of rhetoric and composition on an axis that runs from Aristotle to Gadamer and Ricoeur, and rewriting the history of the human sciences from the early nineteenth century up to the demise of positivist science. Secondly, Schilb's second major critique of the book is apt: Phelps tends to treat the history of both composition and the last 200-odd years of intellectual history as more or less unified by an unnamed "crisis" that is left largely unexamined, both in ideological as well as more material terms.

My purpose in this chapter is to suggest that despite whatever problems readers might have with the selectivity of Phelps's historical analysis or the difficulties they might have with her theoretical approach, there are good reasons to pay close attention to Phelps's project in *Composition as a Human Science*. It may *not* be the case that composition, as it exists right now in the United States in secondary and post-secondary schools, can be seen as a macro-discipline at the juncture of the human and natural sciences that allows a critical examination of the ways in which language and social practice function in the material world. But it *is* true that the study of language's social force has preoccupied many if not most teachers and scholars over the last twenty to thirty years, and that Phelps's intervention into this set of concerns is valuable precisely because it both succeeds and also fails for the same reason: it suggests that rhetoric and / or composition can negotiate a middle way between purely objective knowledge based on systematic observation on the one hand and unexamined practice on the other, a middle ground that is interpretive and contextual. My contention here is that Phelps's attempt to reconfigure the study of language as a model for the human sciences can be shown to exhibit the characteristic hesitation between theoretical knowledge and practical knowledge evident since Plato; but that it also points to the ways in which this hesitation may be put to productive pedagogical use. This hesitation is marked in Phelps's book by an articulation of interpretive or hermeneutic work on the one hand, and scientific (Rorty's epistemological) work on the other. It is an articulation that *favors* the interpretive but that cannot escape being guided by the scientific. In very interesting ways, Phelps's work cannot keep from falling back upon a more or less objective, descriptive view of language *within* which hermeneutics operates on the object of knowledge *and* the objectivist language with which it is described. I will first lay out how Phelps's touchstones – Dewey, Freire, Aristotle and Gadamer – provide the groundwork for her understanding of discursive and extra-discursive material and its effect on human understanding and action; and then I will show how her three-part strategy for a critical practice based firmly in discourse negotiates the relation between scientific and practical wisdom. This relation, however, suffers from the same problems as Rorty's hermeneutics: an inadequate description of the very contexts which constrain hermeneutic analysis in the first place.

The concluding chapter of Phelps's book, "Toward a Human Science Disciplined by Practical Wisdom," invokes two terms which she understands together to form the centerpiece of composition as a discipline: phronesis and praxis. Though it is Gadamer's reinterpretation of the former term that ultimately serves as the guide for her work, it is Phelps' use of the term praxis in connection with the work of Dewey and Freire as it *informs* her theory of phronesis that interests me here. In the epigram that begins the chapter, from a letter to Richard Bernstein, Gadamer says that "I cannot really make sense of a *phronesis* that is supposed to be scientifically disciplined, although I can imagine a scientific approach that is disciplined by *phronesis*." What is most interesting in Phelps's references to Dewey and Freire is that both intimate ways in which practical wisdom and human praxis guide scientific analysis but also in which science (as systematic inquiry for Dewey, as theory or conceptual knowledge for Freire) guides practice.

Dewey and sense-data

Dewey's relation to pragmatism and the positivist tradition is a complicated one. In *Experience and Nature*, one of two works to which Phelps refers in her argument, Dewey does not so much reject the positivist project as redefine it. His work attempts to reintegrate "reflection," a version of systematic and theoretical understanding, with everyday experience so that they merge into something like a critical evaluation of everyday life. Dewey understands sense-experience as the starting point for interaction and communication in human beings, and he sees philosophy and science – as in Rorty's critique of these disciplines – as having abandoned them. As Rorty suggests of Dewey, such a reintegration was supposed to have liberated philosophy from the shackles of a vague theoretism that the Americans had inherited from Europe. Dewey hoped to reintroduce an "experimentalism" into philosophy, one that would involve an examination of everyday events and phenomena in which the observer was involved, and that would then require reflection as a check on those phenomena as "raw experience."

Of course, "raw experience" (or, in keeping with the pseudo-scientific terminology of Dewey, the descriptions of "nature" that are more or less assumed to have to be matched against scientific paradigms) is a difficult term, since for someone such as Rorty it is not something to which we have access except in highly mediated ways. In fact, Dewey occupies an interesting philosophical position somewhere between Rorty, whose hermeneutics attempts to recuperate from science and philosophy a commonsense kernel that cannot be understood analytically, and the more traditional analytic branch of philosophy that works its way back through the Scots and Irish rhetoricians to Locke. Though Locke is not mentioned at all in Phelps's book, and only once in Rorty's *Philosophy and the Mirror of Nature*, it is this connection that I think informs Dewey's desire to reintegrate experience and experiment back into an understanding of language, and thereby in part informs Phelps's desire to do the same.

Locke's initial division of the mind into the will and understanding, inherited from the Cartesian *cogito*, is one of Rorty's bogeys in *Philosophy and the Mirror of Nature* and, at least implicitly, in Phelps's *Composition as a Human Science*, since everything she writes there attempts to merge the divisions of theory and practice, object and subject, into an investigation of the life-world. And yet oddly, Dewey maintains a version of this distinction in much of his work. Locke unhitches language from "the world out there" by linking it instead with ideas; and ideas are the product not of immediate sense-impression – raw sense data – but of the associative principle that allows human beings to relate the characteristics of the objects or phenomena that produce sense-data to categories that work universally. The more elemental the characteristics – and the more general the categorical definitions or sensations – the more universal the idea; and the more universal the idea, then the more apt the word that refers to that idea is to be understood across individuals' uses of it. In the third book of *An Essay Concerning Human Understanding*, Locke goes so far as to suggest that even words arbitrarily assigned to the most universal ideas (derived initially from raw sense-data) apprehended by one individual may be apprehended only partially by another to whom those words are spoken. That is, it is possible to misapprehend even the language associated most closely with the ideas generated by the associative principle in connection to raw sense-data. The same sort of misapprehension is much more likely when less-common experiences – those that are not generated by "nature" but are instead the products of human imagination, or are natural phenomena common to only certain localities – are assigned words. Locke's proposed solution to this problem is to use as clear and concise a language as possible in order to avoid misunderstanding, "to make known one man's thoughts or ideas to another . . . to do it with as much ease and quickness as possible, and . . . thereby to convey the knowledge of things: language is either abused or deficient, when it fails of any of these three" (III.3.23). Much of the tenth chapter of the third book of the essay is a catalogue of how to obtain this kind of clarity.

134

What is important to note here is the relation, in Locke, between raw sense-data and reflection, and the way in which they work together, and how it bears upon Dewey's attempt to return philosophy to a consideration of that relation. It is not so much that the phenomena that act on human perception have a tendency to evoke in perceiving individuals a different range of responses, and therefore a different range of utterances that are intended to communicate those responses. Instead, the most general phenomena are apt to evoke similar (if not the same) responses across individuals, and it is the associative principle – through ideas – to which perceiving individuals *do have* direct access that causes the possibility of misapprehension or misunderstanding through communication. This is one of the reasons Rorty casts Locke as partly responsible for the idea that philosophy has erroneously seen itself as a mirror to nature: the *Essay* was an attempt to cast philosophy as the arbiter of the relation between words and ideas, and between ideas and things, and though the latter was always doomed to failure, it was seen as an imperative anyway. One of the reasons Rorty gives up on epistemology and its attempt to divine a direct relation between the world out there and the sentences we use to describe that world is because Locke (and all subsequent philosophers) have attached discourse to ideas, and that in doing so philosophy has (rightly) divorced itself from the possibility of "seeing the world as it is." And yet what is most interesting about Dewey – and for us, the relation between Dewey and Phelps's notions of rhetoric and phronesis – is that his desire to reattach reflection to sense-data lies somewhere between Locke's bullheaded attempt to work through the problem of the nonequivalence of language, idea and world, and Rorty's complete disavowal of the problem and the attempt to find a third way. Phelps quotes approvingly from a passage in *Experience in Nature*: "The charge that is brought [by me] against the non-empirical method of philosophizing is not that it depends upon theorizing, but that it fails to use refined, secondary products as a path pointing and leading back to something in primary experience" (8; quoted in Phelps, *Composition*, 209). That is to say, Dewey sees his version of pragmatic philosophy as a way to understand reflection as working to guide individuals' understanding of their direct experience, but also to use that understanding of experience to guide reflection. Perhaps more exactly, the moment of critical reflection for Dewey is a moment that links direct experience and reflection in such a way as to "correct" the Lockean problem of misunderstanding by allowing each to inform the other.

And yet it is precisely the relation between "raw sense-experience" and ideas (or, using Dewey's terms, between "doing and suffering" and describing them) that is not theorized. To go back once again to analytic philosophy, both Dewey and Locke understand that there are two relations to be considered, the relation between world and mind, and the relation between the minds of individual humans and the communicative or discursive relations between them in their social life. To be fair to Dewey, in *Experience and Nature* he saw himself only as trying to "behead philosophy" by dethroning epistemology (West, *American Evasion*, 89), and mainly wanted to get philosophers to consider the relation between world and mind, not necessarily to theorize it. But it is ironic, for our purposes, to understand that Dewey saw the project of dethroning philosophy as one that would bring it closer to *the natural sciences* through experimentation, and yet – very much unlike Locke centuries earlier – was unclear about the need for "experience" or "experiment" to guide theory. In "The Need for a Recovery of Philosophy," a work that Phelps does not cite, Dewey says that experience

is a matter of *simultaneous* doings and sufferings. Our undergoings are experiments in varying the course of events; our active tryings are trials and tests of ourselves ... [It is] certain modes of interaction, of correlation, of natural objects among which the organism happens, so to say, to be one. It follows with equal force that experience means primarily not knowledge, but ways of doing and suffering. Knowing must be described by discovering what particular mode – qualitatively unique – of doing and suffering it is. (26, 45)

Again, the problem is that, as I have tried to suggest with Rorty, Dewey does not go far enough to consider the characteristics of the relation between world and idea / word. Moreover, as did Thomas Sheridan – an Irish reader of Locke who went on to write a series of lectures on elocution – Dewey understands at some level that language is a material practice that takes place in the everyday world and has certain effects that must be studied not just reflectively but also practically. But unlike Sheridan – see his sixth lecture on elocution for an example – he does not go on to see how the language of expression, or the language of experiment or of reflection, is likewise a material phenomenon – something akin to "raw sense-experience," which must then be reintegrated into the analysis. This was the charge that has frequently been leveled against Rorty – that he has ignored the extent to which language is intimately tied to the natural world that works in specific and measurable ways – and I would suggest that it could be leveled against Dewey and also, by implication, Phelps: if it is true that Dewey attempts to take "everyday experience itself for the laboratory in which philosophical concepts are tested" (209), it is unclear just what the method used for testing might be, and whether the "praxis" Phelps aims to establish is tied to a more or less normative *scientific* method of inquiry.

But there may be a way out of this quandary, since one strength of Dewey's work (and Phelps recognizes it) is his understanding that raw sense-data has an effect or "makes sense" in terms of its *function*, the way in which it is understood to "work." That is, though sense-data as such cannot be "checked," it can be understood in terms of its effect upon a lived life; and for Phelps reflection must be brought to bear on knowledge in such a way as to *relate* the various sense-experiences as they are brought into combination in complex and non- (or non-uni-) directional ways. "Dewey's experimental method," suggests Phelps,

> reintegrates reflection and experience so that they complement and incorporate each other. Experience is the source for the refined methods and products of philosophy (for which we may read Theory in composition). At the same time, it is the testing ground (praxis) where reflective concepts can be experimentally verified. The process of verification involves taking theoretical concepts as designating abstract meanings that can be tested for their power to illuminate and enlarge primary experience when they are reinserted into personally experienced contexts.
>
> (*Composition*, 210)

Though Phelps fails, because Dewey does, to understand completely the need to articulate a structural relation between raw sense-data as understood by scientific methods of experimentation and testing (regardless of whether or not that method is circumscribed by the institutional and wider political norms of a particular culture), it is also clear that she *could* do so. In the section of "Toward a Human Science" quoted above, experience is seen as a "source" for methods and products of philosophy, as something to which we may not have direct access but which we understand as having a relation to methods and theories derived from them. The relation between theory and practice is recognized as a reciprocal one, but which takes primary experience as that which must be inserted into "contexts" understood as having both an abstract "meaning" as well as a palpable power for "illumination" (or, if you look at it a different way, for change, in Fish's words). We have seen this relationship before in Kuhn and Rorty, but much more clearly in theorists such as Guignon and R. H. Brown, who have begun to work through the relation between the material and measurable effects of language and the extra-discursive on "meaning."

In *The Structure of Scientific Revolutions*, Kuhn never went so far as to say that there is no such thing as direct access to sense-data (or phenomena, or structures), but that our access to those data is through a language established by the institution or community within which one makes systematic (or, if we take Dewey at his word, even unsystematic) observations. There is, for Kuhn, a commonsense division between "neutral observation language" which might be deemed a more or less felicitous description of sense-data or natural phenomena on the one hand, and languages useful for describing how those descriptions make sense in the world on the other. Like Dewey (and Phelps), Kuhn sees the gap between these two ways of producing knowledge as requiring a method for overcoming it, and Phelps takes Dewey (and, though without, perhaps, acknowledging her full indebtedness to his thinking, Kuhn as well) to suggest that it is through praxis – the integration of observation language and the everyday occurrences in one's lived life that allow one's observations both to adhere to and diverge from that language – that we make sense of the gap. Rorty, who *does* fully acknowledge his debt to Kuhn, understands Locke's initial move to obviate the need for epistemology altogether, and goes Kuhn one better: he suggests that

we do indeed need to give up the notion of "data and interpretation" with its suggestion that if we could get to the *real* data, unpolluted by our choice of language, we should be "grounding" rational choice. But we can get rid of this notion by being behaviorist in epistemology rather than being idealist. (*Philosophy and the Mirror of Nature*, 325)

Behaviorism of the kind Rorty advocates means something like paying attention to the particular moments of a lived life, noting the ways in which those moments may hinder the carrying on of a conversation in which the terms of the discussion are understandable by all parties involved, and proceeding in the face of them. What both Kuhn and Rorty have in common, despite the former's adherence to epistemology, is that they are "Deweyan" in the sense that they see a need for taking account of the material dimension of the rhetorical situation.

But neither Kuhn nor Rorty will be of any help to Phelps if we see her as trying to negotiate, for composition, between the human and the experimental sciences in such a way as to allow them to act as guides for one another in a theory of classroom practice. But Phelps's designs for composition might be aided with the help of Brown and Guignon. Guignon notes that even in a hermeneutics like the one advocated by Phelps we need to see the finitude of our rootedness in cultural contexts or institutionally sanctioned methods as part of what constitutes the life-world to begin with ("Pragmatism," 96–7). Brown notes that "society is not only praxis but also practico-inert," and that the practico-inert, "that which cannot be articulated," must nevertheless be brought into either the methods on hand for its analysis or methods that must be constructed for the purpose of doing so ("Symbolic," 328, 331). As suggested earlier, this view of the life-world as at least partly extra-discursive and thus partly dependent for explanation upon more or less scientific methods does not invalidate hermeneutics or the human sciences as a way of understanding human social life. But this view also does not mean that we need to go back to Locke and insist on finding a neutral observation language that gives us relatively unmediated access to the world of raw sense data. Rather, it suggests that we have access to this aspect of the life-world at least in terms of its effects (both discursive and extra-discursive). Moreover, the movement between understanding or reflection on the one hand, and the direct experiential moments of lived life on the other (the integration which Phelps and Dewey say is needed if we are successfully to reorganize philosophy) have to be seen as taking place in a material world that impinges upon any analysis of it. As a result, we have to pay very close attention to the ways in which it does so. As I have tried to suggest, because Dewey fails to do so, Phelps's decision to found praxis on his work is at least in part responsible for her own failure, as John Schilb notes, to acknowledge, despite her own exculpatory remarks, "power and the political dimension of composition and its praxis" (Phelps, *Composition*, xiii; quoted in Schilb, review, 165).

Freire and praxis

One of the reasons that the work of Paulo Freire is valuable for Phelps is that he enlarges the terms "reflection" and "sense data" by placing them in a context that is radically interactive: "Just as Dewey redefines experience as inherently cognitive, Freire redefines true praxis as an inescapable relation between reflection and action" (*Composition*, 211). Phelps goes on to privilege the role of education in human activity, a process that does not simply theoretically provide reflection as a "check" against commonsense data (or, in the case of experimentation in everyday life, a way of guiding experiential work), but rather engages that check constantly through "dialogue." Dialogue establishes an interaction between teachers' and students' praxis, "simultaneously developing [action and reflection] within the students. Dialogue is the means by which reflection creates, recreates, and transforms the knowledge that each side brings to the dialogic situation" (212). If Dewey's praxis is a way of balancing individuals' experiential life with critical reflection and then reintegrating the knowledge produced in those situations into the analysis, in Dewey's words "a process of standing something[,] of suffering and passion" ("Need," 25); with Freire we can investigate suffering as something people not only have in common with one another but also can communicate and do something about.

In the first chapter of *The Pedagogy of the Oppressed*, the text with which Phelps is concerned here, Freire sets up the by-now common oppressor / oppressed dichotomy as one that can only occur in concrete situations – this is no set of theoretical categories, but the pragmatic acknowledgement that it is "the concrete situation which begets oppression," and that it is this situation that must be transformed (*Pedagogy*, 32). It is for this reason that objectivity and subjectivity cannot be separated, but must be treated – pedagogically – as working dialectically: the oppressor (the person or group that holds a disproportionate amount of power in a social situation) is at least in part also oppressed since she surrenders something of her freedom, according to Freire, in maintaining the imbalance of relations. Suffering takes place therefore in social situations, but so, according to Freire, does the possibility of emancipation: "One must make oppression all the more oppressive by adding to it the *consciousness* of oppression thereby making its infamy all the more infamous, in order to make it known" (33, emphasis Freire's; my translation). To make it available to both the oppressor and the oppressed, what Freire calls a "critical consciousness" both "objectifies" and also "acts upon" the life-world, and this critical consciousness takes place in dialogue and in concert with other individuals either in similar situations or who are in a position to understand the nature of those situations.

For our purposes, two points should be made. First, theoretical concerns – reflection – need to be adapted to very specific contextual situations. Freire understands that a praxis must be tied not to theory but to "the teaching community where [it] participates in subtle interchanges, affinities, and oppositions with other models of discourse and teaching" (Phelps, *Composition*, 214). Phelps's addition of Freire to her conception of praxis therefore revises Dewey's desire for a dialectical movement between theory and practice (or between reflection and experience) in favor of a social rather than an individual process. Going back to Dewey's idea of raw sense-experience as that which guides reflection, it suggests two requirements for philosophy – or, for Phelps, a human science. The first is a way to produce knowledge of individual human wills or self-understanding (which presupposes an adequate method of analysis of both how humans interpret their world based on already-held principles, *endoxa*, and the material constraints within which they do the interpreting). The second is a way to produce knowledge of the social interaction in which individual wills are obstructed or deflected. At all points, in other words, at which Dewey would require a constant interaction between reflection and experience, both teachers and students are required to engage in self-understanding as well as something like objective or scientific observation and theorization of the structures within which self-understanding occurs. It becomes clear now that Phelps's praxis, at least as it will inform phronesis, is a rather complicated affair that potentially includes methods from outside what she understands as the human sciences.

The second important point for Phelps is that dialogue for Freire enriches Dewey's analysis because its ability to speak (to "name") an experience – and as such it has a creative capacity – is done from the "built-in" critical dimension of *intersubjectivity*: "it makes the teacher's own praxis reflective and experimental, by extending those qualities into an intersubjective situation . . . The whole may be thought of as a set of interlocking texts, narratives, and their interpretations that are constantly modifying each other" (Phelps, *Composition*, 213, 214). Phelps's use of the term intersubjective in connection with Freire is telling in that it reveals one of the severest limitations to her project. Whether the term is used in connection with phenomenological theories, materialist theories, or in connection with Bakhtin, it is problematic because it describes a process that takes place between subjects, and so is discernable only in terms of the relation's *effects*. That is to say, if Freire's pedagogy is an intersubjective "interlocking of texts" or narratives, it will be possible to produce knowledge of how they interlock only by doing something like reading "between the lines" of the narratives, rather than by reading the narratives themselves: intersubjective analysis takes place after or apart from the reading or analysis of the narratives or texts that are interanimated. The solution to the problem of the effect of the intersubjective is to rely less, perhaps, on *pedagogy* in Freire's "pedagogy of the oppressed," and more on the discursive constructions (and their material effects) of the relations of *oppression*. As I suggested earlier, the omission of these relations is one of the main reasons Phelps's book was so ill-treated by such reviewers as Schilb. It might, however, not be too much – given that Phelps's book could easily be seen as an extended treatment of rhetoric and its connection to praxis and phronesis – to extrapolate in the name of intersubjectivity the same treatment of audience, for example, that appears in the *Rhetoric* and place it inside a broader discussion of the material and discursive construction of polises (as Aristotle does in *Nichomachean Ethics*).

The more troublesome difficulty with the term intersubjectivity is that neither Freire nor Phelps suggests at what point this interanimation of voices will result in knowledge (either as the result of self-understanding or of scientific observation and testing), since "teachers and students participate in an *unrestricted* exchange" (Phelps, *Composition*, 214, emphasis added). In a discussion of another kind of intersubjectivity, in this case Bakhtin's, Michael Sprinker complains that intersubjective negotiation of the the kind championed by Freire and Phelps does not end the problem of the "radical otherness" that potentially exists between teacher and student, or more problematically, between oppressor and oppressed. "Meanings are never completely formalizable because the context of any utterance can never be specified" ("Context," 124). Sprinker's point *apropos* Bakhtin could be made here in connection with Freire and Phelps: intersubjective relations, if they are interanimated texts tied to contexts that are themselves in a continuous process of transformation, are *post*structural, in that, as effects of a complex and overdetermined set of material circumstances which are only available *as* effects, the contexts of dialogue "are without limit. They extend into the deepest past and into the most distant future" (quoted in Sprinker, "Context," 127). At the very moment at which those engaged in the process of what Freire calls *conscientizacao* – bringing to (critical) consciousness – come to some understanding of the nature of the world in which they participate, there is no way to ascertain whether that understanding will translate into action, or whether that action will be emancipatory or regressive. Far from being an "unrestricted" dialogic exchange, the problem of intersubjectivity's boundless context suggests that it is a highly *restricted* exchange. It does not take place in a process "whereby [teachers and students] coconstruct interpretations of Theory and apply these to their own personally experienced models and contexts of discourse"; instead they must constantly check and recheck by whatever methods available – both scientific and hermeneutic – the nature of the constraints that will re-contextualize and perhaps neutralize not only the possibility of producing knowledge but also change.

Phelps's "dialogic ideal," in which a teacher is seen as a subject who mediates between the "systematic knowledge-creation" of a community and "the reflection of learners" (see Phelps, *Composition*, 214) is something she hopes to connect explicitly with an Aristotelian rhetorical situation, in which the "rhetor" or "discourse investigator" moves between knowledge creation in the disciplines and a practical knowledge (which is what, after all, Phelps seems to want here), in which there is movement between "description" and "interestedness." In this scheme, "abstract products of reflection are not reified but re-created in the form of new meanings, new hypotheses and plans for action to be tested in experience" (Phelps, *Composition*, 214). But because these plans for action take place – at least in Dewey – for an individual, it is difficult to see how action translates to an active transformation of the polis, particularly when no theory or practice is suggested whereby the polis as a material entity can be understood. Like Locke before him, Dewey finesses the relations between sense-data and the material world from which these data are formed as effect. And like Locke he is not precise about the material dimension of these relations, which might be amenable not just to interpretive but also scientific analysis. Through Freire, Phelps goes some way toward solving these problems by suggesting that the movement between Theory and experience takes place socially and dialogically / intersubjectively, and by noting the complexity (and potentially overdetermined) character of them *as* effects. But with Freire, the problem is that intersubjectivity complicates rather than simplifies the method of analysis. The problem here with Freire (and by extension Phelps) is that intersubjectivity is a potentially boundless process whereby – even if a method for producing knowledge is put forward – the social movement between teacher and student, or between oppressor and oppressed, is potentially neutralized by this constant wavering back and forth between potential and fact. It is also not clear how Freire's bringing to consciousness *translates into* a method, and whether it is aware of its need for a guiding discipline that sees the social as material and therefore partly "practico-inert" and in need of descriptive explanation. In order to solve these problems Phelps turns to Hans Georg Gadamer and phronesis as a way back toward Aristotle and the systematization of a hermeneutics that works for change through both scientific and practical knowledge.

Gadamer, phronesis, and understanding

Phelps makes a connection between Aristotle's divisions of knowledge in *Nichomachean Ethics*, particularly his divisions between *phronesis* (practical wisdom) and *episteme* (scientific knowledge) and *techne* (technical knowledge), and Gadamer's hermeneutics, and in so doing brings composition – as the study of language and writing to yield understanding – full circle round to a discussion of the human sciences. Aristotle is valuable to Phelps's project because, though he divided the ways of knowing, his scheme did not distance them from either sense-experience or from "truth," though their relation to the truth (as well as from the good) varied somewhat. Gadamer is important because he simultaneously valorizes hermeneutics as a method for human self-understanding in the tradition of the human sciences, while also eschewing method in its classical sense of an unquestioned set of procedures for the examination of an object or phenomenon. Phronesis as Gadamer understands it is a *"form of reasoning as determined by the situation of application* . . . the prototype for a certain relation between knowledge and action, general and particular"* (Phelps, *Composition*, 216). Hermeneutics, then, is a method of understanding human lived lives that sees the situations – contexts – within which understanding takes place as impinging upon, and therefore affecting, the production of knowledge. For Gadamer, as for Aristotle, phronesis as practical wisdom is distinguishable from both scientific as well as technical knowledge since practical knowledge "is bound to context and changed by it" whereas technological use of scientific knowledge "is subsumed under a general law by virtue of its regularity (predictability) according to that law" (*Composition*, 216). Nevertheless, the regularity of behavior of the phenomenon or object will always be contingent upon the situations in which the phenomenon occurs and also that in which it is observed and understood. Gadamer's *Truth and Method* is a highly complex work, but it may perhaps be summed up by suggesting that it understands "bias" or contingency of understanding *not* as the inescapable bane of human knowledge, but as that which makes understanding possible in the first place. Its suggestion, then, is that phronesis and hermeneutics always abut scientific knowledge and force the latter to be reconsidered *in its situations*. Phronesis "requires a weighing" of both the particular and the universal. "Such judgment is not impulsive but deliberate. It . . . requires reflecting and deliberating with oneself. This is phronesis, the virtue of reflective deliberation that determines right application" (Weinsheimer, *Hermeneutics*, 191; quoted in Phelps, *Composition*, 216–17).

Phelps sees Gadamer's method as a "sketch or schema that guides the reflection of the *phronimos* or the wise person" (217), in

145

much the same way that Rorty saw the task for his own version of hermeneutics as one of "edification," the project of finding ways of interpreting – rather than making commensurable – the diverse aspects of our own lives and the lives of others. But the problem that plagued Rorty's hermeneutics is, not surprisingly (since Gadamer is one of the heroes in his hermeneutic pantheon), Gadamer's own from *Truth and Method*, and is in turn one of the reasons why Phelps's own desire to establish composition as a macro-discipline fails along the lines cited obliquely by Schilb. To put the problem in its simplest form is to say that the context within which a particular phenomenon or structure functions may itself be general or specific, but there is no method in place to distinguish between them (and it is an important distinction if we wanted, say, to decide whether something that occurs time and time again is a regularity or a matter of chance); or whether the phenomenon or structure may not be identifiable according to some law, which itself must be formulated according to disciplinary rules. Perhaps more problematically, these phenomena or structures are taken for granted: they simply "occur," and, like Rorty, we are left with the assumption that we understand them only through the mediation of discourse and we therefore also assume that we have to "cope" with them but not necessarily to establish their nature in order to do so. Phelps sees "Theory" as a way to "read different aspects and elements" of a situation (217).

In his discussion of Gadamer and Habermas in *Culture and Domination*, John Brenkman notes several problems that inhere in Gadamer's practical knowledge and hermeneutics, two of which are important to note here. The first (a), is that phenomena are interpretable by dint of something inherent in their structures (but these structures are only visible from our own historically situated times and places); and (b), there is a context within which phenomena and structures have meaning, but this context has to be taken as a given rather than examined. I want to lay these out briefly because they figure importantly in Phelps's attempt to reconcile hermeneutics and praxis to composition as a macro-discipline. Brenkman lists these problems as two of Gadamer's theoretical commitments, and they are:

(1) The cultural tradition is a *universe of meaning* in the strong sense that meaningfulness of transmitted texts is determined by the tradition as a

whole just as the tradition as a whole is a unity comprised of the meaning of the texts transmitted in it. (2) The tradition derives its authoritativeness in the present from the power of transmitted texts to carry meaning forward in time without reference to or dependence upon the social context in which they were originally produced. (Brenkman, *Culture*, 30)

These commitments translate into a method, which for our purposes might be construed as having not just to do with interpretation but self-understanding more generally: that (1) there is a more or less ascertainable relation between the general rule and the specific instance, in that we can see in the instance a hint of the rule that governs it, and in the rule the myriad instances that might be explained by it; and (2) as in hermeneutics, the historical genesis of the text is bracketed, since the coherence of a text can be separated from its originary context. In phronesis the social contexts in which self-understanding and interpretation take place provide knowledge only insofar as they shed light on the more or less coherent phenomenon or structure itself:

Of the first, Gadamer makes clear in *Truth and Method* that the movement of understanding is constantly from the whole to the part [or detail] and back to the whole. Our task is to extend in concentric circles the unity of the understood meaning. The harmony of all the details with the whole is the criterion of correct understanding. The failure to achieve this harmony means that understanding has failed.   (Brenkman, *Culture*, 258–9)

Gadamer concedes that the interpreter arrives at understanding or the unification of part and whole only *approximately*, and may in fact discover that the relation between the whole and the part, the particular and the general, is a disjunction rather than a unity, at which point the interpreter experiences what Rorty might call an incommensurability, and then must seek to "discover in what way it can be remedied" (Gadamer, *Truth*, 261). That is to say, it is perfectly consistent with Aristotle to suggest that there will be incommensurabilities in the attempt of a rhetor (or *phronimos*) to match a description or an interpretation of a situation or set of facts with the audience's knowledge or expectations of the situation in the context of the public good. But such a situation, for Gadamer at least, is also one that suggests that these incommensurabilities can and should be done away with. To go back to where we started, if Phelps sees Gadamer's phronesis as a way to unite Dewey's dialectic, with Freire's socially constructed critical consciousness, her desire to see practical knowledge as unified seems to cut against the grain of her wish to maintain composition as an open-ended human science. It also appears to work against the upshot of the intersubjective character of her method: if inter-subjectivity's biggest problem is the undecidability of a context, it nevertheless carries with it the injunction to continue the analysis by reintegrating the knowledge obtained into the theoretical model and its applicability to situations in the life-world.

One of the central metaphors employed by Gadamer in *Truth and Method* is that of the question and answer, in which the her-meneutic method is seen as a response made by questions put by the past which in turn forms another set of questions that must be answered, but also as a kind of Rortyan "playing back and forth" between knowledges or discourses that eventually finds a unifica-tion in the truth of each individual's lived life. As method, though, the metaphor of question and answer does not solve Dewey's (and Phelps's) dilemma of how we are able to make decisions on the worth or application of knowledge by "testing" sense-data against reflection or vice versa. If language is at least in part useful through the experiential use of it by subjects, and if communication carries with it both a discursive and a material component (that is, if it carries with it something like "meaning" but also a certain power derived from its connection with the political and phenomenal world), then – as Phelps's inclusion of Freire partly indicates – practical wisdom also requires a mode of analysis of both the social and material (phenomenal) world that works alongside under-standing. In one of the salvos in the Gadamer / Habermas debate that began with the publication of *Truth and Method* in English and continued for nearly fifteen years, Habermas takes issue with this aspect of Gadamer's work in the following way:

It makes good sense to conceive of language as a kind of metainstitution on which all social institutions are dependent; for social action is con-stituted only in ordinary language communication. But this metainstitu-tion of language as tradition is evidently dependent in turn on social processes that are not reducible to normative relationships. Language is *also* a medium of domination and social power; it serves to legitimate relations of organized force. Insofar as the legitimations do not articulate the power relations whose institutionalization they make possible, inso-far as these relations merely manifest themselves in the legitimations, language is *also* ideological. ("Review," 360)

As Brenkman has suggested, Gadamer understands ideology as false consciousness and therefore something to be overcome, whereas Habermas sees bias as precisely that which embeds in human social practices the material of its inception – and with evidence of relations of both domination and cooperation. In "On the Scope and Function of Hermeneutical Reflection," Gadamer notes that reality takes place in language and not "behind its back." He is only partly right. Understanding takes place in language, but language has one foot in cognition and another in reality which in fact *does* at least partly take place behind the back of language, if by that I understand that language is derived from understanding and "raw sense data" but is not commensurable with it: understanding is both material and discursive. And the intersubjectivity through which language operates is, as Phelps's Freire implicitly suggests, in conflict with its understandings (and subsequent disseminations) of the world coming into sometimes radical conflict. So Gadamer, rather than moving Phelps's notion of phronesis forward from Dewey and Freire, at least on this account conflicts with it since it suggests that understanding works toward a completed whole that has something like internal coherence.

The second commitment for Gadamer – the bracketing of the genesis of text and, by implication, the possibility of context's ability to shift the ground of analysis – undercuts his own claim that it is precisely the (historical) situatedness of texts and their interpretations that guides understanding. Speaking of the literary text, Gadamer says that "The real meaning . . . does not depend on the contingencies of the author and whom he originally wrote for. It is certainly not identical with them, for it is always partly determined by the historical situation of the interpreter and hence by the objective course of history" (*Truth*, 263). His aim is to expand the cultural value of interpretation by insisting that interpreters understand their activity as fully within and *productive* of contemporary culture. At the same time the contemporary force of the experience of interpretation itself signals that the validity of an interpretation is in part responsible to factors outside its original context. Gadamer here seems to move between granting the context within which understanding takes place a measure of explanatory force, which must therefore be explained or analyzed; and suggesting that self-understandings are valid by dint of their *surpassing* the contextual contingencies of the situation of analysis. In connection with Gadamer's first "commitment," not only are interpretations tacitly coherent, but they are coherent because they do *not* check experience with reflection and vice versa. Brenkman suggests *à propos* this problem that Gadamer's move cuts short "another possible line of inquiry – one that would entertain the possibility that the opposition between an artwork's historical inherence in a past society and its expressive power in the present is an open, complex relation" (Brenkman, 33), and, in connection with practical wisdom, one that would suggest a need for a methodical analysis of the context of the object's interpretation as well as of the object itself, moving between a situation's mappable history and its contemporary importance for an individual's (and polis's) lived life. This other line of inquiry might take the form of an analysis of how the communicative structures of understanding mark its inherence in a set of social practices; of how those structures might reconfigure social practice given the regularities of the social order which a practice will be undertaken; and of how the analysis itself is embedded in a set of practices that likewise must be investigated practically (ethically) and scientifically.

This other line of inquiry is needed, I think, for Phelps to see Theory to be *like* phronesis, a kind of practical wisdom to be guided by both practice and also regulative, systematic theories: teaching as guided by Theory is like phronesis not just in "the uniqueness of the individual case, the indeterminate relation of ends and means, the need for critical judgment, and so on" but also because it "involves activity with practical-moral consequences for others, so that it is not only formed on the model of phronesis (in being hermeneutical), but actually *is* phronesis in the original sense of conduct subject to regulative ideas of right and good" (217). For Aristotle, phronesis as practical wisdom was aligned with scientific and theoretical knowledge on the one hand and technical arts or practices on the other: it also was subject to regulative ideas of "right" and "good" – not just juridical right but also theoretical, logical considerations of the good, which worked in concert with the juridical or institutional – that saw itself constantly forced back to consider the ways that the knowledge it yielded might be reconsidered from the perspective of the other ways of knowing. A hermeneutics wedded to practical wisdom is forced to consider social practice as that which impinges upon it and forces it to inquire about the regularities of that practice. This inquiry must not only "discipline" reflection with sense-experience and sense-experience with reflection, but must also critically examine the relation between practice and theory without underestimating the explanatory capacity of either but understanding them as working simultaneously. In a letter to Richard Bernstein, Gadamer remarks that it is difficult to "make sense of a *phronesis* that is supposed to be scientifically disciplined." Rather than take this comment to mean that the human sciences *as disciplines* should not be organized like the natural sciences, we might instead work towards understanding how in the Aristotelian sense practical knowledge can be *disciplined by* its connection to science.

The making of a practical knowledge disciplined by science

What Phelps takes up in the last section of "Toward a Human Science Disciplined by Practical Wisdom," subtitled "a speculative outline," are three strands in "the texture of application" of a Theory disciplined by practical wisdom (*Composition*, 219–36). Here I simply want to examine Phelps's three-part strategy for making available practical knowledge and see if (and in what ways) it is compatible with an Aristotelian stratgegy (a true phronesis) that works alongside a scientific method as it does in Brown and Guignon, the philosophers of science whose connections to twentieth-century debates in the human sciences seem closely to resemble Phelps's own stated aims.

(1) The first strand is *attunement*, which is seen as something of a first step in any practice. It is "an ongoing state of selective alertness to theoretical ideas encountered or sought out in one's intellectual environment" (220). Phelps suggests that attunement involves two judgments: the first is to sense a match between theory and experience, which is derived (though not explicitly) from Dewey's pragmatism, a match that is never correspondence but rather analogy; the second is to use the articulation to suggest something beyond it. The two moves in attunement are like Gadamer's response to the interpretive question, where the reformulation of the response becomes the next question. Phelps goes on: "If this description [of attunement] sounds familiar, it is

because it follows closely the account that scientists and artists have given of problem solving and creativity, specifically the moments of search and insight" (221). Though derived from Dewey, Freire and Gadamer, the double movement in attunement suggests something like Polanyi's "creativity" in the sciences, particularly in its first step, a suggestion borne out by Phelps's references to his work in *Personal Knowledge*. Though Polanyi's work is at this stage rather dated (it had its heyday in rhetoric and composition studies sometime in the early and middle 1980s, so that even by the time Phelps cites it, it is rather old news), it is nevertheless an interesting connection. In the second section of *Personal Knowledge* ("The Tacit Component"), Polanyi likewise ascribes the common thread that runs between understanding, communication, and mathematical or scientific discovery to something like intuition, a "sense" of a match between theory and practice that leads to further research. In a passage reminiscent of Kuhn, Polanyi suggests that "beliefs and valuations have accordingly functioned as joint premises in the pursuit of scientific enquiries . . . The logical premises of factuality are not known to us or believed by us *before* we start establishing facts, but are recognized on the contrary by *reflecting on the way we establish facts*" (161, 162). For Phelps, as for Polanyi, the first step for a practice of self-understanding is to acknowledge, first, that "factuality," or Dewey's raw sense-data, is only factual to the extent that we can reflect upon the ways in which we establish them (and this occurs discursively); and, second, that the language with which we "name" facts is inadequate for explaining the circumstances of the naming, at which point we need to go beyond discourse to the rules of scientific explanation but with the realization that such explanations will not look like they did before reflection (see Polanyi, *Personal Knowledge*, 160–71; Phelps, *Composition*, 221–2).

Although "attunement" can sound a little like "new-age" leftovers from the shelves of Barnes and Noble, there are reasons why it might work to reconcile some of the difficulties in Phelps's thesis. First, in keeping with her starting point in Dewey's pragmatism, the two components of understanding that are "matched" in the first step of attunement appear to work dialectically. Theory and experience are different categories of knowledge, the latter having to do with the organization of sense-data while the former has to do with the ordering and dissemination of that organized data. If the first is something like description and the second is something like interpretation or phronesis, then there appears to be something like a relative autonomy of the disciplines. Though it is not noted by Phelps, Polanyi's description of the "beauty" of science and the scientist's activity in the discipline because "it is interesting" (Polanyi, 188) again suggests that Gadamer's letter to Bernstein may have been a bit premature: one can see Phelps's work, as a human science or practical wisdom, as being guided by scientific analysis if one understands that these disciplines, though autonomous, are only relatively so, and overlap significantly not just on epistemological questions, but on ontological ones as well.

Secondly, the "match" between Theory and experience will be useful in the same way that it was for Aristotle and (implicitly) for Gadamer; theory folds back onto the operational realm so that the work of critical examination (having, perhaps, both an interpretive and a scientific component) becomes dialectical in nature and, though open-ended, of immediate use in the polises where critical examination takes place. Here again, though it is unacknowledged in Phelps, there is a connection with Polanyi and through him with Gadamer and Aristotle. In "The Tacit Component," in a discussion of science's connection to technology, Polanyi says that

the capacity to perform a useful action presupposes some purely intellectual control over the circumstances in which the action is to take place. Technology always involves the application of some empirical knowledge and this knowledge may be part of natural science. Our contriving always makes use of some anterior observing.   Putting it this way, we become aware of the incommensurability of the two things combined in a technical performance.   (174)

Both kinds of knowledge refer to material things – so they are autonomous relative to their common object – but technology "must . . . declare itself in favour of a definite set of advantages, and tell people what to do in order to secure them" (176). And yet Polanyi goes on to suggest that even the scientific, descriptive task, apart from the ethical moment at which one must divulge the use-value of scientific knowledge, is embedded in the cognitive-ethical dimension. Though the observation and testing of the components of a rare material suggest a use for that material, the rarity of that material, though "it would leave unimpaired the validity of its results," nevertheless "might affect interest attached to their study" (see 176–79; quote from 178). The point here is that the distinction between the relatively autonomous realms of inter-pretation and science is not enough to render them incompatible; and in fact, it requires each of them to "guide" the other: it is not simply that the ethical understanding of a material as "rare" would render interest in its properties for use as small; rather, it requires an investigation into the availability of the material, an investigation that takes the form of an accounting of sense-data (what is this material? where is it found?) of a scientific nature that is what allows us to make a cognitive-ethical interpretation of its "rarity" at all.

It could be asked whether the match Phelps perceives between Theory and experience, derived in part from Polanyi, is – unlike in Kuhn and Rorty – something that can be seen without a full accounting of the provisionality of the knowledge and the lack of immediate access to nature. To backtrack a little, Rorty – and before him Kuhn – took pains to note the inaccessibility of nature to the scientist's (and philosopher's) instruments, and it is partly for this reason that both Rorty and Kuhn have taken so much heat from scientists and philosophers alike: if philosophy (and philos-ophy of science) is simply about interpretation and coping with a world that is made, not found, then the business of both philos-ophy and science would seem a great deal less important than it previously had. And yet it is Rorty's and Kuhn's avowal that nature is a more complex entity than simply something "out there" that contradicts their notion that it is not directly accessible, since it has effects that can be analyzed more or less objectively; and it is precisely Phelps's point – *apropos* Polanyi and attunement – that these effects must be understood both experientially (though perhaps not in their simple, "raw" form) and reflectively. This point deflects the charges (a) that Phelps denies the possibil-ity of saying anything about the world of phenomena, and (b) that her view of nature is too simple. It *may* be the case that the institutional and political norms through which knowledge is organized – both scientifically and also academically – is not adequately acknowledged (and this is most certainly the case in Polanyi's work, since he does not take the care that Kuhn does in enumerating the financial, social, and institutional pressures on the "beauty" of research and the scientist's interest in it). And it may also be the case that some of the weaker versions of social constructivism in rhetoric and composition studies may not adequately understand the complexity of the discursive and material effects of language – constructivisms that ironically have been given credence through Phelps's work on the "rhetorical," "postmodern" turn in language study. But because Phelps moves from Dewey and Freire, whose views of the natural, phenomenal world are a little too simple, to Gadamer, whose view is much more complicated, this charge cannot be unequivocally sustained.

(2) *Critical Examination* is the second strand in Phelps's outline for critical practice (223). If attunement is something like a "felt sense" between Theory and practice, in which each presumably guides the other, critical examination is more firmly grounded in what might be called the "theoretical / experiential." Phelps cites Ricoeur and Gadamer to suggest that it is "the sustained work of analysis (structural description, comparison, imaginative variation, thought experiments) necessary to evaluate Theory at an intellectual level" (223). As a second stage in the construction of knowledge through critical practice, it bears something in common with epistemic knowledge, which is mainly disseminated through the use of demonstrative and apodeictic reason in an attempt to bring those descriptions into accord, as fully as possible, with physical reality. In the Aristotelian scheme, one always assumed that physical reality was at least partially accessible, though the knowledges of such a reality may overlap in incommensurable ways. Phelps recognizes, as I think I have suggested, that this access is not something which we can assume, though it is available through its effects. Again, as in critical examination, Theory and experience work in tandem, in the same way that, though episteme and phronesis are relatively autonomous, they are related by their object of knowledge: "[t]he principle is not to select Theory *because* it is valid in its own terms, but *in view of* those terms and the claims they support, so that application is critical rather than naive" (224).

(3) The third strand in Phelps's model is *experimentation*, which she sees as intertextual. This term is problematic: to what extent should one investigate the specific ways in which the textual aspects of the rhetor's experience defines the object of knowledge?

As Phelps puts it, "One way of conceiving the process of experimentation is as reading researchers in education (influenced by literary theory) have recently begun talking about text comprehension . . . In this view Theory is in a given case not a cognitive schema to be instantiated, but a text to be mapped onto experience" (235). As I tried to suggest *apropos* Freire, this mapping operation may work well if one holds constant at least one of the variables, namely, either "experience" or "text." Since neither of the terms will, in effect, hold still, the map may look rather different depending upon the site or context of the experience or the "interpretation" with which one provides a text. Phelps's connection to Gadamer, however, allows her to *propose* both an interpretation of a text and to *hypothesize* an ethical end that is necessarily connected to a social order within which one does the reading. As we have seen, both Phelps and Rorty (originating with Gadamer) ignore the significance of the extent to which this ethical connection is not simply a matter of "choosing" to read one way or another, but may in several ways be imposed by force or institutional pressure.

Yet the significance of force *may* be proposed by recognizing that both Phelps's practical wisdom and Gadamer's phronesis have their roots in Aristotle, and that Aristotle – writing only a generation after Plato's explicit recognition of the coercive effects of political power – well understood the force of history. And though Phelps does not connect experimentation, or any of the other strands of her proposed structure for rhetoric, explicitly with Aristotle, it is his work (*Rhetoric*, *Politics* and *Nichomachean Ethics*) that serves as the ground for practical wisdom. When Phelps suggests that "[t]here is no reason to believe that what has worked once in one situation will work in the same way, or at all, in the next" because "[e]xperimentation has a historical rather than a determinate function in preparing the way for making decisions in new circumstances" (236), she has in mind a history in which – all things equally tending toward the good – it is possible that the least expedient course of action will be taken. History – like science – is a matter of trying to understand the regularities with which people, groups of people, and their surroundings, interact, but history – like science – is subject to the law of desire and to the law that suggests that desires deflect one another in such a way that they prevent the logical course of action from being followed, even when a persuasive / demonstrative case has been made.

Phelps gives a sense of how the different knowledges in her human science of composition line up and connect with other ways of knowing, and it is remarkable how well her description accords with Aristotle's in *Nichomachean Ethics*. In Aristotle's treatise, the ethical / practical knowledges are those having to do with the activity of lived life, while the intellectual or theoretical knowledges are more contemplative, having to do with the organization of sense experience. These ways of knowing all have their source in sense-data, and all have in common a human source in common knowledge.

Phelps's description is nearly identical to the one provided by Aristotle. "Structural-critical" and "empirical-analytic" knowledges roughly correspond to *nous* (intelligence, which works from first principles to apprehend sense-data) and *dianoia* (sense-perception, which associates inferences linked to sense-data from which syllogisms are built), respectively. "Ethical" and "artistic" knowledges correspond exactly with Aristotle's techne (including rhetoric) and phronesis (ethical wisdom for Phelps, practical wisdom for Aristotle). The pairs, phronesis-techne and empirical-structural (or sense-intelligence) correspond to practically oriented knowledge and theoretical knowledge. All of this so far suggests that Phelps's phronesis, inspired by Gadamer, and Aristotle's, function in very much the same ways: they function dialectically in such a way as to check sense-experience organized conceptually against ethical experience in the life-world. This is consistent with Phelps's beginnings in Dewey and her revision of pragmatism by way of Freire and finally Gadamer.

Most interesting, though, are the areas of inconsistency between Phelps and Aristotle, which occur between the extremes of "doing" and "knowing." The central ways of knowing for Aristotle are theoretical wisdom (*sophia*) and scientific knowledge (*episteme*), which lie somewhere between theory and practice. We saw earlier that even theoretical knowledge in Aristotle is difficult to conceive without reference to the common knowledge which lies at its base, a common knowledge that is always oriented toward an idea of the good, but which idea always has *effects* in definable polises. Phelps, however, has at the center of her ways of knowing a variety of practices – dramatistic, hermeneutical, phenomenological / existential, historical, and ethnographic – that bear very little resemblance to scientific knowledge, and also seem rather distant from Aristotle's *sophia*. The most obvious reason for the absence of, for example, science and mathematics (theoretical and scientific disciplines) in Phelps's accounting of the "types of knowledge applied in composition" is that she is clearly trying to establish composition as a *human* science, distinct from the objective or theoretical sciences: as she puts it near the conclusion of her book:

For some disciplines such as mathematics, praxis is not part of their self-understanding *as* disciplines. This is not the case for composition, whose distinctiveness lies in the experimental relationship it establishes between the general principles of inquiry posited and systematically pursued in science and philosophy, and the normative practice of these principles in ordinary discourse and everyday life. (237)

What we have seen, however, by looking closely at Rorty and before him Dilthey is that the line between the human and natural sciences is *not* the one that runs between theory and praxis but rather between the tools that are specific to each broadly conceived area. And this is because the theoretical and scientific disciplines *explicitly* understand themselves *as* disciplines (though perhaps not at the moment during which their practitioners do their work) through the "experimental relationship" they establish "between the general principles of inquiry posited and systematically pursued . . . and the normative practice of those principles in ordinary discourse and everyday life." It might be fair to speculate that scientific and theoretical inquiry, because they significantly overlap with the practical knowledges and the intellectual knowledges, function "hermeneutically" or "ethnographically," if by that we mean – by restating Dewey by way of Gadamer – that science must be guided or "disciplined" by interpretation and that interpretation must be guided by the descriptive and experimental work of science.

The conclusion of Phelps's chapter (and her book) sounds very much like Aristotle's description of the way phronesis works to create a human social practice. It does so by bringing together the different ways of knowing laid out in *Nichomachean Ethics*, by connecting sense-data and common-sense knowledge to the demonstrative and explanatory function of a science that proceeds

by approximations. This is especially apparent when Phelps tells
us that

Theory in an aleatory science offers historically sensitive explanations of
the past that permit only limited predictions of human behavior (something like weather forecasting), limited both in accuracy and in scope of
application. It provides not prescriptions for practice but a framework for
thinking about it, in terms of meanings, values, and a multidimensional,
stochastic (probabilistic) causality. (236)

Because of what I take to be the uncertainty of Phelps's understanding of the connection between the "natural" and the "human" sciences, the latter of which (I presume) she takes to be
"aleatory," it is worth considering the connection of weather
forecasting to the natural sciences. Forecasting requires the scientific examination of the nature of the atmosphere and its elements;
of the effect of geography on well-established weather patterns; of
the probable effect of wind shear on certain kinds of dwellings; of
the material effects of evacuating a large population in the case of
severe weather. As a result, forecasting is equally guided by
"meanings, values, and a multidimensional, stochastic (probabilistic) causality." In other words, because sense-data is that which
humans have to go on in order to determine the nature of our
world, and because science – like hermeneutics – proceeds in part
by probability, interpretation, and the cognitive rearrangement of
ideas derived from sense-experience, it is likely that Phelps's
desire to see composition as a human science has made her
overlook science's connection with hermeneutics.

It will be the task of the remainder of this book to suggest what
happens when we ignore the need for hermeneutics to be guided
by a stronger view of science's explanatory capacity and for its
connection with social change. Before doing so, I want to make
one final move and suggest that the Theory Phelps tries to outline
in *Composition as a Human Science*, though it bears a great deal of
resemblance to Gadamer's hermeneutics, may actually be closer
to a notion of science and / or conceptual knowledge that sees
itself guided by practical wisdom and yet also sees the need for
ethics to be guided by a systematic description of material and
social reality. In order to lay out this idea of science derived from
the work of Roy Bhaskar and others, we will need to take a detour
through a theory of historical materialism that imbricates Louis

Althusser's dialectical materialism and the emancipatory pedagogies of Paulo Freire and Mas'ud Zavarzadeh. This will, I think,
provide the idea Gadamer cannot conceive, namely, of a hermeneutics disciplined by science.

6

Liberatory pedagogy, conceptual knowledge: toward a practical wisdom disciplined by scientific observation

If it is true that the "rhetorical turn" in the human sciences begun around thirty years ago, based on the work of Dilthey, Gadamer and others and popularized in the American academy by the likes of Thomas Kuhn in science and Richard Rorty in philosophy, was something like a quiet revolution that upended once and for all the superiority of science and forced the scientific disciplines to note how they functioned rhetorically, then the last ten years have seen what might modestly be called a counter-revolution. Where the revolution was marked – by those working in rhetoric especially with something like glee – with announcements that the "sciences of the text," like formalism, New Criticism, structuralism and most Marxisms were shown once and for all to be failures because *science's* claim to special objective status was a false one, the counter-revolution has been marked with cautious reminders that description and observation – though perhaps just as biassed as some of Kuhn's more vocal adherents would suggest – nevertheless cannot be dispensed with even in the most hermeneutical of textual practices. Where the revolution has come close at times to suggesting that the operations of science, because they overlap with interpretation, must ultimately be subsumed by hermeneutics, the counter-revolution has suggested often mutedly, though sometimes stridently, that interaction and not subsumption is what the overlapping of the rhetorical and scientific realms suggests for the work of both the human and the natural sciences. And while the revolution has been seen as a space in which to work for a multiplicity of interpretive views – because ideally no interpretation can be finally said to be better than any other – and thus for the inclusion of voices different from our own (in Graff's words, for "teaching the conflicts" rather than quieting them by consensus), the counter-revolution has suggested that some interppretations *are* better than others, mainly those that are disruptive of the dominant cultural mode and that are critical and different, not part of an *e pluribus unum* patchwork quilt. Not surprisingly, the counter-revolution has been advocated by left cultural critics, many of them cultural and historical materialists that had been silenced by the reigning pragmatisms and humanisms in the thirty year-long ascendancy of the human sciences' hermeneutic realm.

In this chapter, I want to examine two strands of the materialist counter-revolution that have made strong claims for a role for scientific description in a thoroughly antifoundational world: the liberatory pedagogy of Paulo Freire and his American collaborator Ira Shor; and the more radical, emancipatory theory / pedagogy of Mas'ud Zavarzadeh and his sometimes-collaborator Donald Morton. Both of these pedagogical strands begin with a materialist theory whose tradition runs from Marx through Althusser, a theory that does not deny that, as Rorty suggests, language "goes all the way down," but which wonders what language goes all the way down *to*. It theorizes a human subject that is most immediately shaped by social forces that are materialized ideologically, but that is also constrained by extra-discursive material that has an effect upon ideological material and interaction. Finally, it understands itself as at least partly scientific in that it proposes to describe, by successive approximations, the structures and characteristics of the thoroughly ideological world in which humans live and work, and how humans are oppressed and emancipated. Inasmuch as both these strands are partly scientific, they both also suffer from the shortcomings of other scientific practices, including the potential to become moribund and to either overemphasize their capacity for promoting social change or to underemphasize their roles as social interventions.

I begin by examining how the historical and dialectical materialism of Louis Althusser – in such essays as "On the Materialist Dialectic" and "Philosophy and the Spontaneous Philosophy of the Scientist," as well as more commonly read work such as "Ideology and Ideological State Apparatuses" and "Contradiction and Overdetermination" – can be said to be scientific, in order to suggest a relation between ideology, rhetoric, and extra-discursive material. From there I want to move on to Freire / Shor and Zavarzadeh / Morton, to see whether the practical implications of a materialist theory succeed at the task they have set for themselves, and to what degree those tasks might be said to have a scientific component. Finally, I will point to work being done in left critical circles by those such as Roy Bhaskar that successfully integrates a strong objectivist understanding of science within a thoroughly rhetorical and antifoundational world.

Louis Althusser and science

In "Cultures of Discourse: Marxism and Rhetorical Theory," James Arnt Aune does what very few theorists of rhetoric do: he situates Marxist theory in the rhetorical tradition. One of the most interesting lacunae in the essay, however, turns out to be his almost complete omission of any mention of Louis Althusser's work, except to say that it is in a "scientific" rather than "critical" tradition. This is, I think, indicative of the way materialist theory has traditionally been treated by rhetoric in the last twenty years or so. One of the most commonly read texts in the recent western Marxist tradition, Althusser's "Ideology and Ideological State Apparatuses," would seem to be especially ready for adoption by a rhetorical tradition, since it tries to understand the relation between the machinery of state and the production of ideological material – notably, though implicitly, language – a relation which forms the center of the earliest rhetorical tradition. More important, and sometimes overlooked, is the fact that this essay works like something of a pivot for western Marxism, in that it works its way from a discussion of the ever-present nature of ideology to the possibility of constructing knowledge that, while not extra-ideological, is nevertheless conceptually able to describe how ideology functions.

Early on in the essay, Althusser notes that to understand "the reproduction of labour power [one] requires not only a reproduction of its skills, but also, at the same time, a reproduction of its submission to the rules of established order" (132). To put this another way, in order to work a lathe one not only must know how to work the machine but one must also be disposed to work at all, including to be willing to work *for* the person whose lathe it is and to be willing to exchange one's labor for an unspecified return. It is this latter set of relations – in which the members of a culture understand without analysis ("it goes without saying") the "rules of established order," the unspoken structures that organize a social order, a polis – that may take the form of law, but more often than not simply are recognized in the doing.

It is this latter set of relations, what Althusser calls after Marx *the relations of production* that are reinforced and *taught* by the state. At this early stage in the essay, Althusser hints that the means by which the relations of production are taught will be ideology, but he takes one of a number of detours at this point to make clear the different levels of a social whole or polis that must be articulated in order to understand these relations. These are the *"infrastructure,* or economic base (the 'unity' of the productive forces and the relations of production) and the *superstructure,* which itself contains two 'levels' or 'instances': the politico-legal (law and the State) and ideology (the different ideologies, religious, ethical, legal, political, etc.)" ("Ideology," 134). Althusser goes on to note that though these levels or instances are mutually determining and determined, the economic base is determining in the last instance; and that the superstructure and base are "relatively autonomous." These last two principles are important, since taken together they allow that it is possible that the State, a part of the superstructure, is the organ that *regulates* the relations of production, which derive from the economic base. It is this point that is often overlooked when theorists call Althusser's work "determinist" or "functionalist": if the economic base did in fact determine the superstructure in every instance and were not relatively autonomous, the State would not then be required to regulate the relations of production since they also would be determined. These principles suggest that the materials of production – those material objects that are used for the purposes of work, and the material, objective world which constrains work – and the way those objects are understood, interpreted and *worked upon by ideological material* may be seen as separate for the purposes of analysis but must be understood as mutually interanimating. Put simply, the material world and social construction of it each operate according to their own principles and yet function in such a way that they affect one another.

In what appears to be another detour, Althusser suggests that the theory of ideology and the state that he puts forward in this essay is partly descriptive, as opposed to wholly conceptual, and that in order to make the transition to a general, conceptual theory, one must "add something" to the description to give it "a very special kind of obviousness" (139). If there has been a single nagging complaint about Marxist theory, and about Althusser's work in particular, it is that it never does adequately describe the "something" that allows descriptive theory to pass to the stage of general theory. But let us take a detour of our own, and understand the relation between descriptive and general theory in a way similar to Kuhn or Rorty. In that view science (epistemology, for Rorty) proceeds normally by description at times when it has an adequate vocabulary for observing and testing phenomena and structures, and understands "general theory" to be the construction of a paradigm that is able to explain a set of phenomena and / or structures relatively successfully within that vocabulary. In that view, it is also clear that there will be phenomena and structures whose description will *not* adequately be explained in terms of the current vocabulary, at which time there occurs a shift in the general theory, a shift that may take place over an extended period but whose aim is to make sense of all the phenomena that had previously been successfully described *in addition to* the one that to that point had not.

What is important for our purposes is that it is at this point in his essay that Althusser makes a distinction between descriptive and general theory that effectively depends upon the successful integration of descriptions into a system within which the various descriptions may be said to be described *together*, and yet not be "universalized." What Althusser does here, when looking at the sweep of his essay – as a move from the reproduction of relations of production, to organized society or polises, to the regulatory role of the state, to state apparatuses, to the role of ideology, to the constitution of the subject – is to move, as Chaim Perelman does in *The Realm of Rhetoric* from an attempt to build a general theory of a social order and the discursive material in it to a descriptive theory of the individual's relation to language and to her material surroundings. In effect, Althusser's digression here suggests that in order for there to be a theory of effective human interaction (including relations of domination and assent) one needs to construct a social theory that systematizes subjects and systematizes materiality, a theory that ranges from the broadly explanatory and predictive to the narrowly descriptive; and that there is a role for the "addition of something else" to the purely descriptive – what Rorty might call the interpretive or hermeneutic – for such a transition to be thinkable. One needs to *describe* in order to *theorize*; but one also needs to recognize that description *and* theory need constantly to be recontextualized.

One of the places this recontextualization takes place most obviously *within* a state apparatus is in the educational institution itself. Althusser argues that the school, as Ideological State Apparatus (ISA), has taken the place of the Church as the primary site in the construction of assent in the polis. He suggests that recontextualization in the schools, as in all ISAs, takes place as struggle "because the resistance of the exploited classes is able to find means and occasions to express itself there, either by the utilization of their contradictions, or by conquering combat positions in them in struggle" ("Ideology," 147). In a note attached to this last point, Althusser cites Marx's Preface to *The Critique of Political Economy* in order to explain that one needs to distinguish between the economic conditions of production, "which can be determined with the precision of a natural science," and ideological forms in which the struggle – or recontextualization – more properly takes place. He then goes on to say that recontextualization and struggle extend beyond ideological forms into the infrastructure, and it is precisely because the schools are those sites at which the "seams" or contradictions between the materials of production and the relations of production are *taught* and *articulated* that such a recontextualization potentially leads to change. It is important to note that such an articulation of the material conditions of the members of a polis and their understanding of their relations to those conditions takes place not as theory but as praxis. This in turn suggests, as we noted earlier, that the move between descriptive and general theory takes place as a practice that, as in Gadamer's use of the term phronesis, is made manifest by "putting to use" the contradictions or incommensurabilities among the different levels of a culture, one that converges at a (political) site.

This struggle takes place in ideology, and Althusser goes on to describe it and its workings in the next section of the essay. Here are put forward two "theses" on ideology that are important both for rhetoric as well as rhetoric's relation to science. The first is that "it is not their real conditions of existence, their real world, that 'men' 'represent to themselves' in ideology, but above all it is their relation to those conditions of existence which is represented to them there"; the second is that "ideology always exists in an apparatus, and its practice, or practices. This existence is material" (165, 166). Taken together, these theses make two important points. First, ideology has simultaneously a discursive / material component and an extra-discursive / material component that, if we return to Althusser's earlier point about the relatively autonomous relation between ideological material and the base, must be understood separately and yet which function in tandem. If ideology functions by way of representation as Althusser suggests – and he is very careful to note that his description of base-superstructure relations is a metaphorical one – then it can be said to function *rhetorically*. This is because subjects represent to themselves and to one another their relations to the real conditions of existence, and while these representations are made from within material constraints the constraints are not immediately available except through further representations. If ideology's "existence is material," in that it takes place in practices that leave a material trace and which have an effect upon another subject's ability to have an effect upon her world, then ideology functions *practically* (as phronesis), since those effects must not only be recontextualized hermeneutically (that is, ideologically), but insofar as possible objectively, in order to understand their nature so as to be able to predict the possibility of taking action in the future. Because, in other words, ideology functions in both the imaginary and the material registers, any investigation into how it works – the task that historical materialism takes as central – must have an interpretive and an objectivist dimension; it must operate between, as Althusser has hinted, a descriptive theory and a general theory that resists universalizing its descriptions. Language, as it has both an interpretive and objectivist (or material) dimension, is the object of study *par excellence* in materialist theory (see Bernard-Donals, *Bakhtin*, esp. 95–103, 115–20).

As with Rorty *apropos* language, Althusser's subjects are always already interpellated ideologically: each individual understands herself or himself by being defined at least in part by how she or he is understood ideologically by others (see 171), by dint of how she or he follows a set of practices in the life-world. The question for Althusser, as it was for Rorty, is whether there is a position outside of ideology (or language) from which one can examine one's subjection if one is defined already *as a subject*. If such a position is not possible, and we take seriously Althusser's position that, *contra* Rorty, there is a more or less scientific means by which to analyze the workings of ideology, how are we to understand and characterize such a science?

In addressing the first question, Althusser is clear, not just in "Ideology and Ideological State Apparatuses" but throughout his corpus: it is *not* possible to occupy such an exogenous position. To recognize our interpellation as subjects, Althusser suggests, "only gives us the 'consciousness' of our incessant (eternal) practice of ideological recognition – its consciousness, i.e., its *recognition* – but in no sense does it give us the (scientific) *knowledge* of the mechanism of this recognition" (173). Terry Eagleton's gloss on Althusser goes so far as to suggest that such a position makes the latter's subject something like "a form of self-incarceration" (*Ideology*, 146), but Eagleton conveniently forgets that, though in the last instance the economy is determining of the superstructure (and thus ideology's interpellation of the subject), until this last instance superstructure and base (ideology and extra-ideological material; subject and other) act interdependently. The upshot of this point is that the "last instance" is a theoretical necessity (*apropos* the "general Theory") but is for the purposes of descriptive theory unavailable.

As for the second question, on the kind of scientific method, as distinct from ideological analysis (or, in Aune's terms, from the "critical tradition" in Marxist theory), Althusser attempts to answer it in several recently translated works collected in Gregory Elliott's edition entitled *Philosophy and the Spontaneous Philosophy of the Scientists*. In an earlier essay entitled "On the Materialist Dialectic," Althusser equates science with the theory of dialectical materialism, and science's task is to understand the underlying structure of categories that allow us to conceive certain things and that prevent us from conceiving others. In that earlier essay, science (or Theory) is a specific kind of labor, with its own set of procedures, whose aim is the production of conceptual knowledge, and which is demarcated from ideological knowledge by an epistemological break. This break might be characterized by the move from the ability to generalize on the basis of scientific observation and testing to the ability to Theorize (scientifically) a structure which is independent of the human mind's capacity to conceive it but which bears a relation to that capacity. Althusserian Marxism, as I have suggested, has been taken to task repeatedly for failing adequately to theorize this move, and in his book on ideology, Terry Eagleton provides a laundry list of the problems inherent in the position (*Ideology*, see especially 138–9). But even without Althusser's reconceptualization of science as Theory in the "Spontaneous Philosophy" essay (the essay had not been translated by 1990, the date of publication of Eagleton's book on ideology, and there is no evidence in that book that he read "Spontaneous Philosophy" in French), it is clear by now that any understanding of science as the production of conceptual knowledge must understand that while systematic theory-building of any kind *does* provide useful knowledge of the constraints and structures within which human life is lived, it does not operate (like Althusser's history) as a process without a subject, since it is for subjects that knowledge is produced. And about one-third of the way through "On the Materialist Dialectic," it becomes clear in Althusser's definitions of the terms "practice," "theory," "*theory*," and "Theory" that the last term – which is equated with science – refers to the metacognitive process whereby the practices of a field are systematized and critically examined.

It is in the essay entitled "Theory, Theoretical Practice and Theoretical Formulation" where the relation between science and theory becomes most clear, and where Althusser seems to make the greatest concessions to a rhetorical or antifoundational paradigm. At the beginning of that essay, he makes a distinction between a scientific and a utopian doctrine.

[Utopian socialist doctrine] proposes *socialist* goals for human action, yet it is based on non-scientific principles, deriving from religious, moral or juridical, i.e., *ideological*, principles. The ideological nature of its theoretical foundation is decisive, because it affects how any socialist doctrine conceives of not only the *ends* of socialism, but also the *means* of action required to realize those ends . . . Marxist doctrine, by contrast, is *scientific*. This means that it is not content to apply existing bourgeois moral and juridical princples (liberty, equality, fraternity, justice, etc.) to the existing bourgeois reality in order to criticize it, but that it criticizes these existing bourgeois moral and juridical principles, as well as the existing politico-economic system . . . [I]t rests on the *scientific knowledge* of the totality of the existing bourgeois system, its politico-economic as well as its ideological systems.   ("Theory," 3, 4)

Given the distinctions Althusser has already made in "On the Materialist Dialectic" and distinctions he makes later on in the "Spontaneous Philosophy" essay, a couple of points can be made here. In that latter essay, he makes a distinction between philosophy and science, where philosophy proceeds by putting forward theses which can be said to be correct or incorrect, based upon the contemporary context within which those theses are put forward (in much the same way that arguments are said to be more or less correct based upon the contingent political or social situation in which they are made), and where science proceeds by demonstration and proof, based upon whether a phenomenon or structure can be said truly to conform to the scientific theory (see "Spontaneous Philosophy," 74–5). Initially, then, Althusser seems to be proposing a distinction like the one Fredric Jameson draws at the conclusion of *The Political Unconscious*, where he makes plain that Marxism, as a doctrine, will inevitably fail unless its scientific analytical method – whereby ideological material can be examined in order to provide information on how a particular polis functioned politically and economically to provide both blindness and insight in the relations of production – is paired with a utopian, ideological project. In typical Hegelian form, Jameson professes that Marxist theory and practice must, along with scientific analysis, seek "to project its simultaneously Utopian power as the symbolic affirmation of a specific historical and class form of collective unity" (291). Jameson goes on to say that it is a mistake if we think that there is a sharp division between Marxism's analytical function and its utopian, ideological one, and this is quite consistent (Jameson's romantic Hegelianism aside) with a notion of science that overlaps with the ideological to the extent that one cannot proceed without the other.

And it is precisely this point that Althusser makes embryonically in "Theoretical Practice" and much more clearly in "Spontaneous Philosophy," but the point is attended by the same problems we have seen in Kuhn, Rorty, and other philosophers of science since the "rhetorical turn." Althusser makes it clear that Marxism, as a practice, "rests on the knowledge of this ensemble, which constitutes an organic totality of which the economic, political, and ideological are organic 'levels' or 'instances,' articulated with each other according to specific laws. It is this *knowledge* that allows us to define the *objectives* of socialism, and to conceive socialism as a new determinate mode of production . . ." ("Spontaneous Philosophy," 4). This is a complete reversal of the typical way of conceiving the relation between science and ideology: whereas science in the last forty years has seen the need for the guide of hermeneutics or ideology – or, more cynically, whereas science has been unable to extricate itself from the taint of ideological or rhetorical programs – here Althusser suggests that it is the utopian project of socialism (and perhaps any other political or ethical project) that *requires science as a guide*.

Jameson's point that a critical or scientific Marxist project and a utopian one comprise "a unified perspective and not the juxtaposition of two options or analytic alternatives" (*Political Unconscious*, 291) begs the question for Althusser: if it is true that science guides the ideological or rhetorical part of a materialist project, in precisely what ways are they related? To put this question another way, if the scientific project is incapable of positioning its apparatus outside the "bourgeois moral and judicial principles" which it takes for its object, then how does it work – as critique – from within? Ironically, it is a philosophy derived from Kuhn and Rorty that provides the beginnings of a response that is consistent with Althusser's repudiation of a position outside ideology. Here we need to go back to the terms outlined in "On the Materialist Dialectic:" if theory is an individual's categorization of sense-experience in a given polis or community, and that individual's attempt to transform that experience; and *theory* is the distinction between the work that attempts to understand the sense-experience as material occurrence and that which attempts to understand the categories through which that understanding takes place (the work, in other words, of distinguishing between the extra-discursive / ideological and the thoroughly discursive / ideological components of knowledge); then science-as-Theory is the work that generalizes across social and material existence to suggest the structures of human experience and material objects. That is to say, science is the attempt to determine not just the existence and the nature of objects and phenomena, but also the method of inquiry (in both its broadly ideological as well as its narrowly disciplinary forms) and *its* material and ideological constraints. As Phelps and Gadamer found in working with Aristotelian categories of scientific, theoretical and discursive knowledges – and as they likewise discovered the need for a way to theorize the points of intersection between these ways of knowing – Althusser here acknowledges the difficulty of the work of producing scientific knowledge, and the near impossibility of drawing lines of demarcation between them once one understands that "there is no royal road to science, and only those who do not dread the fatiguing climb of its steep paths have a chance of reaching its luminous summit" (Marx and Engels, *Letters*, 172). Althusser goes on to say that science,

far from reflecting the immediate givens of everyday experience and practice, is constituted only on the condition of calling them into question, and breaking with them, to the extent that its results, once achieved, appear indeed as the contrary of the obvious facts of practical everyday experience, rather than their reflection.   ("Theory," 15)

Like the difference between normal and revolutionary science, Althusser's scientific practice aims at working the ideological (political, judicial, socio-economic) material and the results of inquiry located in the individual scientific disciplines against one another to provide not just a constant reevaluation of the paradigm ("the existing bourgeois system") in which inquiry takes place but also the methods (the "'levels' or 'instances,' articulated with each other according to specific laws") of inquiry themselves. Althusser here effectively suggests a parallel or a relation between *theoretical* knowledge (as a knowledge that guides practice, or revolution) and *scientific* knowledge. Moreover, he begins to suggest that theory / science is distinguished by its application of *principles* or laws that work across all instances, but provides the caveat that these laws or principles may be found wanting and in need of supplement or replacement (hence, the desire for revolution). As I have suggested, what one sees in the beginning of this essay is a productive tension between the application of theoretical knowledge as law on the one hand and its ability to "guide" practice (something that seems less definitive – as we saw with Phelps) on the other. The tension apppears again in the "Spontaneous Philosophy" essay, but with different results, as we will see shortly.

Althusser goes on to divide Marxist scientific doctrine into two disciplines, Historical Materialism and Dialectical Materialism. The first, Historical Materialism, concerns itself with history or historical formations, particularly as consisting of economic, political and ideological apparatuses. It sees itself as the intercombination ("organic totality") of the various social formations that are the result of one or another mode of production. "[E]very social totality comprises the articulated ensemble of different levels of this totality," and Althusser, following Marx, outlines the different components of the base and superstructure (which we have seen in the "Ideology" essay) and notes again that each of the various "levels" of a culture is relatively autonomous and so can be studied (provisionally) as separate. The second discipline, dialectical materialism, concerns itself with the production of knowledge, with the real conditions that constitute the history of the production of knowledge. This is Marxist philosophy proper, and it is this which is most close to a scientific operation: it tries to understand the material circumstances under which knowledges are produced at historical junctures but also, like post-Kuhnian science, the circumstances under which it is also delimited by ideological material. The objects of investigation for dialectical materialism and historical materialism are different. For the latter, it is modes of production; for the former, it is modes of thought, modes of the real conditions (the broadly social and material on the one hand; internal to scientific practice itself on the other) of the process of the production of knowledge. Again consistent with post-Kuhnian scientific practice, it is difficult to distinguish between the objects of knowledge – or at least between the extra-ideological material on the one hand and the ideological material on the other – because, going back to the roots of the division between the human and the natural sciences in the nineteenth century, human self-understanding (which takes place for Althusser in ideology) is always constrained by phenomena and structures in the natural world. Consistent, too, with the centuries-old division between the two disciplines is the question of the extent of the difference between the *methods* unique to each discipline (here, historical materialism and dialectical materialism). The speculation in "Spontaneous Philosophy" and "Theoretical Practice" that Philosophy-as-practice proceeds by the establishment of theses whereas Science-as-Theory proceeds by the application of specific instances to "the laws of real processes" (9) begs the question of how the formulation of those laws is related to the real processes themselves.

The significant question thus becomes whether the distinction between science and hermeneutics – like that established by Rorty and some philosophers of science – can be substantiated at all. In "Spontaneous Philosophy," Althusser suggests that

with some distinct exceptions the human sciences are sciences without an object (in the strict sense). They have a false or equivocal theoretical base, they produce long discourses and numerous "findings," but because they are too confident that they know *of what* they are the sciences, in fact they do not "know" *what* they are the sciences *of*: a misunderstanding. (90)

By misunderstanding, Althusser here alludes to the problem that the human sciences attempt to "apply" the methods of other disciplines to their object without investigating either the theoretical consistency of those methods or their own fields. The question – barring the problem of cross-disciplinary "application," which I will talk about briefly below – could be put in the reverse: is it possible that the scientific disciplines, or the broad category of Science-as-Theory, are also at a point where their object is in question, since that object has components both in the extra-discursive / material and the discursive / material which are difficult if not impossible to distinguish?

Althusser notes two problems or questions posed by the existence of Marxism's twin disciplines: "(1) Why did the foundation of historical materialism necessarily entail the foundation of dialectical materialism?" and "(2) What is the proper function of dialectical materialism?" (10). It is the second of these that leads us to examine the relation between science and philosophy, a relation that shifts subtly from one essay to the next. I quote Althusser at length:

We know that knowledge – in its strong sense, scientific knowledge – is not born and does not develop in isolation, protected by who-knows-what miracle from the influences of the surrounding world. Among these are social and political influences which may intervene directly in the life of the sciences . . . In fact, every science – natural as well as social – is constantly submitted to the onslaught of existing ideologies, and particularly to that most disarming – because apparently non-ideological – ideology wherein the scientist "spontaneously" reflects his / her own

174

practice: "empiricist" or "positivist" ideology. [Dialectical materialism is] an absolutely imperative requirement for the very existence and development not only of the natural sciences but of the social sciences . . . [as] the refusal of all ideology . . . [by unearthing] the traps of ideology, in interpretations of historical materialism as well.

("Spontaneous Philosophy," 12–13)

Dialectical materialism provides a way of seeing ideological material attendant to the sciences and their practices *as* spontaneous and co-incident with their disciplinary methods, and as a way to "guide science to action" by allowing them to see those traps as traps and to steer clear of them as much as possible.

The extent to which this *is* possible is what Althusser investigates in "Spontaneous Philosophy," where he explicitly retheorizes not just dialectical materialism but also the relation between it and the objective sciences themselves. There, Althusser first questions philosophy's position as ex-centric to disciplines, wondering whether "the philosopher, by his very *nature*, [is not] the artisan of interdisciplinarity because he is, whether he likes it or not, a 'specialist' in interdisciplinarity" (79). By doing so, he calls into question whether it is possible to engage in interdisciplinary research to begin with, and whether philosophy has a role as the cartographer of the relations between disciplines. Next, he proposes an alternative role for philosophy: "[C]an there be a direction of research [in the sciences]? In accordance with what ought it to be directed? Purely scientific objectives? Or *social* (that is, *political*) objectives (the prioritization of sectors), with all the financial, social and administrative consequences that implies. . .?" (80). Philosophy-as-interdisciplinarity cannot work in connection with science since these questions are directly relevant to scientific work, and do not cross the kinds of disciplinary boundaries we expect to see in the human or social sciences, at least as they're traditionally construed. Althusser, instead, suggests an alternative thesis: since "philosophy is not a science, nor *a fortiori* Science," then philosophy may "intervene [in scientific work] in another way: by stating Theses that contribute to *opening the way* to a *correct* position with regard to these [scientific] problems" (81). It can act to "direct" research. I want to note what Althusser has begun to do here: he has effectively reformulated the science-as-Theory / philosophy-as-ideological practice pair in such a way as to connect philosophy to Theory and science with ideological (or perhaps ideologically driven) practice. This, of course, does not go so far as to completely revise the categories Althusser has set up in the earlier "On the Materialist Dialectic." It does, however, richly and productively complicate those categories in such a way as to make the area of overlap between science and ideology, between demonstration and persuasion, between common knowledge and knowledges specific to disciplines, much broader; and it suggests that the interanimation of the ways of knowing is much more well-defined and much better theorized in Althusser's work than it has been heretofore.

Althusser's third move is to return to the problem of interdisciplinarity: if philosophy cannot establish links between the disciplines (since it does not occupy a position exterior to them, and since the disciplines themselves are related but have methods peculiar to each), then it can be presumed that its function is more clearly to draw distinctions *between* the disciplines. It does so by distinguishing between the scientific – the methods and practices specific to those fields whose aim is to explain the structures and phenomena of the natural and, insofar as possible, the social world – and the ideologies that are attached to them having to do with the "ultimate ends" of the sciences. Philosophy, then, is *sui generis* distinct from both science and ideology, but bearing a double relation to each (see "Spontaneous Philosophy," 83).

There is an important addition that must be made here: the philosophies or ideologies that attach themselves to science are specific to those individual sciences, and are "spontaneous" insofar as they arise directly from the scientific work and are contained by disciplinary ideology. An example of such spontaneity would be what happens when a "discovery" is made that defies current explanations of a particular phenomenon. Kuhn gives us the example of Priestley and Lavoisier and their attempts to understand the properties of dephlogisticated air. The scientific community attempted to explain the anomalous nature of the "discovery" by suggesting that errors had been made in the experimental process, that the wrong sort of apparatus was used, and so on. In short, it was assumed that when one follows a set of procedures, one will get a certain result, and when the result was different from the one that was expected, then something must have gone wrong. For Althusser, these assumptions are the result of a set of spontaneous philosophical premises, spontaneous in that they are not critical of the base set of assumptions – including methodology, the establishment of truth claims, the collection of data, etc. – that drive science in the first place. Philosophy's task is to criticize or dispel such "epistemological obstacles"

by showing that the imaginary solutions they offer in fact conceal real problems. But it is necessary to go still further: to recognize that it is not by chance that these false ideas reign in certain regions within the domain of scientific activity. They are non-scientific, ideological ideas and representations. ("Spontaneous Philosophy," 88)

"[P]hilosophy does not substitute itself for science" in such a process; rather, "it intervenes, in order to clear a path, to open the space in which a correct line may then be drawn" (88). From this Althusser draws the thesis that scientific ideology (or the ideology of scientists) is not only inseparable from scientific practice but spontaneous to it.

If philosophy is that which allows scientists to understand how the spontaneity of the ideologies attendant on their disciplines acts as obstacles to their work, then it is possible to go from Althusser's role for philosophy back to an Aristotelian practical wisdom, whose role is critically to examine practice and to guide not just rhetoric (the persuasive case made in the name of other disciplines) but those other ways of knowing as well. Particularly if we recuperate from Phelps the notion that phronesis is a critically self-reflexive study that proceeds not just by interpretation but also by demonstration and observation, and that it constantly reintegrates the experientially observed and the conceptually theorized, Althusser's understanding of philosophy here as having a double relation both to ideology and to science puts it in the same mediating position as Aristotle's knowledge in phronesis. If philosophy for Althusser clears the ground for the practice of science – or, if we can go so far as to say (Bhaskar, as we will see shortly, does) all socially relevant practice – it should also be seen as activity that works simultaneously *with* science at each of its stages. Given that phronesis for Aristotle as for Phelps is the knowledge of practice and theory and how they interanimate one another, one might go so far as to suggest that Althusser's reformulation of philosophy is not inconsistent with such a knowledge.

The remainder of Althusser's "Spontaneous Philosophy" essay suggests that no scientific practice is without its attendant spontaneous philosophies, and that the role of a philosophical practice, as a way to demarcate the boundaries between methodologies and as a way to force scientists critically to examine the material conditions of their methods, needs to be strongly maintained. Dialectical materialism's role here is to ensure that the spontaneous philosophical convictions of the practitioner stem, particularly during times of scientific crisis, "from the experience of scientific practice itself in its immediacy." It must also ensure that these convictions "allow no room for the philosophical 'doubt' that calls into question the validity of scientific practice" because they maintain

(1) belief in the real, external and material existence of the *object* of scientific knowledge; (2) belief in the existence and objectivity of the *scientific knowledges* that permit knowledge of this object; (3) belief in the correctness and efficacy of the procedures of scientific experimentation . . . capable of producing scientific knowledge.

("Spontaneous Philosophy," 132–3)

Since the tendency in idealist reactions to scientific crises leads scientists to go "outside" science for ways to reconcile them – by suggesting that an aberrant tendency or object is the result of "error" or "bad science" rather than the sign for the need to characterize the object of knowledge differently – dialectical materialism may not oblige the scientist to abandon idealism but instead perhaps to balance an idealism with a spontaneous philosophy that is critical of the scientific description without forcing the scientist to relinquish it altogether. It does so by critically examining the conditions that have brought about the reaction in the first place. The upshot of Althusser's work here is that he has established the need for a strong, objective view of science and observation – one that even though it is working alongside ideological material and is therefore subject to the forces of domination, still works by successive approximations to conceptually (and constantly) reconsider the relation between material and discursive (i.e., interpretive) data derived from the life-world.

Liberation, Emancipation, Pedagogy

If it is true that a materialist notion of theory and practice in the human and natural sciences is, if not commensurable, at least compatible with a strong objectivist understanding of phronesis and practical wisdom in the Aristotelian sense, then it remains to examine the practice – especially the pedagogical practice – of such a materialism. Since the task of this book is critically to examine the connection between materialism, pedagogy, and rhetoric as part of a strategy to produce knowledge, we need to look at some contemporary examples of materialist *teaching* practices that take as their aim (as Aristotle's rhetorical project did) the promulgation of political freedom and the elimination of political domination.

At the moment there are two predominant ways of thinking about pedagogy and rhetoric that might loosely be called liberatory or emancipatory. Since the publication in 1970 of *Pedagogy of the Oppressed*, Paulo Freire's critique of the banking concept of education has been something of a commonplace in humanities divisions (despite, perhaps, the lack of follow-through by teachers of that critique). That book and others that have followed have gained Freire a surprisingly devoted following in the United States, surprising because of the explicitly radical, political and emancipatory edge of his work. One of Freire's most ardent supporters and sometimes-collaborator, Ira Shor – someone who is otherwise marginalized in the world of English studies and rhetorical theory – has extended some of Freire's work to the American context. The biggest complaint about Freire's pedagogy is that it is not emancipatory *enough* because it fails to grant students the wherewithal to produce *conceptual knowledge*, or at least understand that the human sciences within which most of Freire's and Shor's North American students work produce ideologically unself-conscious philosophies, Althusser's spontaneous philosophies, that further mystify instead of lay bare the contradictions of those disciplines. One of the loudest and most consistently scientific critiques of the Freirean "ludic" academy has been that of Mas'ud Zavarzadeh and his sometimes collaborator, Donald Morton. I want here to examine the debate between the ludic and the radical since both take something like an Althusserian starting point, namely, the call for a critical pedagogical practice that reserves a strong role for objective description and the creation of a broadly conceptual view of knowledge in the move toward emancipation.

Freire tells us early on that his intention is to construct a pedagogy that at once "liberates" both the person in the position of oppression as well as her oppressor. He says that this will happen only "through the praxis and the [oppressed's] quest for [liberation], through their recognition of the necessity to fight for it . . . [which] will actually constitute an act of love opposing the lovelessness which lies at the heart of the oppressor's violence, lovelessness even when clothed in false generosity" (*Pedagogy*, 27). Self-liberation is particularly difficult since "the very structure of [the oppressed's] thought has been conditioned by the contradictions of the concrete, existential situation by which they were shaped." Though Freire does not use the term in the same way Althusser does, he seems to be talking here about the materiality of ideology and the hegemony it exerts. Freire talks about "models of humanity," in which the oppressed want to "be men," but where such an ideal necessarily carries with it the contradictory condition of their own subjugation: because the relations of production require class divisions, and because the oppressed understand those relations, including the hierarchical one in which the *campesino* does not own the means of production whereas the landlord does, as "natural," then the oppressed's desire to be "a man" is the desire to be a man occupying a higher class position, namely that of the oppressor. Freire is interested here in the ways in which thought is "structured" in human activity and in discourse through *prescription*, the unstated but very palpable law in accordance with which subjects are interpellated, and also in the relation between praxis and liberation (or emancipation, or autonomy; see 29). In regard to the first point, Freire understands much in the way as Althusser does that ideological state apparatuses, like the schools, are sites at which those rules are disseminated most nakedly, but also those sites at which hegemony can be turned into resistance. One can see *Pedagogy of the Oppressed* as something like a handbook for how to use the schools as such a contestatory site. In regard to the second point, what is most interesting – and perhaps most problematic – about Freire is his desire to see praxis as a drive for an autonomy or a state of agency that is almost mythical in its lack of constraints. Much in the same way that Habermas's ideal speech situation – and like Althusser's "last instance' – is conceivable but historically unavailable, Freire understands a connection between a real, historical struggle that takes place at the level of discourse and material existence and a theoretical and perhaps unavailable state.

The problem of transformation in Freire is like that encountered by Althusser: "Just as objective social reality exists not by chance, but as the product of human action, so it is not transformed by chance. If humankind produces social reality (which in the "inversion of the praxis" turns back upon them and conditions them), then transforming that reality is an historical task, a task for humanity" (*Pedagogy*, 33). Social relations have both an ideological and a material component, and in the same way that ideology interpellates human subjects within the constraints of the materiality of those subjects' surroundings, praxis also requires not just social transformation at the ideological level but also at the material level. As in the work on "Spontaneous Philosophy," Freire is aware that there is the need for a form of consciousness that has a double relation both to science (as the method with the material dimension can be studied) and ideology. Freire calls this relation *conscientizacao*, the perception of "social, political, and economic contradictions" (17n). But *conscientizacao* requires the subject "to take action against the oppressive elements of reality," which suggests that that is not enough, then, to make "real oppression more oppressive still by adding to it the realization of oppression."

It is the transformative dimension of praxis, given the implicit distinction – and difference in register – between the materiality of a lived life that can be described and studied scientifically and the discursive nature of that life that requires an interpretive method, that is most attractive to rhetoricians who see pedagogy as by definition transformative. But it is this same dimension that is also what is most difficult to theorize in Freire. For praxis, as liberation, to be "the action and reflection of men and women upon their world in order to transform it," four elements are required. The first is an objectively verifiable knowledge of the oppressor / oppressed contradiction. In the first stage of Freire's pedagogy, this includes the "making oppression more oppressive" by uncovering the mechanisms by which oppression operates. It is unclear, both in this work and in Freire's other writing, the degree to which such knowledge is scientific. By looking back to Phelps and her appropriation of Freire for rhetoric, it is possible to say that it *does* include such a descriptive moment, since any theory of transformation based upon practical wisdom requires the actor /

agent to understand the situation common to speakers in its social and material dimension. The second requirement for praxis is a "critical confrontation" with the objectively real. If we go back to Althusser's definition of philosophy as a "meta-knowledge," a knowledge of the material conditions of the production of knowledge, then such a confrontation (a) cannot take place outside ideology and (b) must be continuous and recursive. In the same way that philosophy's retheorization of Theory acknowledges that the "objectivity" of such meta-knowledge is also contingent but nevertheless a valid way of approximating the conditions in which critical investigation takes place, Freire's critical confrontation is likewise a continuous and self-reflexive process that – like "dialogism," Freire's third requirement for praxis – is potentially boundless. We have already considered the potential boundlessness of dialogism (as an intersubjective process), but it bears repeating here that Freire's dictum that we should "recognize 'other' persons as persons" is rather more complicated than he might suggest. If ideological interpellation takes place at the material as well as the discursive level, then one wonders whether understanding one's interlocutor as a "person" does not obfuscate rather than critically confront the *material* dimension of the circumstance of subjectivity since persons have a certain cohesion and identity in time and location that a subject – constantly reinterpellated dialogically – does not.

When these three conditions are met, suggests Freire, and the praxis involved in liberation through pedagogy begins, the oppressor will eventually disappear because the condition of oppression will have been ameliorated. Inasmuch as the praxis Freire advocates here is pedagogical through and through – in that it involves dissemination of a critical method for understanding one's material and ideological involvement in the production of a life – it also acts as something like Althusser's philosophy of guidance, in that it attempts to clear the ground for work of self-understanding, the traditional province of the interpretive sciences, as well as for a reorganization of technological transformation of the infrastructure – the reapportionment of land, the ownership of the means of production by the workers, the reallocation of labor in families, etc. – that has traditionally been examined by the social (in connection with the natural) sciences. Unless the obstacles to each of these transformative "crises" is met with a critical (or, for Althusser, philosophical) discipline rather than with a spontaneous reaction, the pedagogical revolution cannot be borne out.

As I have suggested, despite the positive program of Freire's pedagogy – and despite that pedagogy's connection, as I have tried to briefly outline here, with a materialist tradition that can be thought of as consistent with a rhetorical / practical one – it has a number of critics, particularly from inside the materialist camp. One of Freire's most constructive critics is Ira Shor who, far from disagreeing with Freire's more or less humanist liberatory pedagogy, attempts to revise some of the difficulties in the earlier work. In broad outline, the four topics on which Shor finds the need to revise Freire are on the structure of ideology, on resistance, on the social nature of liberation, and on the possibility of Althusser's conceptual knowledge.

With regard to the first point, Freire suggests that because all individuals, oppressors and oppressed alike, have access to "the word," then everyone also has the same potential access to change: because "within the word we find two dimensions, reflection and action . . . [t]here is no true word that is not at the same time a praxis. Thus, to speak a true word is to transform the world" (68). Freire goes so far as to include a note with the following equation:

$$\left. \begin{array}{c} \text{Action} \\ \text{Reflection} \end{array} \right\} \quad \text{word} = \text{work} = \text{praxis}$$

The point here is that there is a direct relationship between human social activity and language, and that when one utters the word in dialogue with another person, one transforms not just the relation between those two speakers but the speaker's "personhood" or subjectivity as well as the world – material and social – within which those speakers enter into relation. In effect, because the act of "naming the world . . . is an act of creation and re-creation" (70) – because along with transforming or recreating the relation between the object named and the name *one also creates a new object* – Freire seems to suggest that praxis has the ability to create a world out of whole cloth.

What this means is that, perhaps *unlike* common knowledge made accessible through rhetoric, there is no necessary connection between discursive material and extra-discursive material. But this would seem to prevent rather than promote change. If all that is required to transform one's lived life is to reorient it in language and yet that language is not connected to social reality at all (and we are leaving aside for the moment the question of whether Freire gives us any scientific, or other, method with which we can examine that reality), then change in one does not mean change in the other. One can imagine a session in the US Congress where creating a piece of legislation to shift funding for Aid to Families with Dependent Children from Federal authority to the jurisdiction of the states is seen as both bringing the budget into balance and providing more effectively for single-parent families. In the reality of the l04th Congress, it appears clear that such a move may well change nothing at all, and may in fact have a harmful effect on individuals who are constrained not by discourse or "the word" but by material and social conditions that are promulgated in part discursively / ideologically but which bear a highly complex relation with the material / real. In *Critical Teaching and Everyday Life*, a book that is now over a decade old but which is highly relevent today, Shor suggests as much in a chapter entitled "Interferences to Critical Thought." In a long earlier chapter Shor outlined the culture schooling in which he worked during the early l980s; here Shor observes that the "operation of the interferences [to critical thought] are complex." He goes on to suggest that there are several material and ideological elements – the architecture of the community college, largely the result of the campus revolutions of the l960s; a narrow vocationalism connected to a service-sector economy; the gender, race and class hierarchies established to maintain order in a non-traditional student population, among others – that contribute to what he calls a "self-dehumanization" of students through their own resistance to such a culture. Shor goes some way toward extending Freire's understanding of ideology's connection to the infrastructure, though he perhaps does not provide the method for studying that infrastructure but only the philosophical / practical "guide" for clearing the ground so that study can be done. Whereas Freire's "critical confrontation" was difficult to conceive because his notion of ideology is not well developed, Shor's analysis of the complexity of the relation between "word," "work," and "praxis" – and the overdetermined structural relation between discourse and socio-economic reality – brings it more in line with a rigorous materialist theory.

A shortcoming of Freire's work is his understanding of "liberation": to what extent are the oppressed *freed* when taught in Freire's revolutionary fashion, and what are they free *from*? Early on in *Pedagogy of the Oppressed*, Freire sets up several dichotomies:

The conflict lies in the choice between being wholly themselves or being divided; between ejecting the oppressor within or not ejecting them [*sic*]; between human solidarity or alienation; between following prescriptions or having choices; between being spectators or actors . . . (30)

In valorizing the first item in each pair, liberation would seem to be the freedom from oppression, alienation, spectatorship, and freedom to "be oneself." Liberation, then, consists in finding that which is authentic, free from ideological constraint and false consciousness; in short, liberation is the emergence of an unfettered agency and of a unified subject.

The story changes, though, further on in the book. In the second chapter, where Freire begins systematically to distinguish between the "banking concept" of education and a truly liberatory pedagogy, he suggests that a problem-posing education, "as the practice of freedom," denies "that man is abstract, isolated, independent, and unattached to the world; it also denies that the world exists as a reality apart from the people." "Education as the practice of freedom" evokes a response in students "to the challenge [which in turn] evokes new challenges, followed by new understandings; and gradually the students come to regard themselves as committed" (*Pedagogy*, 62). In this description of the end of a liberatory education, the process by which students become liberated or "freed" is more complicated and continuous. Rather than providing a passage from inauthentic to authentic understanding of one's life-world, education's end-point is *commitment*, not knowledge. Here freedom is a practice rather than a goal of education, something which Ira Shor is much more clear about in *Critical Teaching*. Though he understands ideology as a Lukacsian "false-consciousness," he nevertheless does not understand critical teaching as that which allows students to emerge from ideology into the light of the real, or even from false consciousness to class consciousness. Rather, in a statement that sounds like Freire, Shor suggests that those features of mystifying ideological rhetoric that are challenged through the practice of critical education "may be more oppressive that before, because the consciousness of oppression will have been raised" (*Critical Teaching*, 83). What is important to note here is that with both Freire and Shor's corrective, it is unclear whether the material constraints – the fact of the distractions at Shor's College of Staten Island or any other institutional (or non-institutional) setting – are changed even through a continuous process that does not also involve understanding the nature of those constraints.

A related question to which Shor responds with a more satisfactory answer than does Freire concerns the emancipatory nature of liberation. The question has to do with the extent to which a critical consciousness allows students – or anyone else – to construct knowledge of the structures (both natural and social) of ideology that contribute to oppression or freedom, structures that are at least in part objective but perhaps ultimately inaccessible, and it finally circles back to Althusser: to what extent does Shor, more than Freire, account for those material circumstances which may act as very real obstacles to the liberation of (an authentic) subject, and which may lead student subjects to acknowledge the teacher's idea of critical education while nevertheless understanding that it sounds a lot better than it really is? The answer is that Shor *to some extent* is better on this question than Freire. While Freire does implicitly acknowledge the deadening effect ideology has by naturalizing a subject's own understanding of her place in a world ordered hierarchically, he tends not to stress that effect during the process of *conscientizacao*. Shor, on the other hand, is quite clear: "in the class or on the job, [students] know how to sabotage any process which alienates them. They have ways to set limits on their own dehumanization. They can be unproductive while looking busy, they can be clever while playing dumb, they can scheme against the boss while looking honest," and this kind of cynicism is the result of traditional education's failure to present students with "a vision of alternatives" (*Critical Teaching*, 53). Shor calls this a passive resistance, in contrast to an active one that provides students with the knowledge of the regularization and naturalization by which ideology works to produce a closed circle of understanding. Shor here hints at the ability of a critical education to enable students to posit a structure for the relations that prevent their education, which in passive resistance leads to cynicism and which in active resistance leads to revolution. Like Althusser's revised notion of science – and unlike Freire's dichotomous view of authentic versus inauthentic selves – Shor suggests the need to understand as much as possible the causes for cynical consciousness while also acknowledging the dialectical nature of conceptual or scientific knowledge by which that understanding is reached. While Freire is rather hopeful that liberation is the freedom to act according to those rules which have been set up once the established order by which ideology functions have been thoroughly changed, Shor is rather less sanguine about the possibility of wholesale revision, at least in part because whatever new set of rules – ethical, political, economic – is set up will bring with it its own consciousness and its own material effects which may in turn be understood as obstacles to the production of knowledge.

Part of the reason Shor is rather more precise on this point – and more consistent with Althusser – than Freire is because he acknowledges the thoroughly *social* nature of ideological interpellation, and thus of liberation. In making what Shor calls a "democratic future," the liberatory class can "investigate the economic laws and mediations which are responsible for the making of everyday life" at the level of a culture or a society, not just how individuals' understandings are created economically and rhetorically. Mass culture "is hydra-headed," says Shor in one of his more Adornian moments, yet what he suggests is quite true: students must understand the sociological and historical – read contradictory and overdetermined – dynamic that prevents individualist renderings of ideology because of the multiply- determined centers of interpretation and the multiple interpretations that will in turn be supplied for them. This is *not* true because of the faintly Rortyan proposition that a lack of objective foundations allows multiple interpretations and cannot prevent any one interpretation from overwhelming any other. It is true, rather, because the process by which objective knowledge is produced – scientifically, conceptually – is accompanied by spontaneous philosophies, ideologically-produced, that combine to ensure its use-value, its applicability to a world understood in conventional, institutional terms. The "economic laws and mediations" by which social structures function can be objectively established, but they are also ideologically implemented for use. This does not

render them tainted or biassed, but does suggest that their implementation – rather than, perhaps, their *sui generis* establishment –
is what a student's "real" is comprised by. This makes Slavoj
Žižek's point – that the illusion of reality rather than knowledge of
the reality itself (which is inaccessible at any rate) is that which
produces agency – all the more relevant here (Žižek, *Sublime
Object*, 28–35): cynical reason is what constructs students' understanding of the educative (and emancipatory) project in the first
place, and it is also that which gives impetus to the project of
emancipation when it can be deployed successfully, since it is the
knowledge of the structures (or "causes") of the illusion insofar as
it can be seen in its effects that might be called the "object of
knowledge" in a liberatory pedagogy.

But liberatory pedagogy – on either Freire's or Shor's account of
it – is not liberatory enough for some materialist practitioners, in
part because it continues to play into the hands of the "ludic
academy," an academy that understands the self as unified and
whole, and that still sees – claims, not to mention research,
oriented toward the left notwithstanding – the goal of education
as the replication and enforcement, not the critique, of humanism.
In particular, the ludic academy has compromised the emancipatory goal of Althusserian theory and practice by joining forces
with a watered-down American version of poststructuralism
which, for all its work in the last twenty-five years questioning the
enlightenment model of the self and reason, nevertheless retains
the basic premise of "'uncertainty' about the (representational)
reliability of knowledge" (Zavarzadeh, "Reading," 21). This uncertainty has a tendency to do away with notions of class struggle
or the possibility of constructing more or less scientific or conceptual knowledges. Worse still, there is a strand left over from the
1960s that suggests that the goal of a critical education is not
critique or even a poststructural reorientation of marginal and
central, but democracy, which for such radical left theorists as
Mas'ud Zavarzadeh, Donald Morton, Adam Katz and others is
simply another mystification at the service of the ruling class. For
Zavarzadeh, in particular, Freire and Shor fall into this category,
with *The Pedagogy of the Oppressed* holding a central place in the
canon of sixties leftovers.

In the introduction to their collection on radical-left teaching
entitled *Theory/Pedagogy/Politics*, Zavarzadeh and Morton lay

out the terrain that they see in the critical academy in the last decade of the twentieth century. What they call a humanist pedagogy, which "inculcates obedience to authority in the free subject" through the "practice of textual interpretation" and "the 'interpretive essay,'" allows for "individual variation [on the part of students' work] but insist[s] on the central truth of the text, ... reif[ying] the subject as free but at the same time obedient to the authority of the great mind of the author" (*Theory*, 3, 6). This pedagogy has slowly given way to a more active interrogation of authority through "critique," the investigation into the conditions of the discursive practices of the humanist academy itself. Like Freire's critical pedagogy or Shor's problem-posing education, Zavarzadeh and Morton wish to "demystify 'authority' (that of the author and of those whom the author represents in the symbolic order of culture). In undertaking a critique, rather than writing an interpretive essay, the learner also discovers that the text is not inherently meaningful, but that meaning is an effect of the signifying practices and codes with which he is familiar" (7). They go on to suggest that there exists a structure or "grid of intelligibility" that is available to students through the deployment of a critical Theory, a grid that is more or less the objective marker of the "cause" of the contradictory effects that are the cultural artefacts we call texts as well as the conventional (and more often than not unspoken but assumed) reading practices embedded in the academy and popular culture. But as soon as they note that such a structure is available for Theory to map, Morton and Zavarzadeh suggest that there are two ways to approach such a structure. What they call "ludic" postmodernism assumes that such a structure is available and corresponds to the left-hand term in the pairs right / wrong, good / bad, white / black, and so ludic postmodernism eventually falls back into the same humanist rut that traditional pedagogy was bogged down in. Without saying so, their ludic postmodernism looks much like the result of Stanley Fish's antifoundational rhetoric, which – though it tries to argue to the contrary – establishes an antifoundational foundation which begins by saying "my interpretation is not any less valid than yours is" but ends by adding "so it might as well be *more* valid," effectively producing a totalitarianism of interpretive brutishness: whoever argues loudest and longest wins (See Farmer, "Thuggery"; Rorty, "Thugs," 564–80).

Morton and Zavarzadeh see the way to resist this ludic tendency to "domesticate" theory as the production of conceptual knowledge, the constant retheorization of theory by way of practice, practice by way of theory in a dialectic reminiscent of the (problematical) process recommended by Phelps. Two tendencies in the contemporary academy that do this are "textual studies," which "basically defines 'politics' as those reading activities that 'delay' the connection of the signifier to the signified," in effect also delaying the political implications of such a strategy, and "cultural studies," which is defined by a "focus on the politics of production of subjectivities rather than on textual operations, [which] understands 'politics' as access to the material base of power / knowledge / resources." This latter tendency is divided into the experiential camp – which looks like a multiculturalism, focusing on how the experiences of different groups cannot be commensurated – and a critical camp, which sees its task as forging a totality of new relations, both political / economic as well as – insofar as possible – material, the work of which must in part also be the revolution that such emancipatory knowledge produces.

It is in this context that Zavarzadeh put forward his "The Pedagogy of Pleasure 2: The Me-In-Crisis," an essay that takes the form of a letter to one of his students which models by implication the emancipatory, left pedagogy that he has in mind to replace Freire's and Shor's and which he suggests is closer to the aims of a scientific / Theoretical practice scouted by Althusser. That essay created something of a firestorm of responses in *College Literature*, the journal in which it was published, and it is in those responses that many of the underlying assumptions of Zavarzadeh's (and Morton's) strategy of emancipation come clear. I was part of that firestorm – I had been a referee for Zavarzadeh's submission, and Jerry McGuire, the managing editor of *CL*, asked me to respond to Zavarzadeh in print, and he in turn responded to me and the others who were asked to respond. It was interesting to see the wide range of opinions on the article, not just by the initial reviewers but also by those who responded to the context of the review process itself. For me, both at the time I refereed the piece and now, Zavarzadeh is right on target in insisting that pedagogy is in great need of theorization, particularly as regards classroom practice which still makes many of the same humanist assumptions Zavarzadeh and Morton complain about in their collection in spite of the theoretical work that has gone on for nearly twenty-five years. It was also interesting to note that the responses to Zavarzadeh reflected a general unease about politically (or, much the same thing, theoretically) charging pedagogy. The essay's fourth reader, Alan France – to whom Zavarzadeh does not respond at all, possibly because that reader was the only one to recommend publication – is precisely right when he notes that the pedagogy of pleasure does identify a frustration many teachers have with what goes on in their classes. Students *are* often too willing to take what goes on at face value; too willing to avoid questions that make visible the contradictions of the academy and of "liberal" education; and too unwilling to challenge a teacher and to respond to a teacher's "oppositionality." This is in part due to the complicity of poststructuralism with the ruling academic ideologies that reify knowledge (only now in terms of "misreading" or "abyss" rather than the old-New Critical terms, "irony" or "metaphor"). And Zavarzadeh's point is that conceptual knowledge, as "scientific," is that which is required to break the intellectual ground that makes praxis possible.

But France's last comments reveal the single biggest problem in Zavarzadeh's program for a revolutionary pedagogy (and, incidentally, one of the reasons I did not recommend the piece for publication in *College Literature*). In his review, France asks for "a better (more literal) idea of the status of his / her absent interlocutor. . ." ("Symposium," 18). In "The Pedagogy of Pleasure 2," as well as in the introduction to *Theory/Pedagogy/Politics*, there is little mention of the student to whom the putative author of the "comment" writes other than as a second-person addressee or as someone who has apparently not done the work expected over the course of a semester. The interlocutor really *is* absent. It was this absence that – at least in part – characterizes a strand of post-theoretical (read here "post-poststructuralist") pedagogy one often sees in essays on how to theorize the teaching of English studies, a strand that might be connected to Althusser's notion of the objectivity of conceptual knowledge: the work is explicitly political / theoretical but pays little attention either to the students that presumably labor in the classroom, or to the ethical goal of their attendance in the first place.

To anticipate at least one criticism of this last assertion: revolutionary pedagogy is precisely "about emancipation from the regime of exchange and exploitation" ("Symposium," 33) and oppositionality in the classroom is meant "to provide people with a historical knowledge of the social totality, thereby helping to produce members of a vanguard party fighting for a society of economic equality." This is perfectly in accordance with Althusser's attempts to reorganize theoretical practice as the production of objective knowledge of the (otherwise inaccessible) structures whose effects are domination and exploitation naturalized by ideology. Yet what we have seen in Althusser is the acknowledgement that such a knowledge comes attendant with spontaneous ideological formations that allow it to have a use-value that is not commensurable with the language in which that knowledge comes encoded. That is to say, though he does so in a much more theoretically sophisticated argument than does Freire, Althusser recognizes that the access subjects have to conceptual knowledge is partial, and that it requires both scientific investigation as well as an interpretive moment at which scientists find themselves trying to explain the relevance of their work to a polis. This is not to say that science is rhetorical; rather, science functions alongside rhetoric since their purviews overlap. Zavarzadeh tells us that "objective knowledge is possible: its occlusion is the outcome of class relations and is not ontological" ("Reading," 28). But what is required in order to understand with any degree of scientific rigor the character of those class relations is scientific observation, which is likewise occluded. Zavarzadeh is right to suggest that objective knowledge is possible; but his suggestion that a critique that takes place in the classroom can give us access to it is only partly right, since the relations that teacher and student attempt to map continue acting on the mapping operation in spite of the theoretical work taking place. This tends to undermine the implied point in Zavarzadeh's essay (as it did in Althusser's philosophical tracts), that science (conceptual knowledge) begins with a vanguard that has access to the levers of knowledge, particularly given that such a vanguard class will most likely originate – as it seems these days – in the largely white, upper-middle class (i.e., ruling-class) student body that gains entrance to universities because the institutions keep raising the bar to keep "underprepared" students out. At least as important is that Zavarzadeh can hardly be surprised that some of his students – many of whom, at Syracuse especially, are white, upper-middle class, traditionally-educated eighteen- and nineteen-year olds – will resist not just the content of the course but the revolutionary pedagogy itself. Given the tone of disappointment of Zavarzadeh's essay – a "letter" to the student who had not turned in her / his final paper assignment – it is clear that the student was unwilling to read much of what was assigned for class, and was unable (or unwilling) to write the paper at least in part because this resistance was fostered, not neutralized, by what comes across as a highly adversarial pedagogy. Again, this should not come as a great surprise to Zavarzadeh given the implications of Althusser's spontaneous philosophy and its effect on scientific investigation.

My assumption about the adversarial nature of pedagogy comes of reading "The University and Revolutionary Practice: A Letter toward a Leninist Pedagogy," an essay written by Adam Katz – who, at the time he wrote that essay, was a doctoral student at Syracuse responding to criticism by a philosophy professor of his participation in her class – which is included in Morton and Zavarzadeh's *Theory/Pedagogy/Politics*. Katz, taking the oppositional stance to classroom practice derived from Althusser by Zavarzadeh, has been called "Trotskyist," "adversarial," "gladiatorial," and "masculine," among other things by his professor and by fellow students. Katz goes on to argue – as Zavarzadeh does in "Reading my Readers" – that such terms are symptomatic of an "individualist" stance to teaching, in which the teacher fosters a democracy in the classroom that is made up of various "free individuals" who "express themselves," and in which all knowledge constructed from such "free subject positions" is equally valid. Such a classroom, Katz suggests, actually works to mystify the authority of the teacher who is here working to interpellate her students as individual "producers" of knowledge in the economy of the institution which functions as a microcosm for the consumer economy of capitalism, which needs good "workers" who see themselves as valuable – but individual – parts of a production machine. Better, says Katz, to "make [contradictions and antagonisms] concrete in material practices," and for the teacher "to stand at the 'extreme' end of students' statements and positions that bear some emancipatory potential, and by taking them to their 'logical' conclusions, to pressure and enable these students to move beyond the structural limitations of such positions and statements towards even more emancipatory, radical, and revolutionary subjectivities" ("University," 237).

The "essay" Zavarzadeh has written by way of "commenting" on his student's letter (a letter in part designed to exculpate her / himself) was therefore meant to continue such an oppositional stance that, consistent with Althusser (as well as with Shor's interpretation of Freire's work), does not rely on an institutional structure or set of rules but which must be built into the practice of a lived life. But like the letter to Katz, in which neither the teacher's own position and set of assumptions about the academy nor Katz's own strategy in the course of a sixteen-week seminar, not only is there a great deal we are not told about the student to whom the letter is addressed, but there is also a great deal about the practice of revolutionary pedagogy that we're not told from reading "The Pedagogy of Pleasure 2." Many things are assumed – among them, that the readers of *College Literature* practice the pedagogy of pleasure (or practice any explicitly theoretical pedagogy at all); that we know what revolutionary pedagogy looks like when it is done properly in a course; that we can tell what students do (or do not do) in such a classroom and what kind of resistance they exhibit; what sorts of things a teacher (such as Zavarzadeh or Katz) does to overcome such resistance. None of this gets said, and so the reader is left to infer a great deal about the student in question, and the rest of the students in the course. What we do get is a great deal that comes off as complaint: that the student has not bothered to read, that the student is making excuses, that the student assumes that her/his own little world is the single most valuable experience s/he can talk about or bring to the class. Much more clearly, the reader learns about Zavarzadeh's understanding of radical pedagogy as it works against the pedagogy of pleasure, his code word for poststructuralist theories and pedagogies that wittingly or unwittingly reduce the world to discourse and hold up the "free subject" as the originator of that discourse and thus knowledge.

The question about the student is in effect a question about the material conditions of the classroom that both do and do not accord with the theoretical perspective that Zavarzadeh (and, by implication, Althusser) outline as both conceptual and emancipatory. If the student had not bothered to read the assignments throughout the term – which is what Zavarzadeh implies – and if

– as it is also implied – that the "letter" is being written at the end of the semester in response to the student's failure to produce an adequate final project, then one is forced to ask about the extent to which the teacher in this course had contact with his students not just in the classroom and not just in responding to their work, but also outside the classroom and in producing something like ethical knowledge that would enable him to catch on to this student's "failure." The question that one needs to ask that has to do with the understanding of a polis that has at its disposal the common knowledge that allows it to understand the language of the rhetor – and the ethical question that accompanies it about the production of the rhetor's subject of enunciation – is this: how well did Zavarzadeh here investigate the (practical and scientific) knowledge available to the members of the polis before he began to engage them critically? If the teacher's stance in the classroom – like Katz's – is characterized by its belligerence, authoritarianism and confrontational style, then it does not come as a surprise to me that the student here felt cowed by the teacher all term and may have felt completely unwilling or unable to complete the year-end assignment. One does not need to engage in a pedagogy that is wholly "affective" or expressive in order to plumb the abilities of one's students and to find the degrees of mystification that they are under.

Like Zavaradeh and Katz, I have tried over the course of my (relatively short) career to politicize my classroom, and to engage questions about the constructedness of discourse, the politicization of knowledge and the complicity of the academy with the ruling class. But I also know full well that if I enrage my students, if I scare them, if I am too confrontational or if I fail to understand the knowledge my students have and as a result talk over their heads and then get angry because they do not get it, one of two things will happen (and I say this from experience, not conjecture), and both can be explained in terms of cynicism and the spontaneity of student response. First, the student may simply drop the class. Unless you work at a place such as Syracuse where many students are (presumably) reading off the same sheet of music when they enter a classroom (I presume, from Adam Katz's article, at least, that even at Syracuse not everyone agrees about the pedagogy best suited to produce emancipated subjects), different students act differently, as do different teachers. The result is that if a student feels antagonized or threatened by the teacher or the subject matter of a class (not to mention the appearance of the teacher or of the classroom), she may well leave and take something more to her taste. This defeats the purpose of the revolutionary classroom, since it is those students most in need of being confronted with the structural limitations of their positions that would leave most quickly. Secondly, students could very well stay in the class, learn the language of the course – learn what "hegemony" and "power / knowledge" and "praxis" mean and use them properly in sentences – and perhaps engage in the give-and-take of the classroom. But such evidence of participation does not mean that the student is becoming emancipated. Quite to the contrary, it may mean that – in order to survive the class and maybe get the grade they think they (or maybe their parents) can tolerate – they will play the radical teacher's game and look like they are learning when in fact they are only doing what Žižek suggests (and Fred Pfeil and others have made clear in everyday terms): taking the cynical stance. These students are, in Žižek's terms, recognizing "the particular interest behind the ideological universality, the distance between the ideological mask and the reality, but [finding] reasons to retain the mask" (*The Sublime Object*, 29). The hegemony of ruling-class ideology is extremely pervasive. It may be that revolutionary pedagogy is one way to resist this hegemony. But it is not clear whether Zavarzadeh recognized what his students were doing or what they were *not* doing (reading the material, snickering behind his back) so his "comment" about the student's me-in-crisis strikes me as ineffectual at best (and counterproductive – since these comments might have been of much more use at the point the teacher got the sense that the student was not reading – at worst). As I have tried to suggest, though it is not explicit in Althusser's essay on spontaneity, it is easy to reach the conclusion that the work of (scientifically) describing the effects of social and economic relations and the work of understanding how those descriptions function in a larger social order are extremely complicated in the way that they overlap and function together. The scientist needs also to understand that in order to keep from falling into the trap of believing one's own practice is immune to critique, she needs to guide science theoretically, and guide theory scientifically. Cynicism is the logical outcome of pedagogy in a world considered ideological through and through: of course the illusion is what produces agency, since there is no way to understand any element of the life world except in terms of a false consciousness. This was part of the problem with Freire: one only has recourse to either true or false consciousness, with the former being a utopian aim. Zavarzadeh's theoretical practice is scientific to the extent that any other theory is scientific, but whereas Althusser suggests that dialectical materialism, as science, also must be wary of its own spontaneous philosophies, Zavarzadeh seems blind to the possibility that his student's cynicism is the result of his own ideological blindness which itself keeps him from recognizing the results of his work in a world that does not match his understanding of it.

In my response to Zavarzadeh in the *College Literature* forum, I mentioned Tompkins and Freire as potential correctives to his conceptual pedagogy ("Pedagogy"; also see Ohmann, *English*, especially 178–81, 184–6). I did so not because I particularly buy Tompkins's individualist rendering of Freire, or that I do not find problems in Freire's own work, as I have tried to show here. (Nevertheless I find it odd that Zavarzadeh should reject Friere out of hand since, rather than simply validating the experiences of the Brazilians he works with, he provides a way to conceptualize that knowledge, which is the first move in clearing the ground for praxis.) But what Freire does – and Zavarzadeh fails to – provide in very explicit terms is a description or even an idea of what goes on between the students and the teachers in the classroom. *How* or in what terms does confrontation work? What sorts of assignments work (or, in the case of this student, don't work)? What do you read? How does the course fit the institutional (i.e., department and university) aims? And how do these aims become objects for study? Instead, the questions Freire asks about the very specific instances of his students' situations – about what prevents learning, about the very material instances of a student's position in a class-layered culture – and that Shor asks about his students' day-to-day lives as commuter students at the City College of New York and about their boyfriend / girlfriend problems cannot be the *only* ones teachers asks. If they were, teachers would lapse into the individualist, intersubjective theoretical position which Louise Phelps risks occupying in her analysis of composition. But these interpretive questions – about lives not our own that cannot be commensurated into our own terms – are the ones that must situate any rigorously descriptive analysis of class or institutional-ization of knowledge or the relation between race and gender; and they are also the ones that must likewise be subjected to that very same rigorous analysis in scientific terms in order to explore how, for example, assumptions about gender on the politically conser-vative wards on Staten Island function in more or less regular fashion. In effect Alan France, has it right when he says that "The Pedagogy of Pleasure 2" "articulates . . . the 'political uncon-scious' of a nagging amorphous complaint about our students (and our teaching) . . ." at a time when we have the means available to do more than characterize these complaints but in-stead explore their determinants.

Bhaskar and strong objectivity

Those means are available in a philosophy of science articulated most strongly by Roy Bhaskar – but found also in work by Sandra Harding, Donna Haraway, S. P. Mohanty, and others – that in rough outline is not content with the suggestion that the necessary description of phenomena and structures must be contingent. In short, a realist view of the sciences does not conflate the contin-gency of description (an epistemological question) with the con-tingency of the object of description (an ontological question); does not see the natural sciences as rendering the human sciences redundant (or vice versa) but rather sees a role for each in the work of what Bhaskar calls "underlaboring" for practical work in the world; and understands a connection between the ability to produce knowledge of objects and structures that in effect pro-duce and guide human life, and the possibility for humans to become emancipated from those structures that render them un-free. It will be my task in the remainder of this chapter to draw the broad outlines of a realist philosophy of science, while noting its connections to a theory of rhetoric that does not compete with science but rather works in tandem with it as a theory to describe and possibly change the world of human relations, a theory that is consistent with a materialist understanding of ideology, the real, and the structural relation between the two.

In a chapter of *Reclaiming Reality* entitled "Realism in the Natu-ral Sciences," Bhaskar defines realism as "the theory that the ultimate objects of scientific inquiry exist and act (for the most part) quite independently of scientists and their activity" (12). In effect, realism is an ontological position in philosophy, not an epistemological one. It requires, according to Bhaskar, that scientists establish a philosophy of science in such a way that scientists see what they are doing as gathering information about the nature and behavior of the world as though they were not there to observe it. Realism, in other words, is metascientific in that it requires of scientists to undertake their work as delineated by the conventions of the paradigm within which they perform it while understanding that work to have no effect upon the behavior or nature of the objects under investigation. Realist philosophy of science works in the same way that Althusser insists philosophy *must* work in connection with the work of the sciences themselves: it must "draw a *line of demarcation* between interdisciplinary ideology and the effective reality of the process of the mutual application and constitution of sciences" (Althusser, "Spontaneous Philosophy," 87), between the structures observed and described by the sciences and the ideological and necessary work of understanding those descriptions in a social life-world. As Bhaskar puts it, "philosophy distinguishes itself from science by its *method*, and more generally by the kinds of considerations and arguments it deploys[:] . . . both the premises and conclusions of philosophical arguments remain contingent facts, the former but not the latter being necessarily social (and so historical)" (Bhaskar, "Realism," 14). The premises of philosophy are hypothetical, in that they propose for the work of scientific description that the world must be structured and differentiated, but it does not suggest the method for science by which these regularities might be tested, explaining the contingency of those premises. The results, however, tested by the methods established by science – and, importantly, guided by metacognitive theory – are not contingent, in that they bear out or disprove the regularities put forward by the premise. Going back to Althusser, philosophy "clears a path" for scientific work to proceed, since – as we have seen in our discussions of Kuhn and Rorty *apropos* hermeneutics – scientific work does not always understand how to proceed in the face of impasses (or, for Althusser, crises) that arise when an object of phenomenon refuses to operate in the way a paradigmatic description of it suggests it should. What is important for us here – and what distinguishes a realist philosophy of science thus far from the position Zavarzadeh stakes out regarding conceptual knowledge – is that Bhaskar insists upon both the existence of a mind-independent reality that has a structure and can be differentiated as to its component parts; and the need to describe that reality insofar as possible with the aid of a philosophical, meta-cognitive "standpoint," a set of propositions about the world that are contingent and interpretive, but which do not call into question the validity of science's descriptions.

Science describes the object's or phenomenon's structures through experimental activity, in which scientists co-determine or are causally co-responsible for patterns of events. By carefully controlling the conditions under which they produce these patterns, scientists are able to identify the ways in which these events operate. So, for example, a scientist will hypothesize the behavior of a virus under certain conditions in the human body, and will manipulate a number of these conditions in a set of experiments in the lab in order to observe the pattern of events exhibited by the virus under each of the conditions tested. The scientist understands her activity as co-producing a set of phenomena that replicate a finite set of related phenomena that would occur whether she did the experiment or not. The results of her observations thus do not translate directly into the "laws of nature," or a set of explanations for the ways in which that virus behaves under all circumstances in the natural world or in the human body. As Bhaskar suggests, the objects of scientific inquiry are not the events observed and the constant conjunctions co-determined by the scientist, but rather – because the conjunctions of events in an experiment both replicate but also predict future behavior, because there are finite numbers of variables the scientist can use if the experiment is to give any indication of a natural phenomenon – the "structures, generative mechanisms and the like (forming the real basis of causal laws), which are normally out of phase with them" (16). The descriptions which scientists make about the organism must be *applied* to a system of organisms (in this case, the single family or species of virus) that is open (where constant conjunctions, controlled patterns of events, do not occur). Realist philosophy, then, suggests that

if [experimental] activity is to be rendered intelligible, causal laws must be analysed as tendencies, which may be possessed unexercised and excercised unrealized, just as they may of course be realized unperceived (or undetected) by anyone. Thus in citing a law we are referring to the transfactual activity of mechanisms, that is, to their activity as such, not making a claim about the actual outcome (which will in general be co-determined by the effects of other mechanisms too). ("Realism," 16)

One of the problems in Zavarzadeh's view of conceptual knowledge as providing a way for his students to clear a path for the revolutionizing work of liberation is that the open system – the worlds in which they lived and worked – seemed to be operating behind the teacher's back. Zavarzadeh was content to observe the "constant conjunction" of his classroom, and to transform the conditions of learning he saw there – and complained bitterly when those conditions did not change in the ways he anticipated – which led to him to "make a claim about the actual outcome" of the event rather than to do the ideological, interpretive work required to see the *failure* of the "experiment" as a tendency in that open system, and to reconsider the method of observation according to what he observed. Of course, Freire errs on the side of interpretation, without explicitly outlining the need for the work of observation, causing him to uncritically equate word and world without the intervention of Theory (or, in Bhaskar's terms, philosophy).

Bhaskar marks the difference between the "intransitive" dimension – the open system of the world that exists independently of our ability to describe it – and "a *transitive* dimension or epistemology" which we need to constitute in order "to complement the intransitive dimension or ontology already established" ("Realism," 18). The production of scientific knowledge is contingent – as is the production, traditionally, of rhetorical knowledge – insofar as it is a social process whose aim is to furnish descriptions of the *mechanisms* of phenomena in the natural world; but it is objective insofar as its philosophy gives us a way to understand how one set of descriptions is superior to another through the first's ability to describe phenomena that the second could not. So, for example, if one has two incommensurable theories describing the behavior or structure of an event, and one explains most of the phenomena comprising the event while another describes the same phenomena plus other phenomena *not* otherwise described by the first, one can say that the second theory is preferable to the first because of its explanatory capacity.

It is not enough to suggest that both theories are contingent and therefore suspect because of their incommensurability, since the hypothesis that enables constant conjunctions of events to take place – that the world is structured in such a way the constant conjunctions are possible – is borne out by the experimental method itself. It also is not enough to say that incommensurability renders the need for scientists to discard science altogether and find a third method for negotiating the two theories, since "to say of two theories that they conflict, clash or are in competition presupposes that there is something – a domain of real objects or relations existing and acting independently of their (conflicting) descriptions – *over* which they clash" (19). Zavarzadeh fails to understand this when he refuses to recognize that the impasse he has reached with his student is something like a clash of incommensurable theories, but one over a part world shared in common by both. In such a case, Zavarzadeh would be forced to adopt Freire's understanding of teaching – something like a constant conjunction since it combines observation of the natural (and the social) world with a testing of those theories in practice, and then reorganizes the results through further observation – that forces teachers to account for each student's materially constrained position as having an ontological dimension with epistemologically (and contingently) explainable effects. In other words, Zavarzadeh fails to see the incommensurability of his and his student's understanding of the institution and its rules as at once an ontological and an epistemological problem.

The implications of all this for the natural *and* the human sciences are at least the following two. First, the human sciences take as their object of study the mechanisms and structures of human social relations, which do not render themselves available to constant conjunctions (i.e., experimentation) in the same way as the natural sciences, thereby limiting the descriptive capacity of the human sciences to explanation rather prediction. That is to say, because human agency deflects the direct influence of individuals on their material surroundings and upon one another – differently from natural objects whose behavior remains relatively constant because those objects are not active agents – we are not able to predict human behavior through constant conjunctions as we are able to predict the behaviour of natural objects. Bhaskar notes that this "means that any social science must incorporate a historically situated hermeneutics; [and that] the condition of social science is a part of its own field [and so] it must be self-reflexive, critical and totalizing in a way in which natural science is not" ("Realism," 24). This also means that human social relations are also objectively real, and also behave according to certain laws and structures, and that these laws and structures are the objects of knowledge for the human sciences, which are also to be gleaned by establishing premises deriving from them conclusions founded upon observation. The self-reflexiveness required by the human sciences nevertheless does not render the ontological existence of the structures of human social relations negligible. Rather, it means that the philosophical guide required of the natural sciences as implied by Althusser must be much more rigorously applied in such a way that the human sciences, by providing an historically situated hermeneutics, ask at each point in human scientific inquiry in what ways that inquiry might differ if the *position* from which the hypotheses and observations are made were changed. The second implication is intimately tied to the first: "the possibility arises that the behaviour of higher-order (biological) entities, such as human beings, might both be explanatorily irreducible to (or emergent from) and yet entirely consistent with, lower-order (physical) laws" (24). The implication, in other words, is that there are many points at which the human sciences – and practical wisdom – overlap with the natural sciences (and their methods).

Bhaskar goes on to suggest that though the human and the natural sciences are distinct methods, each with distinct objects (the tendencies by which natural objects behave for the natural sciences, the tendencies by which human relations operate for the human sciences), what binds them together is the notion that one can move from the production of knowledge in the transitive dimension through observation and testing of events in the natural (and social) world to conclusions about the properties in the ontological dimension of those events as indicators of their tendencies in larger systems. These tendencies must then be observed, followed by the production of hypotheses about component aspects of the object, and so on. In a central chapter of *Reclaiming Reality*, Bhaskar debunks both social and individualist theories of social relations, suggesting instead that people, in their conscious human activity, for the most part unconscious-ly reproduce (or occasionally, transform) the structures that govern their substantive activities of production. Thus people do not marry to repro-duce the nuclear family, or work to reproduce the capitalist economy. But it is nevertheless the unintended consequence (and inexorable result) of, as it is also the necessary condition for, their activity. (*Reclaiming Reality*, 80)

In the same way that realist science does not take as its object of study constant conjunctions but rather the generative mechan-isms for the events tested by them, social sciences do not take human behavior as their object but rather the relations and the mechanisms that generate it: relations between people and each other, their products, their activities, nature and themselves. Pay-ing attention to these relations *in addition to* the material objects (or lower-order, physical entities) and understanding them *as tenden-cies to be studied* suggest that, like the intransitive ontological dimension in the natural sciences, it is these relations (and their replication and transformation) that must be studied "rather than the actual complex motley of particular social forms" (81–2). Even though the human sciences have an exclusively explanatory rather than a predictive role, because the mode of application of laws is the same in both the human and natural sciences' "sys-tems," and even though the need to rely on explanatory criteria may affect the confidence with which we hold social scientific theories, "if we have independently validated claims to social scientific knowledge (on explanatory criteria) then we are just as warranted in applying our knowledge as in natural science" (83). The transcendental realism Bhaskar is here proposing both for the human and the natural sciences – "transcendental" because it understands the ontological real as existing independent from the epistemological capacity to explain it – suggests that the concep-tual knowledge proposed by Althusser for Theory (and, by impli-cation, dialectical materialism) may square the interpretive di-mension of the study of human interaction, and its manifestations in language, with a rigorous scientific method involving the ob-servation and testing of human interaction with the natural world. This will always necessarily involve a philosophy – a science of science – that is so constantly vigilant that the frustra-tion of a Zavarzadeh or the idealism of a Freire does not mark the end of the road for the transformation of social structures.

At this point I want to say very briefly how Bhaskar's transcendental realist philosophy of science provides a way for rhetoric to understand itself as a materialist theory of description that mediates between the world of hermeneutics (or abnormal description, on Rorty's terms) and a world of scientific description (or normal description). Much of this ground is covered in a chapter in Bhaskar's *Reclaiming Reality* and in a subsequent book mainly on Rorty entitled *Philosophy and the Idea of Freedom*. Turning the tables on Rorty, who proposed hermeneutics as an alternative philosophical strategy to epistemology, Bhaskar instead proposes transcendental realism as an alternative to hermeneutics, which he understands as entailing a theory of the nature of being of the objects of investigation in both the human and natural sciences as co-existing with their explanations. That is to say, Bhaskar understands the danger of a position such as Rorty's as suggesting that when one changes one's description of an object or of an explanation, one has also changed that object's ontological status. Though science's constant conjunctions take place in closed systems, their objects of knowledge are the structures and generative mechanisms by which they operate and which are "out of phase with them," which is to say that they do not occur in the same context as they would in the natural world. So we produce, in experiment, not the laws of nature but rather their empirical grounds. We produce "causal laws," which are descriptive of the mechanism in question. This bears on the juncture of the human sciences and the study of rhetoric in several ways. It is not necessarily true, for one thing, that descriptions or redescriptions of phenomena or mechanisms are purely contingent, as Rorty and others move quite close to saying. We may well be able to describe a phenomenon with which we have access – in Zavarzadeh's class, we remember that his student wrote about his experiences – by determining the forms such experiences take (and we can do this both in terms of the generic constraints of narrative as well as the event's conceptual content), and by describing particular component parts or elements that comprise that experience. We can do all of these things without equating the transitive descriptions one makes with "the world," or "the way the world works apart from our understanding of it." Written descriptions one produces in a class, like the production of knowledge that results from scientific observation and testing, are the results of work in a closed system.

But they may also be taken as tendencies exhibited by phenomena or mechanisms outside our direct capacity to observe them, outside, namely, the constraints of the material and social world within which we operate. So, though what we, or Zavarzadeh's or Freire's students, may observe or write may not provide us with direct access to Rorty's "world out there," written descriptions produced in conjunction with those observations nevertheless can be said to redescribe in the transitive dimension tendencies of objects in the intransitive dimension whose effects may be observed and tested scientifically, and which may be said to operate according to verifiable laws.

Scientific investigation can be seen as a "three-phase schema," in which a phenomenon is identified, explanations for the phenomenon are constructed and empirically tested, thereby identifying (or describing) the mechanisms at work. The explanation then becomes the phenomenon to be tested and so on. If, in the first phase of the schema the observer notes a regularity through experimentation, it is the result of some operative mechanism (generated theoretically), and what is imagined in the second phase is not simply *imaginary* but can come to be known, through the replication of the event through further testing, as the "real." This point, I think, is crucial for bringing the study of language in "the realm of the contingent" – in, that is, the contemporary antifoundational paradigm – around to recognizing its compatibility (and, in fact, its necessary connection) with theoretical and experimental science founded on observation and testing. One's descriptions – in writing, in speaking, in the formulation of observation language created as we try to understand our surroundings – are not imaginary, though they are derived from the imagination (as scientific description also is). In the schema described above, there is a progression from description of a state of affairs limited to a specific instance to a description of broader mechanisms, both human / social and objective / natural; the essence of the progression lies "in the *movement* at any one level from knowledge of manifest phenomena to knowledge, produced by means of antecedent knowledge, of the structures that generate them" (Bhaskar, "Realism," 20). Knowledge inscribed linguistically can be thought of as knowledge derived from descriptions of phenomena, which were previously described as structures that generated that knowledge, and so on. Literary or hermeneutically generated knowledge has everything to do with the material objects and structures that exist independent of the capacity to describe them, and it is the scientific generation of knowledge of these structures or objects (social as well as extra-social; either descriptive or predictive knowledge) that must not be left out of a rhetorical theory.

We must bear in mind, warns Bhaskar, that we do not only observe scientifically produced experiments (or, in a rhetorical analysis, a situation in which certain components may be described as the object under discussion) and record them *as if* they reflected the way the world works, since on this view people are just passive sensors of given facts who record their constant conjunctions or, as Bhaskar says, "passive spectators in a given world" (23). Rather, people – rhetors, interlocutors taking part in a communicative act – should be seen as active agents in a complex, open world, in which the phenomena science describes, and the inquiry that science produces, are highly complex and ordered. The same sort of investigation is available for the human sciences since human activity is at least in part material activity, and inasmuch as Freire (and, for that matter, Rorty and Kuhn) are right to suggest that there is an imaginative, extra-scientific component to such investigation, it must be acknowledged that such a component cannot be isolated from the world of brute material reality whose impact can be discerned and understood conceptually as impinging upon human behavior. It is highly probable, Bhaskar tells us, that human behavior cannot be reducible to, yet may be emergent from, the behavior of lower-order physical objects and the laws derived to understand their mechanisms.

Bhaskar's realist philosophy of science implies a dialectical relationship between the human and natural sciences in a much more explicit way than even the dialectical pedagogies derived from materialist theory, and certainly more clearly than Rorty or Kuhn. The relationship here requires that scientific inquiry be understood as having a social component, as with Rorty and Kuhn (and not unlike Freire); but that the social component must be understood scientifically, which would serve as a corrective to Zavarzadeh's combative conceptual stance, in that it would allow his students to guide, rather than stand in the way of, his theoretical inquiry. This move implies the possibility of having a realist social science that at once understands knowledge as mediated (the central tenet of contemporary thought), but also understands that some knowledges explain certain things better than others. We discover ways to "*make* facts and, in experimental activity, closed systems; but *find* out about (i.e., discover, identify and investigate the nature and properties of) things, structures, and causal laws," and we do so in open systems (Bhaskar, *Philosophy and the Idea of Freedom*, 10). Contrary to the theorists we have discussed so far, it is necessary to understand not "how writing changes things" in the world, but to understand that writing does not simply have a social dimension, but that it also has a material dimension apart from its rhetorical one but inextricable from it, and that in order to change the world we need to understand and attempt to transform the mechanisms and structures by which material objects, no less than social entities, operate.

On many of the accounts we have dealt with so far – including Rorty's, but also implicit in Freire and Zavarzadeh – redescription is a valuable human act because it has the potential to lead to human emancipation. Freedom becomes, "through our capacity to *redescribe* [the] world (or relevant bits of it), something which is both positive and humanistically more recognizable – namely, the capacity to create, and choose between, different vocabularies" (Bhaskar, *Philosophy*, 63). By making a new, incommensurable description of herself stick, an individual makes it so. She creates her self over, "which is to say, 'overcomes' her previous or past self" (65). In the rhetorical phase of discovery – in the terms used by contemporary composition studies, when a writer finds out what one has to say – the writing or speaking subject reworks the contexts of previously uttered discourse in order to desribe a contemporary instance; in orienting the language differently, the writer has effectively redescribed or changed the self.

Yet this is hardly freedom, since it does not do much to change the material constraints within which one does the uttering. As I have tried to suggest thus far – in this chapter and in others – unless there is a way for human subjects to determine how to adjudicate between competing and incommensurable descriptions, one cannot tell just what it is they are (re)describing. Unless one theorizes science as adequate to the task of fixing the status of material reality then all redescriptions are equally satisfactory, with the result that each redescription (including, in Zavarzadeh's terms, the most conceptual, potentially emancipatory knowledge produced in the agonistic classroom) is going to be overturned by some other, incommensurable redescription, thus voiding the emancipatory properties of the previous one. It is no wonder that Zavarzadeh is frustrated by his student's failure to "get it," to change his mind: without understanding how that student's material situation structures his ability to produce knowledge (conceptually or otherwise), all he can change is the student's language, but as Zavarzadeh has amply shown, this has not made the student any better at using that language to change his material surroundings which, after all, he does not have the ability to understand.

Bhaskar has helped to pinpoint one of the biggest inherent dangers in an easy (read here "non-realist") antifoundationalism, particularly as it pertains to the study of language. We cannot but acknowledge that the paradigm shift described by Rorty and others has complicated our ability to match our descriptions of the world to the mechanisms of that world. Particularly in the field of rhetoric studies (including the study of writing in the academic disciplines roughly called composition studies), a great deal of exciting work has been done in the years leading up to Louise Phelps's attempt to understand that work as reorienting the broad field of the human sciences, work by people such as Jim Berlin, John Schilb, Pat Bizzell, Greg Myers and others who have tried to understand the problems inherent in squaring writers' material conditions to the methods available for understanding them. The risk we run, in paying attention to the ways in which descriptions are incommensurable or potentially liberating, is that of losing sight of *what* writers are producing knowledge *of*. In an essay on the reform of the study of writing in the wake of the contemporary reorganization of knowledge, Greg Myers tells us that we need to examine the very "limitations" that give "structure to our thought," and to see them as "whole systems of ideas that people take for granted and use to make sense of the world. One cannot escape from one's economic interests and ethnic background [!!], but one can try to understand how they shape one's thinking and social actions" (Myers, "Reality," 169). But even this is difficult to pull off unless one can systematically and scientifically analyze "economic interests and ethnic background" insofar as they are both produced by and independent of the ideologies generated, in

Althusser's terms, spontaneously by the norms imposed by the disciplines within which one does the analyzing. The pedagogies generated by rhetoric and composition studies in recent years have stressed the collective work of students to form consensus and the generation of essays on topics that interest them, but Zavarzadeh is right when he tells us that this leads students into the "me-in-crisis" thinking that forces them into the microscopic world of independent, free subjects when nothing could be farther from the actual conditions within which they operate. And yet without understanding the mechanisms that help generate the ideological double-bind of cynicism, Zavarzadeh also cannot leave students anything but frustrated, since the chasm between the teacher's dialectic and the student's me-in-crisis cannot be articulated without understanding the limitations of the student's own field.

One way to navigate this treacherous middle passage is to understand rhetorical analysis as a realist investigation into the social and material structures that impinge upon agency. To do so, I want to simply point back to Aristotle's stratification of knowledge and suggest – as I did earlier in connection with Phelps and Althusser – the points of convergence for the construction of a materialist rhetoric that sees itself as a dialectical engagement of scientific and interpretive knowledge. To recall *Nichomachean Ethics* (and I refer back to the discussion in the second chapter), Aristotle proposes the pair *nous*, the faculty with which humans grasp sense-data and first principles, and *dianoia*, the faculty that associates thoughts to form syllogisms. At the first level of contemporary scientific inquiry, scientists identify the phenomenon to be investigated (through sense-data) and attempt to produce an invariant result or constant conjunction by formulating a premise or hypothesis, which must be tested logically through its component parts. Aristotle's *episteme* is roughly the equivalent of scientific knowledge, which – through observation of the mechanisms reproduced through testing, "represents the real." As Bhaskar puts it,

[g]iven such an invariance, science moves immediately to the construction and testing of possible explanations for it. If there is a correct explanation, located in the nature of the thing or the structure of its system, then there is a reason independent of its actual behavior for that behavior. Such a reason may be discovered empirically. And, if we can

deduce the thing's normic behavior from it, then the most stringent possible criterion for our knowledge of natural necessity is satisfied. For example, we may discover that copper has a certain atomic or electronic structure and then be able to deduce its dispositional properties from a statement of that structure. If we can do so, we may then be said to possess knowledge of natural necessity *a posteriori*. (Bhaskar, "Realism," 21)

Aristotle's third realm of inquiry was *sophia*, which is directed toward those elements of being that are eternal and changeless, like the formation of a definition. This may be likened to the expression of a phenomenon's structure in an attempt to define that process (or object, or phenomenon): these are the causal laws, which then appear as the tendencies of natural – and social – objects, realized under closed systems. This does not put an end to inquiry, but provides "a stepping stone to a new process of discovery in which science seeks to unearth the mechanisms responsible for *that* level of reality" (Bhaskar, "Realism," 21). In other words, the definition or law devised to explain what a scientist has observed in closed systems is then enlarged – as a definition – to explain hitherto untested bits of reality in the open system of the object at hand, and further testing then begins. The fourth and fifth realms in Aristotle's sytem are *techne*, including rhetoric and dialectic, which produces common-sense knowledge that results from the first three levels of inquiry, such that one can begin to see the practical implications of scientific discovery in the political world, implying in turn a social knowledge that also proceeds from the first three levels of inquiry; and *phronesis*, which puts common-sense knowledge into practice, roughly equivalent to the technologization of the products of scientific discovery, or the implementation of a hypothetically constructed politics in the world of brute material constraints. This is what Freire has called *praxis*, though it is clear at this point that it cannot be implemented without a fully developed scientific method of social and natural entities and structures.

Students and practitioners of rhetoric alike must understand that the inquiry involved in using language – what for Rorty is hermeneutics, and what for materialism is the dialectic – has both an interpretive and a scientific dimension, and that each is structured and relatively autonomous. To understand this is to understand that redescription as the rhetorical deployment of argument in a world of social and material constraints depends upon investigation at all previous levels. To separate interpretation and science – to suggest that scientific or conceptually constructed knowledge is simply a different kind of knowledge from literary knowledge – implies that so-called natural phenomena only affect human social understanding insofar as the humans involved are directly affected, and understand them explicitly and at all times. Such a separation implies that writing – and rhetoric – are largely a private affair, in which meanings and the production of writing are important only insofar as one says they are. To subsume one realm of inquiry beneath the other – regardless of which one does the subsuming – *equates* the world with the language used to describe it (one of Freire's problems), leading to the dangerous and plainly false conclusion that if we (or our students) could simply "rewrite" their situation everything else will be rewritten to their advantage. What Bhaskar's transcendental realism suggests to us – deriving from materialist theory – is that though there is a complex relation between the transitive, epistemological dimension in which we describe the world, and the intransitive, ontological dimension in which the real operates independently of our descriptive capacity, it is necessary for us to conceptually link the two, even though this link can be established only with the understanding that it may be temporary, and only with the constant vigilance afforded by the metatheoretical discipline Althusser would have as Philosophy. What we have learned, in the last few years of this century, is that despite the antifoundational revolution, science proceeds apace; and that even if naysayers complain that common-sense wisdom has eroded, it has not so completely that we are unable to say with relative certainty when someone's utterances have gone too far: giving the poor laptop computers will not bring the underclass into the twenty-first century, as House Speaker Gingrich told us after the 1994 elections, if for no other reason than that they may have no place to plug them in. Changing communication technology – changing what we say – will not change the world in which that technology works unless we systematically explore the complexities of the material world in which such cummunication takes place. The implications of the false assumptions of a Gingrichite epistemology for pedagogical, social, and writing theory will be the subject of the next section of this project.

7

Toward a materialist rhetoric: writing the conditions of the incommensurable

With the publication of Richard Rorty's *Philosophy and the Mirror of Nature*, antifoundationalist thinkers could legitimately claim that, with the overthrow of epistemology, hermeneutic analysis could give us the best and most useful information about "the world." Our understanding of the world is created – linguistically inscribed in a process of "redescription" – rather than "discovered" scientifically. So, the antifoundational object of analysis is the *vocabulary* used by people trying to describe their surroundings. It is useless trying to analyze the surroundings themselves, because you can never escape their mediated nature: they are always *descriptions*, and as such all we have to go on are the linguistic schemes that the various interlocutors have at their disposal. What this thesis fails to account for, though, is the object of knowledge, the object of all the descriptions that Rorty sees as so important. We may be able to reconcile competing normal descriptions (that is, abnormal discourse) by finding a "third vocabulary" with which to make descriptions, but the fact remains that there is something that is being described and is (one would think at least in part) responsible for the difference of opinion. Moreover, redescribing something is not necessarily going to change it, nor is redescription necessarily an adequate tool for analysis.

The rioting that occurred in Los Angeles during the last days of April and the first days of May 1992 after the announcement in the Rodney King police-beating case appears to me to be a perfect example of an event (or, if you prefer, object of knowledge) that cries out for some kind of "redescription." My point in this chapter will be that the Los Angeles riots of April and May 1992 in the wake of the Rodney King verdict cannot be adequately accounted for (or described) conventionally or normally; and that any reconciliation of competing normal discourses (which could be called, in Rorty's paradigm, an abnormal conversation) that does not account for the event's complex overdetermined nature, will create a "description" that will be useless in setting an agenda for social praxis. In looking at the mainstream print media's descriptions of the event, we may be able to see "other human beings as 'one of us,' rather than as 'them,'" and we do this through redescription, and in so doing to either "give us the details about the kinds of suffering being endured by people to whom we had previously not attended," or to "give us the details about what sorts of cruelty we ourselves are capable of" (Rorty, *Contingency*, xvi). But these same descriptions have in most cases obfuscated the complex material forces at work in the riots, and rather than allow "moral change and progress," have worked, to the contrary, for moral complacency and social retrogression.

The first task of this chapter, after a brief recapitulation of Rorty's version of antifoundationalism and some of its attendant problems, is to summarize the mainstream print media's accounts of the riots that followed the King verdict on April 29, 1992. The main source for these descriptions is the coverage by the *New York Times* (and, as backdrop, the three major networks) of the events immediately following the verdict. I chose these sources because they are the vehicles by which the majority of the general public receives its news of day-to-day events. (I chose the New York, rather than the Los Angeles, *Times* in part because of its status as a national newspaper.) In elucidating the descriptions from the media, I will suggest that because of the nature of the events they were covering, they could do nothing but "normalize" what was a thoroughly abnormal series of events, and that they sought to "make commensurable" their accounts of material events that were difficult, if not impossible, to understand linguistically. I want to show how the normalization of these descriptions has served, on the one hand, to disseminate information about the riots and conditions in south-central Los Angeles, but on the other hand, to ignore the difficult and complex material conditions that preceded and fueled the events, thereby in effect stalling, not promoting, the social change that Rorty wishes he could encourage. Finally, I want to suggest, since Rorty's pragmatic approach to the contingency of langauge does not seem to work in the way he wants it to, an alternative analysis that could be used to analyze the riots in Los Angeles, one that accounts for its "descriptions" while not discounting the material conditions it purports to describe.

Richard Rorty argues in *Philosophy and the Mirror of Nature* that epistemology is obsolete because it has failed, since Plato and the sophists, adequately to theorize the relation between human cognition and the objects of knowledge. He sees language theory as a way to reestablish some of that lost ground by giving philosophy and / or theory a way to consider how language works, but does not presume to understand the way the world works outside of considerations of language. Rorty's champion in this enterprise is Donald Davidson, whose "pure" philosophy of language rests on the idea that correspondence is a relation "which has no ontological preferences – it can tie any sort of word to any sort of thing" (cited in Rorty, *Mirror*, 300):

> In giving up dependence on the concept of an uninterpreted reality, something outside all schemes and science, we do not relinquish the notion of objective truth – quite the contrary. Given the dogma of a dualism of scheme and reality, we get conceptual relativity, and truth relative to a scheme. Without the dogma, this kind of relativity goes by the board. Of course truth of sentences remains relative to language, but this is as objective as can be. In giving up the dualism of scheme and world, we do not give up the world, but reestablish unmediated touch with the familiar objects whose antics make our sentences and opinions true or false. (Cited in Rorty, *Mirror*, 310)

Pure language theory is, as Rorty puts it, a way of "coping" with the world.

Rorty claims that philosophy's recourse to a "world without mirrors" (that is, a world without an overarching epistemology) is to establish hermeneutics, or "an expression of hope that the cultural space left by the demise of epistemology will not be filled – that our culture should become one in which the demand for constraint and confrontation is no longer felt" (315). As opposed to epistemology, which proceeds from the assumption that all contributions to a given discourse are commensurable, hermeneutics begins from the assumption that the set of rules under which such a discussion could be settled on every point where

215

statements seem to conflict is not always possible, and is never finally determinable. Hermeneutics is based on a model of discourse, in which interlocutors "play back and forth between guesses about how to characterize particular statements or other events, and guesses about the point of the whole equation, until gradually we feel at ease with what was hitherto strange" (319). "What was hitherto strange" is "abnormal discourse." Normal discourse is discourse of whatever kind – including scientific discourse – that is conducted within an agreed-upon set of conventions about what counts as a relevant contribution. "Abnormal discourse is what happens when someone joins in the discourse who is ignorant of these conventions or who sets them aside" (320).

Rorty suggests that we operate scientifically when the conversation is taking place in normal discourse, and operate hermeneutically when the conversation takes place abnormally. Using Gadamer as his hero, Rorty notes that when there is no common ground on which to enter into a normal discourse, then – hermeneutically – "all we can do is to show how the other side looks from our own point of view. That is, all we can do is be hermeneutic about the opposition – trying to show how the odd or paradoxical or offensive things they say hang together with the rest of what they want to say, and how what they say looks when put in our own alternative idiom" (364–5). But restating things "in our own language" does not change the ground – impossible in Rorty's view – on which we stand to do the talking.

In Rorty's view, then, freedom becomes, "through our capacity to *redescribe* [the] world (or relevant bits of it), something which is both positive and humanistically more recognizable – namely the capacity to create, and choose between, different vocabularies – that is, to speak or write 'abnormally'" (Bhaskar, *Reclaiming Reality*, 170). By making a new, incommensurable description of herself stick, she makes it true, according to Bhaskar. Thus she creates herself, "which is to say 'overcomes' her previous or past self" (171).

For our purposes, one here needs to ask whether Rorty's distinction between normal and abnormal discourse obviates the existence of what Roy Bhaskar calls "intransitive" objects of knowledge, those objects *about which* we form descriptions and which exist independently of our constructing those descriptions.

That is, if on the one hand one conducts science against a background of agreed-upon principles of observation, or on the other one introduces a new paradigm with which to produce observations, neither case suggests that there is nothing upon which to agree, but – on the contrary – both suggest a need for a way to describe and observe *something* that exists ontologically. Moreover, Rorty suggests that there is no way to discern whether revolutionary science is in fact progressive, since there is nothing objective (extra-ideological or extra-linguistic) to which one can appeal in order to make such a judgment. But in response to this, Bhaskar notes that, though human explanations and interpretations of extra-ideological material may be by necessity constructed and therefore contingent, those explanations may be called progressive – by dint of their broader explanatory capacity – since the observations may be repeated and the results reproduced. In a sense, there is no need to suggest that simply because explanation of material objects and phenomena must be contingent, then the objects of that knowledge must also be called contingent.

At issue here is how (or whether) the act of redescription affects the material world in whose midst a subject stands.

[T]here is more to coping with social reality than coping with other people. There is coping with a whole host of social entities, including institutions, traditions, networks of relations and the like – which are irreducible to people. In particular, it would be a mistake to think that we had overcome a social structure, like the economy, state or family, if we were successful in imposing our description of it on the community.

(Bhaskar, *Reclaiming Reality*, 175)

If there's going to be some change beyond simply changing the description of one's relationship to material (that is, extra-ideological) entities – given that these exist, though for Rorty it is hard, if not impossible, to theorize them – then we need a way not just to understand how subjects are formed through discourse but also how they are affected by material constraints – hunger, disease, wealth or poverty, leisure or work, various economic conditions and so on – that also enter into the way humans engage with one another and construct their subjectivities. We are not necessarily completely determined by such material constraints, but they *are* imposed and we do need to account for them. Real freedom involves understanding how one's ideological surroundings are constructed in the best way one knows how, and the ability to transform – by actively transforming the ways in which those ideological surroundings work – the ways in which the material conditions affect the subject.

At this point, we need to look at how the mainstream print media – one of the channels through which a large portion of the American public understands its relation to the events in Los Angeles in the Spring of 1992 – came to "inscribe" the aftermath of the King verdict. One of the most interesting aspects of their "interioriz-ation" or "normalization" of those events is that the language used to describe the riots and the reasons behind the rioting is that the language of the newspaper articles, almost without exception, follows Rorty's pattern of making the incommensurable (that is, the visceral reactions of Angelenos to the announcement that the four police officers had been acquitted on all but one count of the indictment, a reaction that was in many cases extra-verbal) com-mensurable by changing the contexts of the discussion (in some cases, to suit the electoral politicking that was going on in the approach to the Democratic and Republican conventions that summer), thereby changing the tenor of the discussion and thus of the "events" themselves. Within a few days of the first violence, the *New York Times*'s writers had largely framed the discussion of the riots in terms of race (not class) and in terms of presidential politics (not community-level social relations), and made Los Angeles out to be a kind of racial "war zone" – terms quite familiar to readers of the *Times*, many of whom are urban and Anglo – without considering the lived life of Angelenos living in South Central. What came to be reported in the *Times* – and in a number of other mainstream print media – was the story of "senseless" violence, while what was occurring in Los Angeles during the weeks of late April and early May 1992 made a very peculiar kind of sense, but one that many people reading accounts of it in the papers, did not have access to. I will have more to say about how to "make sense" out of the riots shortly. For now, I want to take a look at the print media, particularly the *Times*, and suggest how it "normalized" the riots, and what this normalization leaves out.

The front-page lead from the *Times* on April 30 was given a three-column headline "Los Angeles Policemen Acquitted in Taped Beating," over a photograph of officers Wind and Powell embracing while officer Koon looks on, with the hint of a smile on his face. The text of the article reads, in part:

Four Los Angeles police officers were acquitted of assault today in the videotaped beating of a black motorist that stunned the nation. The verdicts immediately touched off a storm of anger and scattered violence in the city.

As residents set scores of fires, looted stores and beat passing motorists in the downtown area and pockets of predominantly black south-central Los Angeles, Mayor Tom Bradley declared a state of emergency, and Gov. Pete Wilson said he would send in the National Guard.

. . . Immediately after the verdict, an unusually impassioned Mayor Bradley appeared on television to appeal for calm in a city where the videotape has come to symbolize complaints about police brutality, racism and street violence.

"Today the system failed us," the Mayor said.

Immediately apparent in this excerpt are the conflicting depictions of what is occurring in Los Angeles and why. There is no causal connection established in the two sentences that begin the article between the announcement of the verdicts and the "storm of anger and scattered violence," though the following paragraph reinforces the notion that it is the violence that is quickly becoming the "story," not necessarily the acquittal itself. What is notable, though, in the refusal to establish a connection between the violence and the verdicts is also the confusion established by the article's author, Seth Mydans, in Mayor Bradley's television appeal after the verdict. On the one hand, he appeals for calm in an "unusually impassioned" plea; on the other, he notes that "Today the system failed us." The clearest part of Bradley's statement is that the "system failed us," referring almost certainly to the acquittal of the four officers who, by way of the videotape that captured them beating King, became part and parcel of the "complaints about police brutality, racism, and street violence." His statement, though, is much like the one I heard the night the verdict was announced issued by Benjamin Hooks, who was speaking to a largely African-American audience at Mississippi State University: "this is a joke, a tragedy." That is, coming from a mayor who – along with the Governor – is in charge of "keeping the peace," the visceral reaction to the verdicts reported in the *Times* by the mayor is incommensurable with his plea for calm, and expresses an anger and bewilderment that cannot, apparently, be made sense of in his public capacity as mayor. Likewise, the connection between the rioting and the announcement of the verdicts, while understandable (it was, presumably, anger over the verdict that caused the violence as a pre- or extra-verbal expression of that anger), refuses, in Mydan's article, the linguistic link.

What Mydans, in this article, is depicting is – on Rorty's terms – a phenomenon or set of phenomena (namely, the violent incidents that occurred in areas of Los Angeles immediately following the King verdict) that are thus far (that is, on April 30, 1992) outside of a conceptual scheme. What Mayor Bradley, and Benjamin Hooks, and Seth Mydans and the video newscasters were doing was attempting to understand – again, in Rorty's terms, to "cope" with – those phenomena with various "languages" that are incommensurable because the events (the rioting) so far have not been sufficiently placed within a "scheme" or context with which they can be discussed. Rorty suggests that it will be impossible to reconcile the phenomena (and their descriptions) to some state of affairs upon which everyone can agree, and as regards the violence in Los Angeles during the Spring of 1992 I think it is patently obvious that there was absolutely nothing – no philosophical structure, no apparatus with which to verify the objective "truth" of the cause of the riots or their understandability – outside of our descriptions of it with which to make sense of it. Rorty, though, goes a step further and says that it *is* possible to reconcile competing *descriptions* of events or phenomena in order to make them available for discussion and understanding. To do so, says Rorty, we "play back and forth between guesses about how to characterize particular statements or other events, and guesses about the point of the whole situation, until gradually we feel at ease with what was hitherto strange" (*Mirror*, 319). And this is what the *New York Times* reporters already had begun to do as they reported the LA riots, and what they continued to do more and more successfully as they began to more satisfactorily "cope" with the riots by inscribing them in "normal" language.

In the same edition of the *Times*, Mydans wrote another article entitled "Verdicts Set Off a Wave of Shock and Anger," one that characterizes the violence that was spreading through certain parts of the city in much different terms than his front-page article. In section D of the national edition of the paper, after noting the similarity to the 1965 Watts riots, he writes:

Mobs of young men rampaged through the streets [of south-central LA] overturning and burning vehicles, smashing windows and spraying graffiti. Police officers, firefighters and news helicopters reported being shot at.

. . . [The violence] began moments after the reading of the verdicts, in which a suburban jury with no black members acquitted Sgt. Stacey C. Koon and Officers Laurence M. Powell, Timothy E. Wind and Theodore J. Briseno of assault charges.

. . . Helicopter and news cameramen showed gripping scenes of vicious beatings of motorists by groups of thugs, startling evocations of the videotaped footage of the beating of Mr. King.

This time the language has been more "normalized." This is not the language of surprise; this is the language of recognition. The biggest difference between this article and Mydans's first is that there is a direct relationship established between the reading of the verdicts and the beginning of the violence. Not only does the reading of the verdict and the beginning of the violence all appear in a single compound sentence, but there is the addition of an important fact: it was "a suburban jury with no black members" that acquitted the four police officers of "beating and kicking a black motorist." What this article begins to do, in a way that the section-1 article (the one readers would see first; it would take them some page turning to get to Mydans's second article) did not, was begin to frame the incident as a racial issue. This is hardly surprising: for the year between the beating and the trial the papers and television news had cast the beatings as racially moti- vated, including a rumor that one of the officers had made a remark about King "looking like an ape," a rumor that itself nearly caused violence in April and May of 1991. However, what is equally troubling is that not only are the riots connected to what appeared to be a racially motivated beating and an equally racial- ly motivated acquittal, but the rioters are characterized as "mobs" of young men, and as "thugs." This kind of characterization became even more prevalent in the next day's edition, particularly after the April 30th beating of truck driver Reginald Denny, a beating that was different in at least one respect from the beating of Rodney King: it was televised live. In a page-1 article by Jane Gross entitled "Smell of Fear in Los Angeles" (which was placed directly below a photograph of nearly two dozen African- Americans lying face-down in the street with their hands cuffed behind their backs while helmeted police guard them against a background of a graffiti-sprayed wall), one finds the following:

Throughout the sprawling metropolis, even in neighborhoods far from the epicenter of the violence, Angelenos sensed that the next car that passed might carry hooligans waving crowbars and axes, that the next store to burn down could be the one on their corner. This was not a disturbance with a clear perimeter, they came to understand, and while some street corners were safer than others, there was really no place to hide.

The roadways were emptier than usual, but chaotic as a bumper-car ride as nervous motorists navigated a shifting maze of barricades and craned their heads skyward to track the newest plume of smoke rising in the heavy haze. The drivers' eyes darted from side to side, taking the measure of the stranger in the car beside them, plotting new routes as streets and highways closed and reopened, and gazing in horror at the ravaged and smoldering stores that dotted the city.

It is precisely "fear" that is the organizing principle – the "conceptual scheme" in Rorty's terms – in Gross's article, but a fear that is somehow familiar to readers of the paper. This is no longer the language of reportage, of pastiche. Rather, Gross here seems to be drawing a picture, setting the perimeters of the discussion, by drawing on a language that makes readers think of, say, Soweto or Kuwait City, where there are "plumes of smoke" and "barricades," where "hooligans wav[e] crowbars and axes." What is true of South Africa and of Kuwait – that there are clearly good guys and bad guys, that in general terms the violence that exists can be portrayed in dichotomous pairs (Blacks versus the white government, bad-guy Saddam versus innocent Kuwaitis) – seems to be true here. It is most certainly shocking that discourse that newspaper reporters have been using in South Africa and during the Gulf War, not to mention Sarajevo and Peru, can be used to "normalize" the situation in Los Angeles. But it is more interesting that, in connecting racial division to the rioting on the same ground that division has been "inscribed" on racial and religious grounds in "other," foreign situations, Gross and Mydans and others at the *Times* have begun to use the problems of race as a way to make sense of what was going on in Los Angeles, as the "explanation which satisfies our need to tell a coherent causal story about our interactions with the world" (Rorty, *Mirror*, 341).

Probably one of the most cynical "redescriptions" of the riots and their causes reported by the *Times* was the one put forward by the presidential candidates (notably, George Bush and Bill Clinton) in the heat of the primary election season. As was the case with Mydans's and Gross's pieces on the violence, the candidates went from trying to "cope with" a complex phenomenon and its various inscriptions, both in the visual media as well as in the press, to making these various inscriptions "commensurable" – and glossing over the dissonance that resulted from its material complexity – by casting it in a political language. The president is reported as using "words that reflected Americans' reactions to both the verdict and the rioting that followed it" when he noted that "Yesterday's verdict in the Los Angeles police case has left us all with a deep sense of personal frustration and anguish. Yet it is important that we respect the law and the legal processes that have been brought to bear in this case." One can discern here the attempt to normalize the riots and their refusal to be inscribed. By the time these words had been uttered, Reginald Denny had already been pulled from his truck in a south-central street and beaten nearly to death, and the images of that event, as well as others, had been broadcast live to much of the nation. Presumably, this latter beating had been an expression of "personal frustration and anguish" by those who stopped and beat Denny. Asked why he thought Denny had been beaten so severely, Bobby Green – who had helped drive Denny to the hospital after having seen the beating on television – said "Because he is white" (Stevenson, "Blacks," A21). To the men who beat Denny, it may have been the case that, because he was white and so unaffected by what was going on in LA, to be driving though south-central, he gave the outward appearance of being out of place, something or someone unrecognizable: something "other." In the same way that the beating of Rodney King was indescribable to the point of having to let the videotape "speak for itself" in the trial, and in the same way that television anchors had to struggle to find words or else simply let videotape roll on the screen while they sat wordlessly, the appearance of Denny in his truck on that street was abnormal, and so the young men who beat him were attempting to "cope with" the phenomenon with an equally abnormal – and pre-verbal – action. That Mr. Bush could be said to speak in words that "reflected" the reactions seems incongruous at best and just wrong-headed at worst. It is simply the case that the attempt to normalize the riots in terms that Americans can understand is simply impossible, and it does not reflect what was going on out on the street. To then follow this "reflection" with the statement that we ought nevertheless to "respect the law and legal processes that have been brought to bear in this case" is a tremendous contradiction, one that hermeneutics – in which the "hope of agreement [among possible conversations, or, at least, exciting and fruitful disagreement] is never lost so long as the conversation lasts" (*Mirror*, 318) – cannot easily accommodate.

The political normalization of the aftermath of the King verdicts took, as Michael Wines put it in an article on p. 22 in the May 1st edition of the *Times*, a "partisan turn" (see also Wines, "White House Links the Riots to Welfare"; Apple, "Bush Says Largesse Won't Help Cities"):

> ... As the day progressed, the President moved further from his initial expression of "frustration" about the King verdict and began condemning the rioters. In his last appearance of the day at a fund-raising even in Columbus [OH], the President did not mention the verdict at all. "We must condemn the violence and we must make no apology for the rule of law or the need to live by it," he said.
>
> ... "I would hope that he would at least acknowledge that the facts of the case as evidenced by the film lead a lot of Americans, and not just black Americans, to wonder about the accuracy of the verdict," Mr. Clinton said [in response to Bush's earlier remark].
>
> He contended that the violence had been worsened by "more than a decade of urban decay" caused by lowered Federal spending in cities. ...
>
> [Clinton later said in a speech to an integrated crowd in Birmingham, AL] "No nation would permit what's going on in Los Angeles tonight, where the automatic and semi-automatic weapons in the hands of lawless vandals who are using this King verdict as a simple excuse to go wreak violence and shoot people are running unchecked in the streets. And it is wrong."

In Seth Mydans's May 1st article, he notes that "the verdict itself seemed mostly forgotten in the energy of the vandalism and looting that continued throughout the day and into the night" of April 30. It appears, similarly, that for both Clinton and Bush, the verdict – or, at least whatever it was that "caused" the rioting – was forgotten amidst the discourse that tries desperately to move the force of the events that are taking place away from the largely unverbalizable, uninscribable and toward a rhetoric that valorizes the law which, in the words of Ronald Dworkin (an antagonist of

Rorty and Fish), inscribes "innumerable decisions, structures, conventions, and practices [which] are [its] history" (159). Although it could be argued – and Dworkin does – that it may *not* be the case that there is a beginning to the "chain" of decisions that produce the law's history, the language of the law (and here Fish and Dworkin agree) still "articulates consistency" (quoted in Fish, *Doing*, 385). And it is this consistency that is particularly problematic, since it was the "rule of law" that could, in the eyes of many, be seen as directly responsible not only for the "failure" of the jury to convict the four police officers who beat Rodney King, but for the beating itself. The convenience of terms like "lawless vandals" or, in another article, "thugs," does reconcile two irreconcilable phenomena – the apparently lawlessness of the verdict and the equal disregard of the law that establishes public tranquility – but to use it on the same day that the president asks the residents to obey and respect the "rule of law" empties it of all its power to signify, to normalize, the context of the discussion taking place in the *Times*.

As I have tried to show, redescription in antifoundational terms does work to reconcile incommensurable descriptions of "the world," like the riots in Los Angeles in the Spring of 1992. But those descriptions – *because* they attempt to discursively bridge the gap between complex understandings of the world – make it difficult to understand the *objects* of those descriptions, namely, the material conditions of existence in LA and the rest of the country after the acquittal of the officers accused of beating King. I will not dispute the Rortyan / Kuhnian thesis that scientific (or in fact any systematic) accounting for phenomena is contingent, or that those accounts are inextricably bound with the socially constructed linguistics accounts of the same phenomena. Bhaskar's project, though, does dispute what on Rorty's account of things turns out to be a subsumption of scientific investigation to hermeneutic constraint. Rather than suggest that science operates hermeneutically, Bhaskar proposes realism as an alternative to hermeneutics, which entails a theory of "the nature of the being ... of the objects investigated by science – roughly to the effect that they exist and act *independently* of human activity, and hence of both sense-experience and thought" (13, emphasis added). While it is a worthwhile project to understand how to create a language through which humans can engage in a conversation about, say, the LA riots, it is equally – if not more – important to understand how (or to what extent) we can understand the objects of knowledge in such an event and the ways in which those objects *resist* becoming "normalized" in such a "conversation of mankind."

Bhaskar's analysis of phenomena such as the LA riots is modeled on scientific experimentation, in which humans "co-determine, or are causally co-responsible for, a pattern of events" (15). As they experiment upon objects or phenomena, scientists meticulously control the conditions they work under to identify the mode of operation of structures, mechanisms and processes which they do not produce." When successful, experiments make intelligible causal laws, patterns of events and so on. What is important in such a model is that, through creating "constant conjunctions" such as these, scientists are "redescribing" phenomena that *do not* take place in constant conjunctions. We can reproduce a sequence of events to produce a particular mechanism, but this mechanism can (and does) occur through the same sequence of events *not* produced through human interference, but rather "in nature." These mechanisms (we can think of them as "tendencies") are "intransitive objects of scientific inquiry," objects that act independently of their identification by human beings. "Causal laws" are descriptive of the mechanism. The "transitive" dimension – or epistemology – is the specific historical and social form of knowledge (i.e., description) that we have of such objects or mechanisms or phenomena.

The implication of this for the purposes of examining an event like the LA riots – and in the investigation of linguistic events more generally – is that it is not necessarily the case that "descriptions" or "redescriptions" of phenomena or mechanisms (in this case, the King beating verdict and the riots that followed it) are purely contingent. We can describe the verdict and the riots (i.e., the event to which we have access); we can inscribe those events with a vocabulary to which we also have access; in so doing we can determine the forms that the riots take on (in terms of genre – newspaper reportage, war correspondence, framed narratives – and in terms of material *content*); and, perhaps most importantly, we can describe the particular component parts or elements that comprise the riots (that is, their political, legal, social "spins"); and we can do all of this *without* equating those descriptions with "the world," or "the way the world works apart from our under-standing of it." What we – or Seth Mydans, or Bill Clinton or Benjamin Hooks – may observe and write about the riots may not be "the way it is out there," those written descriptions neverthe-less can be said to "redescribe" in the transitive dimension (in potentially varying ways) those things that take place as intransi-tive objects of knowledge, objects that *are* subject to scientific investigation and which *do* operate according to verifiable laws. That is, though the language we use to attempt to normalize or contextualize the rioting that took place in 1992 will undoubtedly allow vastly different communities to engage in a "conversation" about the riots and the potential causes of the riots, that language will *necessarily* fail to account for the phenomena themselves because it occurs in closed systems (vocabularies). What is re-quired is another kind of investigation into the phenomena that takes place outside the "conversation" and which first looks at those places at which the conversation explicitly fails to make commensurable certain aspects of that conversation.

This other kind of investigation is precisely *scientific* investiga-tion. It should be seen as a "three-phase schema," in which a phenomenon is identified, explanations for the phenomenon are constructed and empirically tested, thereby identifying (or "de-scribing") the mechanisms at work. This explanation then be-comes the phenomenon to be tested and so on. If, in the first phase of this schema we get a regularity through experimentation, it is the *result* of something, and what is imagined in the second phase is not just imaginary but can come to be known as the "real." The descriptions of people such as Seth Mydans and Michael Wines of the destruction caused by the riots are absolutely not "imagin-ary," though they are derived from the imagination (just as any *scientific* description is). But you can move from "knowledge of manifest phenomena to knowledge, produced by means of ante-cedent knowledge, of the structures that generate them" (Bhaskar, 20). Thus knowledge inscribed linguistically (like the knowledge that we gather as we read the *New York Times* or *Time* or *Ebony*) can be thought of as knowledge derived from descriptions of phenom-ena (i.e., the King beating and the verdict and the rioting), phe-nomena that can be and have been described as structures that generated that knowledge and so on. Linguistic knowledge has a direct relation to knowledge of phenomena, that is, knowledge that we can think of as being *scientifically derived*, and this relation cannot be left out when we try to understand the resistance phenomena exhibit in written communication.

What is at stake is the degree to which people can change their material circumstances through a redescription of those circumstances. The realist philosophy of scientific inquiry, over and against the pragmatic world-view, implies that scientific inquiry must be understood as having a social component; but that the social component must be understood scientifically: phenomena like the riots, and the inscription of such phenomena, are not simply a function of the social. The social function is also material, and we need to understand how material objects and entities work. For antifoundationalism, redescription (reinterpretation) is a valuable human act because it leads to human emancipation. By inscribing the complex events that comprise the riots in Los Angeles, the newspapers "created" the riots, at least insofar as the reading public had access to them in a language that would allow them to take part in the descriptive act themselves. But such redescription does not change the material constraints by which you are bound because in antifoundationalism's view science is inadequate to the task of fixing, once and for all, the nature of material reality. So even if we wanted to say something about the relations of those descriptions to "scientifically determinable reality," science's redescriptions are equally in flux, and so any redescription (that produces "emancipation" of the subject doing the redescribing) is apt to be overturned by some other incommensurable redescription, thus voiding the emancipatory properties of the previous one. What you end up with is a "redescription" of the riots in Los Angeles, and of the beating that was presumably its proximate cause, but with no way of seeing how changing that "scheme" is going to change anything else.

I would like to cite one more example of the media's normalization of the events in Los Angeles "as a way to discuss not only what antifoundationalism *cannot* do but also to begin a discussion of an alternative way to examine the language used to inscribe the riots as well as the riots themselves. This final example – a set of descriptive pieces in the *Times* narrating the looting of several stores, in which a number of the looters were "interviewed" by reporters – serves, I think, to show, on the one hand, how even the voices of those taking part in the riots and lootings are themselves "normalizations" but are further normalized by the reporters inscribing the events; but on the other hand how the inscription of the polyvalent languages here can be seen as effects of social structures which are complexly overdetermined and must be described not merely in hermeneutic terms as "voices in a conversation," but also as having a material (i.e., physical) aspect and material constraints. As Bhaskar notes,

social structures are concept-dependent, but not merely conceptual. Thus a person could not be said to be "unemployed" or "out of work" unless she and the other relevant agents possessed some (not necessarily correct or fully adequate) concept of that condition and were able to give some sort of account of it. But it *also* involves, for instance, her being physically excluded from certain sites, definite locations in space and time. (*Reclaiming Reality*, 174)

What is required is, first, the "ontological tenet," in the words of Paisley Livingston, "that there is a mind-independent reality having entities that take part in causal interactions," and an "epistemological tenet," which holds that "these things are knowable, albeit partially and by successive approximations" (*Literary Knowledge*, 90). Science is the way to redescribe the tendencies exhibited by agents and structures, a redescription which functions both in the transitive dimension (that is, whose descriptions are socially constructed) as well as upon intransitive objects of knowledge. It is by suggesting how the utterances that narrate the Los Angeles riots are descriptions of real objects and real utterances that we can get past the pragmatist impasse and begin to articulate a positive praxis based on the knowledge that such an investigation yields.

In his article dated May 1, Seth Mydans reports that "it was clear from the words of the rioters, as well as black elected officials and others, that their anger ran far deeper than reaction to the acquittal" of the four officers. In the same article, though, his choice of words is telling: though "entire blocks of buildings were left in ruins," some other parts of town "took on the atmosphere of a street party as black, white, Hispanic and Asian residents mingled to share in a carnival of looting." I do not think I am pushing things here by suggesting that Mydans's use of the term "carnival" evokes the Bakhtinian connotation: an overturning of traditional or sanctioned behaviors with an aim of outwardly mocking (and subverting) the dominant ideology. What is interesting, though, about the article is that it does not suggest what the "deeper" causes of the riots are. Though certainly sparked by the riots, community leaders and the rioters themselves suggested that there was more to it than simply letting off steam at the injustice of the jury verdict. And yet, at least in this article, there is no way to read the riots except by understanding them as a kind of carnival in which the dominant ideology – in this case, the one that has established the legal system and the state which "provides police protection" – is attacked with something like glee. What I am trying to suggest is that, though Seth Mydans at the *Times* – and though community and city leaders in Los Angeles – understand that there is more going on than just the venting of anger over the announcement of the verdict, they are having a hard time understanding the complexity of it. Describing this situation by calling it a "carnival" in the antifoundational paradigm that conflates redescription with scientific observation (the epistemic with the ontic) runs the risk of obfuscating the complexities involved in the "carnival" atmosphere as simply one of many possible observations of the rioting. But I would like to suggest, along the lines of Roy Bhaskar, that there are material as well as ideological "constraints" to such a description, and it is these constraints (particularly the material ones) sacrificed by pragmatism, which are crucial to a materialist analysis of the riots themselves.

Such an analysis entails understanding that there are at least two "redescriptions" involved in the narratives that "tell" the riots. The first is that of the rioters themselves. Bobby Green's assessment of the cause of Reginald Denny's beating, "because he was white," is one way to understand the highly abnormal event: in his "normalization" of it, you can make sense of the beating by providing it with a rather simple equation: Reginald Denny was white, and those who beat him were black; Rodney King was black, and he was beaten by white police officers; because the white officers were granted a certain license to beat King (and presumably other black motorists) by the verdict, then the young men who beat Denny had a license to beat him because of his race. Taking into account the other "normalization," the question which frames Bobby Green's response to the question he was asked (why do you think Denny was beaten so severely?), this "conversation" casts the LA riots – or at least this particular episode – as racially motivated. Both interlocutors are attempting to cope with the utterance (and in this case, actions) of other humans by asking and answering questions that are highly complex, but whose responses belie that complexity. Now, it is true that for any one person on the street who one would ask about the causes of the riots (or of King's or Denny's beating), one would get several different responses. But these responses are the effects of certain physical states and read tendencies which are similarly complex but which are, far from "descriptions," responsible in varying degrees for the utterances themselves, and which must be investigated – regardless of how "partially or by successive approximations" – in order to move past simple redescription and on to some positive praxis. To do so, one would, for example, have to examine the social forms that sanction the "carnival," and how the forms of the carnival take can be seen as effects of certain social forms which in turn must be mapped scientifically.

Reading Michael Marriott's article dated April 30 where the inability to "speak" the riots becomes most clear, you can begin to see not only the Rortyan impasse but also ways to move beyond it. Entitled "The Sacking of a Neighborhood," the article describes some of the looting along Western Avenue. Among its descriptions are interviews with one young man looting a supermarket, and another walking in the center of Western Avenue. It is not so much the way in which the interviews are couched, but rather the words of those being interviewed themselves, that speak to the problems inherent in the view that it is the contextualization and understanding of discourse that should occupy the time of people analyzing language events. These words defy contextualization:

Near the ABC supermarket, a young man who would only identify himself by his last name, Master, made several trips through a shattered window with arms full of groceries before discovering that he had a problem. He had grabbed so many boxes of a breakfast cereal, Cinnamon Mini Buns, that he could not close the trunk of his car.

"I don't even eat this stuff," he said. "I'm going to give it away to people who don't have any food."

But that, he said, was not why he stole the food. Speaking in hyper-animated gestures, his voice a piercing scream, Mr. Master explained that he looted because he wanted white people across the United States to know how angry blacks were about the acquittal of four white police officers in the beating of Rodney G. King, and about their general condition in this country.

"This is the 90s," he screamed. "They killed the first King," he said, referring to the assassination of the Rev. Dr. Martin Luther King. "Now they want to mess over the second King," he said, referring to Rodney King. As looters packed their goods in their cars with the unhurried ease of weekend shoppers, Mr. Master looked up from his car's trunk and whispered, "We have been cool too long."

So do these:

> . . . Along Western Avenue a stocky black man in knee-length shorts and a blue cotton shirt paraded along the median line. Wearing dark glasses and a cap that said "DESERT STORM," he aimed to look menacing.
>
> As cars passed, he would raise his right arm up in a clenched fist, while his left hand rode threateningly close to his waistband where he had pocketed a pistol. Its outline could be clearly seen.
>
> "All of this is a statement of unity," said the thirty-three year old man who refused to identify himself. "This," he said as he scanned the tangle of firefighters and looters against a backdrop of burning storefronts only yards away, "is about the black community coming together.'

In each of these two descriptions, one can see two vastly different "impulses" at work. The first is the impulse that might be characterized as the ideological. In Rorty's words, it is the attempt "to find the proper set of terms into which all contributions should be translated if agreement is to become possible" (*Mirror*, 315). This is the impulse of the writer of the article, the rational attempt to make sense of the language of the unnamed or partially named interviewees (the man with the trunkful of cereal identifies himself as "Master"). In the first description he moves from the language of the first utterance ("I'm going to give [the food] away to people who don't have any food") to the second ("This is the 90s. They killed the first King") with a transition that may or may not have been uttered by Master himself, a transition that marks the connection between the injustice evidenced in the acquittal of the four white police officers and the injustice implied in the hunger of those living in south-central Los Angeles. There also exists the link between the two "Kings," which is established by Master, but which is bolstered not only by Michael Marriott, but also by other writers for the *Times* who refer to the riots that erupted after the assassination of Dr. Martin Luther King in 1968. In the second description, the unnamed man walking the centerline of Western Avenue is even more explicit: "this is a statement of unity," he yells, though it is unclear what "this" refers to. In the language of both the authors of the articles and of the interviewees themselves, you can see the attempt to "find the proper set of terms" with which to justify looting and protest, and by which to understand the decades-long oppression of an underclass.

But this other impulse – the one working against "newspaper writing" or "justification" or any other attempt to rationalize the phenomena described – is one that is largely extra- or pre-verbal, one that defies categorization or contextualization and thereby pulls away from agreement altogether. The most obvious sign of the ambivalence in the descriptions is in the gestures not only of Master but also of the gun-toting man on Western Avenue. Master is "speaking in hyper-animated gestures," an odd mixture of voice and the body, with his voice sounding, to Michael Marriott at least, a "piercing scream." But in his use of the assassination of Dr. King to justify his looting of the ABC supermarket for food he does not eat, he also inscribes two widely divergent and apparently contradictory desires. It is an expression of anger: the city of Los Angeles, whose legal system let the four officers go and whose police state allowed them to beat a man senseless, must see the rage that such an unreasonable set of actions produces: "he looted because he wanted white people across the United States to know how angry blacks were about the acquittal" and "about their general condition in this country." It is a reaction to Master's immediate circumstances – he is a black man who, in the words of James Buford, president of the Urban League of Greater St. Louis, felt "powerless and disgusted, betrayed . . . by an American dream he had believed in" (Wilkerson, "Acquittel," 23) – that is *not* reasonable if you look for a causal or necessary relationship between the *expression* and the phenomenon that caused the expression. If the looting is in fact a carnival of violence, it is an inversion of the power police officers have in relation to those presumed guilty or violent, one that transgresses the license the state has to control its subjects. But if it is a carnival, it is also highly contradictory expression that refuses translation or "normalizing strategy:" Master's actions are at once destructive and meaningful, sanctioned (normalized by the media as expressions "like those that followed the assassination of Dr. Martin Luther

King" and observed and "contained" by riot troops patrolling the city) and revolutionary. And it also speaks to the material conditions perceived by Master, in which "people . . . don't have any food" and would be happy to get any food they could, even if it is, ridiculously, Cinnamon Mini Buns cereal.

It is these material conditions – the "objective constraints that operate on humankind in society and in nature" – that require investigation in order to understand the events in Los Angeles and to (possibly) prevent them from happening again. The contradictions exhibited in the language of Master, of the unnamed man walking Western Avenue's centerline, of the presidential candidates and the others trying to "cope" with what took place in Los Angeles in the Spring of 1992, are the result of structures that are likewise contradictory and complexly overdetermined. The law that protects the residents of Westwood against looters is the same law that allowed four white police officers to be acquitted for the beating of Rodney King. The anger that began against what was perceived as the "system" that favored whites quickly turned to anger against Korean-American shopkeepers who were perceived as biased against African-Americans, Korean-Americans whose parents may have purchased their stores from the parents of some of the looters (see Kim, "Korean-American Perspective,"). The "statement of unity" for the black community that the looting suggested to the man walking Western Avenue was also a statement that reflected the demise of the black community's belief in the "American dream," as expressed by James Buford, president of the St. Louis chapter of the Urban League.

What you see, in these passages from the *Times*, is the breakdown of the impulse to make reasonable those things that appear "abnormal" and the emergence of what Homi Bhabha, in another context, calls "nonsense:" inscriptions that "baffle the communicable verities of culture with their refusal to translate" ("Nonsense," 204). To paraphrase Bhabha, the descriptions here of the events on Western Avenue in south-central Los Angeles display an "alienation" between the totalizing language that attempts to make sense of those events in terms of "riots" or "violence" or "carnival" and the function of language as expressing those things which are inexpressible, that in Rorty's terms are "incommensurable" but which, in our attempt to make them commensurable by providing them with a new context, slip away into something else. We need not a way – either in writing the language of the events surrounding the riots or in theorizing it – to express those impulses but rather to examine – if only with the knowledge that any data we gather will lead to contingent conclusions – the physical constraints that make for the different discourses in the first place.

Realist philosophy sets down four principles, which might be followed by antifoundationalism, and which can serve as a way to see how scientific analysis can help generate data on the events in Los Angeles. First, we must recognize, as Bhaskar suggests, the *sui generis* reality and causal efficacy of social forms, on a strictly physical criterion, in terms of their making a difference to the state of the material world which occurs in any event (*Reclaiming Reality*, 174). It is, after all, scientists who produce the constant conjunctions through which scientific laws are formulated, just as it is people who work for the *Times* or *Newsweek* or those who read the presses or watch the news reports on TV who observe and redescribe "the world." It is those redescriptions, both scientific and non-scientific, that are then reformulated, retested, and redescribed. We need to understand that reinscriptions of the riots in terms of class, of race, of politics and power are not just "made-up" ways of seeing the world, but that they in fact have a *physical* aspect to them, and that "redescribing" these aspects is not simply a matter of recontextualizing the conversation – letting us talk about it in more or less commonsense terms – but in fact is having a physical effect on those doing the talking, just as watching the beatings of Rodney King and Reginald Denny had a physical effect both on the viewer as well as on the individuals themselves. In writing and in the negotiation involved in reading this writing, what they are in fact doing is renegotiating – in the scientific sense, re*formulating* – that social (and by definition physical) reality, and in doing so, that social whole will in turn make a difference within the larger (material) social whole.

Secondly, we must grant the existence of objective social structures, "dependent on the reproductive and transformative agency of human beings" (*Reclaiming Reality*, 174). These structures are not created by human beings, but instead preexist us, and their existence "is a necessary condition for any intentional act" (174). Inasmuch as we are born into families, or classes, or neighbor-

hoods (south-central Los Angeles or Kennebunkport or Colum-
bus), and inasmuch as we are born physically male or female, we
are to this extent always already inside social structures. And to
the extent that we redescribe our material surroundings, we do so
as a condition of our being circumscribed thus materially. Put
another way, social life always has a material dimension (and,
according to Bhaskar, leaves some physical trace), and it is these
physical traces that can and should be examined scientifically
along with linguistic traces. One of the headlines for an article in
the *Times* on May 2 read as follows: "38 Bodies at the County
Morgue Reflect the Diversity of a Torn City" (A7), and noted that,
in the morgue that morning there were the bodies of 15 African-
American, 11 Hispanic, 5 white, 2 Asian, 5 people of "unknown
ethnic origin." Aside from the ugly irony of the milquetoast word
"diversity" linked to thirty-eight dead bodies, even just the headline on this article suggests that we are not just dealing with words
here: thirty-eight people from perhaps thirty-eight different families living thirty-eight separate lives ended sometime before May
2, 1992, and that there are aspects to those lives – the "physical
trace" – that must be examined in order to get past the mystification offered by the language that the article offers. More to the
point, there exist social and economic "tendencies" that are material, and that preexist our understanding and "description" of
them, and these also must be accounted for as objects that may
disrupt the capability of describing them. Antifoundationalism
often leaves unexamined the very material constraints that in
many ways determine what gets written and what gets seen.

Thirdly, Rorty's notion that social interaction consists of "coping with other persons" needs to be reformulated, since we cope
not just with persons but also with social structures and the
physical world in which they reside. We need to "find and disentangle webs of relations in social life, and engage explanatory
critiques of the practices which sustain them" (175). In reading the
Times, or any description of the world, for that matter, we need to
see language not simply as a medium through which to redescribe
"the world," but also as a metalinguistic reformulation of a real
set of events or phenomena of which the author has (physical)
experience. As a result, we examine not just "the world" as a set of
objects of knowledge, but also the author as an agent of social
practices which can be examined and analyzed materially and

scientifically. What we have seen in the preceding analysis of some of the reports of the riots that were written in the *New York Times* are instances of breakdowns in the narrative which was supposed to make sense or translate physical occurrences into terms readers could recognize. Instead of suggesting that this breakdown is inevitable, particularly in cases of "abnormal" events which appear by definition to be extra- or pre-linguistic in origin, we should see the language as the product of active agents, agents that, in uttering these reactions, are producing a materially and socially real set of circumstances that can be examined scientifically. Moreover, we also need to reformulate "coping with nature," because we redescribe the social world *within* the natural world and the ways it works, and we may need to recognize some of these "absolutes" (like the fact of the non-renewability of natural resources like oil; or like the fact that an underclass exists and has certain characteristics, etc.). The social world and the physical world, both subject to investigation, are inextricably intertwined. By changing one you inevitably change the other.

Fourthly, Bhaskar notes that the social sciences are not rendered redundant by writing as "redescription," since we need to be aware of not just motivation and skills (which writing presumably talks about) but also of "unacknowledged conditions and unintended consequences," both of which can be discussed in scientific as well as in "hermeneutic" terms (177). We may be able to rewrite or redescribe the circumstances that may immediately change by uttering "thugs must respect the law," or by critiquing, say, enterprise zones in urban areas. But there are other material circumstances that change as a result that we just won't be aware of, and these circumstances – because we are unaware of them – cannot be examined hermeneutically, but certainly can be observed and tested scientifically.

Bhaskar suggests a fifth principle: to paraphrase, insofar as human agents desire freedom, it will involve trying to understand (or explain) the character of socially-conditioned entities in order that those entities might be changed. That is, it involves "a theory of those constraints [of those entities] and, insofar as freedom is feasible, a practice of liberation or liberty preservation" (178). That is, what we need to do is not only understand the linguistic constraints upon human agents, but the physical ones as well; and we need to formulate a theory of change *based upon* such an

237

understanding. Charles Hagen writes in a feature on the video images of the King beating that

> ... [A]s the verdict in the case demonstrates, the videotape remains open to interpretation. While most Americans still regard the tape as irrefutable evidence of police brutality, the jury that acquitted the indicted officers obviously saw it differently. This puzzling fact goes to the heart of the matter: that photographic images of all sorts remain essentially ambiguous, and must be anchored in a convincing narrative before they take on a specific meaning. And most images can be made to fit into a number of widely disparate narratives.

"People see what they are conditioned to see," says one wag (Alter, "'Fireball'," 43), and this is just the point: narratives of the same object of knowledge differ. It is not enough to simply try to find a way, hermeneutically, to continue the conversation in order to get as many individuals to participate as possible, because you end up with statements like this, from a *Newsweek* article: "Was the trouble in LA a 'riot' or an 'uprising'? Both, actually, but it takes common language and trust to say that." More than "common language" and "trust," we need to understand the reasons for doing so through not just the transformation of descriptions, but also through "the transformation of structures rather than just the amelioration of states of affairs" (Bhaskar, *Reclaiming Reality*, 178). Only in this way can we get past seeing the riots, or any human activity or event, in terms of redescription and onto suggesting how we can transform the structures that lead to them. Only in this way can we get beyond pragmatism – which clearly is not up to the job – and understand the rhetorical as having social and transformative force.

Works cited

Alter, Joseph. "TV and the 'Fireball.'" *Newsweek* May 11,1992:43.
Althusser, Louis. "Ideology and Ideological State Apparatuses: Notes
    Toward an Investigation." *Lenin and Philosophy*. New York and
    London: Monthly Review Press / New Left Books, 1971, 127–86.
    Essays in Self-Criticism. London: Verso, 1976.
    "Contradiction and Overdetermination." *For Marx*. London: Verso,
    1977, 87–128.
    Philosophy and the Spontaneous Philosophy of the Scientists. London and
    New York: 1990.
Apple, R. W. "Bush Says Largess Won't Help Cities." *New York Times*
    May 7, 1992: A1+.
Aristotle. *Nichomachean Ethics*, trans. Martin Ostwald. New York: Bobbs
    Merrill, 1962.
    Rhetoric, trans. W. Rhys Roberts. New York: The Modern
    Library / McGraw-Hill, 1954, 1984.
    The Prior Analytics, trans. Robin Smith. Indianapolis: Hackett, 1989.
    The Posterior Analytics, trans. Jonathan Barnes. Oxford:
    Clarendon / Oxford University Press, 1975.
    Politics, trans. Carnes Lord. Chicago: University of Chicago Press,
    1984.
    Topiques, trans. Jacques Brunschwig. Paris: Société d'Edition, 1967.
Arnhart, Larry. *Aristotle on Political Reasoning*. Carbondale: Southern
    Illinois University Press, 1984.
Aronowitz, Stanley. *Science as Power*. Minneapolis: University of
    Minnesota Press, 1988.
Aune, James Arnt. "Cultures of Discourse: Marxism and Rhetorical
    Theory." David Cratis Williams, Michael David Hazen and J.
    Robert Cox, eds. *Argumentation Theory and the Rhetoric of Assent*.
    Tuscaloosa: University of Alabama Press, 1991, 157–72.

Bakhtin, Mikhail M. *Rabelais and His World*. Bloomington: University of Indiana Press, 1968.

Barilli, Renato. *Rhetoric*. Minneapolis: University of Minnesota Press, 1989.

Beiner, Ronald. *Political Judgment*. London: Methuen, 1983.

Bernard-Donals, Michael. Rev. of *Doing What Comes Naturally*, by Stanley Fish. *minnesota review* 34 / 5 (Spring / Fall 1990): 135–40.
  Mikhail Bakhtin: Between Phenomenology and Marxism. Cambridge: Cambridge University Press, 1994.

Bernstein, Richard J. *Beyond Objectivism and Relativism: Science, Hermeneutics and Praxis*. Philadelphia: University of Pennsylvania Press, 1983.

Bhabha, Homi. "Articulating the Archaic: Notes on Colonial Nonsense." Peter Collier and Helga Geyer-Ryan, eds. *Literary Theory Today*. Ithaca: Cornell University Press, 1989, 203–18.

Bhaskar, Roy. *The Possibility of Naturalism*. Brighton: Harvester Press, 1979.
  Scientific Realism and Human Emancipation. London: Verso, 1986.
  Reclaiming Reality: A Critical Introduction to Contemporary Philosophy. New York and London: Verso, 1989.
  Philosophy and the Idea of Freedom. Oxford: Blackwell, 1991.
  Dialectic: The Pulse of Freedom. London: Verso, 1993.

Bitzer, Lloyd. "Political Rhetoric." Dan Nimmo and Keith Sanders, eds. *Handbook of Political Communication*. Beverly Hills: Sage, 1981, 225–48.

Bizzell, Patricia and Bruce Herzberg, eds. *The Rhetorical Tradition: Readings from Classical Times to the Present*. New York: Bedford / St. Martin's, 1990.

Black, Edwin. "Plato's View of Rhetoric." *Quarterly Journal of Speech* 44 (1958): 361–74.

Bourdieu, Pierre. *Toward a Theory of Practice*. New York: Cambridge University Press, 1977.

Brenkman, John. *Culture and Domination*. Ithaca: Cornell University Press, 1987.

Brown, Richard Harvey. "Symbolic Realism and the Dualism of the Human Sciences: A Rhetorical Reformulation of the Debate between Positivism and Romanticism." Simons, ed. *The Rhetorical Turn*, 320–40.

Burke, Kenneth. *A Rhetoric of Motives*. Berkeley: University of California Press, 1969.

Cantor, Paul. "Rhetoric in Plato's *Phaedrus*." Kenneth W. Thompson, ed. *The History and Philosophy of Rhetoric and Political Discourse*, vol. II. Lanham, MD: University Press of America, 1987, 1–21.

Davenport, Edward. "The Scientific Spirit." Joseph Natoli, ed. *Literary Theory's Future(s)*. Urbana: University of Illinois Press, 1989, 267–91.

Davidson, Donald. "On the Very Idea of a Conceptual Scheme."
Proceedings of the American Philosophical Association 47 (1973–4):
5–20.

Dewey, John. "The Need for a Recovery of Philosophy." Richard J.
Bernstein, ed. *On Experience, Nature, and Freedom: Representative
Selections*. New York: Bobbs-Merrill, 1960.

*How We Think: A Restatement of the Relation of Reflective Thinking to the
Educative Process*. Chicago: Regnery Press, 1971.

Dilthey, Wilhelm. *Introduction to the Human Sciences*. Rudolf Makkreel
and Frithjof Rodi eds., Michael Neville et al. trans. *The Collected
Works of Wilhelm Dilthey*, Vol. I. Princeton: Princeton University
Press, 1989.

Dummett, Michael. "What is a Theory of Meaning?" Samuel
Guttenplau, ed. *Mind and Language*. Oxford: Oxford University
Press, 1975. 97–138.

Dworkin, Ronald. "How Law is Like Literature." *A Matter of Principle*.
Cambridge: Cambridge University Press, 1985, 142–59.

"Truth and Meaning." *Synthese* 7 (1967): xx.

Eagleton, Terry. *Walter Benjamin; or, Towards a Revolutionary Criticism*.
London and New York: Verso, 1981.

Literary Theory: An Introduction. Minneapolis: University of Minnesota
Press, 1983.

Ideology: An Introduction. London: Verso, 1991.

Farmer, Frank. "Foundational Thuggery and the Rhetoric of
Assumption." [unpublished manuscript]

Fish, Stanley. *Doing What Comes Naturally: Rhetoric, Change, and the
Practice of Theory in Literary and Legal Studies*. Durham, NC: Duke
University Press, 1989.

Fox Keller, Evelyn. *Reflections on Gender and Science*. New Haven: Yale
University Press, 1985.

Freire, Paulo. *The Pedagogy of the Oppressed*, trans. Myra Bergman
Ramos. New York: Continuum Press, 1970, 1993.

Gabin, Rosalind J. "Aristotle and the New Rhetoric: Grimaldi and
Valesio: A Review Essay."*Philosophy and Rhetoric* 20.3 (1987):
171–82.

Gadamer, Hans Georg. *Truth and Method*. London: Sheed and Ward, 1975.
Philosophical Hermeneutics. ed. and trans. David E. Linge. Berkeley:
University of California Press, 1976.

Gaonkar, Dilip Parameshwar. "Rhetoric and its Double: Reflections on
the Rhetorical Turn in the Human Sciences." Simons, ed. *The
Rhetorical Turn*, 341–65.

Garfinkel, Harold. *Studies in Ethnomethodology*. Englewood Cliffs, NJ:
Prentice-Hall, 1967.

Garver, Eugene. "Aristotle's *Rhetoric* as a Work of Philosophy."
Philosophy and Rhetoric 19.1 (1986): 1–22.

Works cited

"Aristotle's *Rhetoric* on Unintentionally Hitting the Principles of the Sciences." *Rhetorica* 6/4 (Fall 1988): 381–93.

Gosling, J. C. B. *Plato*. London: Routledge & Kegan Paul, 1973.

Graff, Gerald. *Beyond the Culture Wars: How Teaching the Conflicts can Revitalize American Education*. New York: Norton, 1992.

 Professing Literature: An Institutional History. Chicago: University of Chicago Press, 1987.

Grassi, Ernesto. *Rhetoric as Philosophy: The Humanist Tradition*. University Park: Penn State University Press, 1980.

Grimaldi, William M. A., S.J. *Aristotle, Rhetoric I: A Commentary*. New York: Fordham University Press, 1980

Gross, Alan. *The Rhetoric of Science*. Cambridge, MA: Harvard University Press, 1992.

Gross, Jane. "Smell of Fear in Los Angeles." *New York Times* May 1, 1992: 1+

Guignon, Charles B. "Pragmatism or Hermeneutics? Epistemology After Foundationalism." Hiley, et al., eds. *The Interpretive Turn*, 81–101.

Habermas, Jürgen. "A Review of Gadamer's *Truth and Method*." Fred Dallmyr, and Thomas McCarthy, eds., *Understanding and Social Inquiry*. South Bend, IN: University of Notre Dame Press, 1977, 34–51.

Hagen, Charles. "Photography View: The Power of a Video Image Depends on the Caption." *Sunday New York Times* May 10, 1992: H32.

Haraway, Donna. *Primate Visions*. New York: Routledge, 1988.

Harding, Sandra. *The Science Question in Feminism*. Ithaca: Cornell University Press, 1986.

 "Rethinking Standpoint Epistemology: What is 'Strong Objectivity?'" *Centennial Review* 36/3 (Fall 1992): 437–70.

Harstock, Nancy. "The Feminist Standpoint: Developing the Ground for a Specifically Feminist Historical Materialism." Sandra Harding and Merrill Hintikka, eds. *Discovering Reality: Feminist Perspective on Epistemology, Metaphysics, Methodology, and the Philosophy of Science*. Dordrecht, Holland: Reidel, 1983.

Havelock, Eric A. *The Liberal Temper in Greek Politics*. London: Cape, 1957.

Heidegger, Martin. *Being and Time*, trans. J. Macquarrie and E. Robinson. New York: Harper and Row, 1962.

Hiley, David R., James F. Bohman and Richard Shusterman, eds. *The Interpretive Turn: Philosophy, Science, Culture*. Ithaca: Cornell University Press, 1991.

Hunt, Everett Lee. "Plato and Aristotle on Rhetoric and Rhetoricians." *Studies in Rhetoric and Public Speaking*. New York: The Century Company, 1925, n.p.

Hunter, Lynette. *Rhetorical Stance in Modern Literature.* New York: St. Martin's, 1984.

Jameson, Fredric. *The Political Unconscious: Narrative as Socially Symbolic Act.* Ithaca: Cornell University Press, 1981.

Kasteley, James L. "In Defense of Plato's *Gorgias.*" *PMLA* 106/1 (January 1991): 96–109.

Kennedy, George. *The Art of Persuasion in Ancient Greece.* Princeton: Princeton University Press, 1963.

Kim, Elaine H. "Home is Where the *Han* Is: A Korean-American Perspective on the Los Angeles Upheavals." Robert Gooding-Williams, ed. *Reading Rodney King / Reading Urban Uprising.* New York: Routledge, 1992, 215–35.

Kinneavy, James. "William Grimaldi–Reinterpreting Aristotle.' *Philosophy and Rhetoric* 20/3 (1987): 183–200.

Kuhn, Thomas S. "The Natural and the Human Sciences." Hiley, et al., eds. *The Interpretive Turn,* 17–24.

   The Structure of Scientific Revolutions. Chicago: University of Chicago Press, 1962, 1970.

Leff, Michael C. "Modern Sophistic and the Unity of Rhetoric." John S. Nelson et al. eds.*The Rhetoric of the Human Sciences.* Madison: University of Wisconsin Press, 1987, 19–37.

   "The Habituation of Rhetoric." Joseph Wenzel et al. eds. *Argument and Critical Practices: Proceedings of the Fifth SCA/AFA Conference on Argumentation.* Annandale VA: SCA Publications, 1987, 1–18.

Levins, Richard and Richard Lewontin. *The Dialectical Biologist.* Cambridge: Harvard University Press, 1985.

Livingston, Paisley. *Literary Knowledge: Humanistic Inquiry and the Philosophy of Science.* Ithaca: Cornell University Press, 1988.

Locke, John. *An Essay Concerning Human Understanding.* ed. A. Campbell Fraser. Excerpted from Patricia Bizzell and Bruce Herzberg, eds. *The Rhetorical Tradition.* New York: St. Martin's Press, 1990.

Lloyd, G. E. R. *The Revolutions of Wisdom.* Berkeley: University of California Press, 1987.

Longino, Helen. *Science as Social Knowledge.* Princeton: Princeton University Press, 1990.

Marriott, Michael. "The Sacking of a Neighborhood: An Orgy of Looting, a Carnival of Crime." *New York Times* May 1, 1992: A21.

Marx, Karl and Friedrich Engels. *Letters on* Capital. London: Harmondsworth, 1983.

Mohanty, S. P. "Us and Them: On the Philosophical Bases of Political Criticism." *Yale Journal of Criticism* 2/2 (1989): 1–31.

   "The Epistemic Status of Cultural Identity: On *Beloved* and the Post-colonial Condition." *Cultural Critique* 24 (1993): 41–80.

Mydans, Seth. "Los Angeles Policemen Acquitted in Taped Beating." *New York Times* April 30, 1992: 1+.

243

"Verdicts Set Off a Wave of Shock and Anger." *New York Times* April 30, 1992: D22.

"23 Dead After 2d Day of Los Angeles Riots." *New York Times* May 1, 1992: 1+.

Myers, Greg. "Reality, Consensus, and Reform in the Rhetoric of Composition Teaching." *College English* 48/2 (February 1986): 154–73.

Neel, Jasper. *Plato, Derrida, and Writing.* Carbondale: Southern Illinois University Press, 1988.

Norris, Christopher. "Right You Are (If You Think So): Stanley Fish and the Rhetoric of Assent." *Comparative Literature* 42/2 (Spring 1990): 144–82.

Ohmann, Richard. *English in America.* New York: Oxford University Press, 1976.

Okrent, Mark. "Hermeneutics, Transcendental Philosophy, and Social Science." *Inquiry* 27 (1984): 23–49.

Pecheux, Michel. *Language, Semantics, Ideology: Stating the Obvious.* New York: St. Martin's, 1975.

Phelps, Louise Wetherbee. *Composition as a Human Science: Contributions to the Self-Understanding of a Discipline.* New York: Oxford University Press, 1988.

Plato. *Gorgias,* trans. Walter Hamilton. London: Penguin, 1960.

    Gorgias, trans. Terrence Irwin. Oxford: Clarendon/ Oxford University Press, 1979.

    Gorgias: or, On Rhetoric, Refutative, trans. W. R. M. Lamb. Reprinted in Patricia Bizzell and Bruce Herzberg, eds., *The Rhetorical Tradition.* New York: Bedford / St. Martin's, 1990, 61–112.

    Phaedrus: or, On the Beautiful, Ethical, trans. H. N. Fowler. Reprinted in Patricia Bizzell and Bruce Herzberg, eds. *The Rhetorical Tradition.* New York: Bedford / St. Martin's, 1990, 113–43.

Plochmann, George Kimball and Franklin E. Robinson. *A Friendly Companion to Plato's* Gorgias. Carbondale: Southern Illinois University Press, 1988.

Polanyi, Michael. *Personal Knowledge: Toward a Post-Critical Philosophy.* Chicago: University of Chicago Press, 1958, 1963.

Putnam, Hilary. *Mind, Language and Reality.* Cambridge: Cambridge University Press, 1975.

Quine, W. V. O. *Pursuit of Truth.* Cambridge, MA: Harvard University Press, 1990.

Reinhold, Robert. "Surprised, Police React Slowly as Violence Spreads." *New York Times* May 1, 1992: 1+.

Rorty, Richard. *Philosophy and the Mirror of Nature.* Princeton: Princeton University Press, 1979.

    Consequences of Pragmatism. Minneapolis: University of Minnesota Press, 1982.

Works cited

"Epistemological Behaviorism and the De-Transcendentalization of Analytic Philosophy." Robert Hollinger, ed. *Hermeneutics and Practice*. Notre Dame, IN: University of Notre Dame Press, 1985, 115–42.

"From Logic to Language Play." *Proceedings and Addresses of the American Philosophical Association* 59 (June 1986): 742–59.

"Thugs and Theorists: A Reply to Bernstein." *Political Theory* 15 (November 1987): 564–80.

Contingency, Irony and Solidarity. Cambridge: Cambridge University Press, 1989.

Rouse, Joseph. *Knowledge and Power: Toward a Political Philosophy of Science*. Ithaca: Cornell University Press, 1987.

"Interpretation in Natural and Human Science." Hiley et al., eds. *The Interpretive Turn*, 42–56.

Sanders, Robert E. "Discursive Constraints on the Acceptance and Rejection of Knowledge Claims: The Conversation about Conversation." Simons, ed. *The Rhetorical Turn*, 145–61.

Schilb, John. "Review of *Composition as a Human Science* by Louise Wetherbee Phelps." *Rhetoric Review* 8/1 (Fall 1989): 162–6.

Self, Lois S. "Rhetoric and *Phronesis*: The Aristotelian Ideal." *Philosophy and Rhetoric* 12/2 (Spring 1979): 130–45.

Sheridan, Thomas. *A Course of Lectures on Elocution*, ed. G. P. Mohrmann. London: Augustan Reprint Society, 1969.

Shotter, John. *The Cultural Politics of Everyday Life*. Toronto: University of Toronto Press, 1993.

Simons, Herbert, ed. *The Rhetorical Turn*. Chicago: University of Chicago Press, 1990.

Sloterdijk, Peter. *Critique of Cynical Reason*. Minneapolis: University of Minnesota Press, 1987.

Sokel, Walter H. "Dilthey and the Debate Between the Human and Natural Sciences." *The History and Philosophy of Rhetoric and Political Discourse*, Vol. I, ed. Kenneth W. Thompson. Lanham, MD: University Press of America, 1987, 1–22.

Solmsen, Friedrich. "Dialectic without the Forms." *Aristotle on Dialectic: The Topics*, ed. G. E. L. Owen. Oxford: Oxford University Press, 1968, 49–68.

Sprinker, Michael. "Boundless Context." *Poetics Today* 7/1 (1986):117–28.

"Knowing, Believing, Doing: Or, How can We Study Literature, and Why Should We, Anyway?" *ADE Bulletin* 98 (Spring 1991): 46–55.

"The Royal Road: Marxism and the Philosophy of Science." *New Left Review* 191 (1991–2): 122–44.

Stevenson, Richard W. "Blacks Beat White Truck Driver as TV Cameras Record the Scene." *New York Times* May 1, 1992: A21.

Stewart, J. A. *Notes on the Nichomachean Ethics*. Oxford: Clarendon / Oxford University Press, 1892.

245

Works cited

"Symposium: The Subject of Pedagogical Politics / The Politics of Publication." *College Literature* 21/3 (October 1994): 5–118.

Taylor, Charles. *Philosophy and the Human Sciences*. Cambridge: Cambridge University Press, 1985.

"Overcoming Epistemology." K. Baynes J. Bohman, and T. McCarthy, eds., *After Philosophy: End or Transformation?* Cambridge, MA: MIT Press, 1987.

"Thirty-Eight Bodies at the County Morgue Reflect the Diversity of a Torn City." *New York Times* May 2, 1992: A7.

Tompkins, Jane P. "The Reader in History." Jane Tompkins, ed., *Reader Response Theory: From Formalism to Post-Structuralism*. Baltimore: The Johns Hopkins University Press, 1980, 201–32.

"The Pedagogy of the Distressed." *College English* 52/6 (October 1990): 653–660.

Vaida, Clifford. "The Relevance of Plato's *Gorgias*: Rhetoric, Architectonic Arts, and the *Kosmos*." *Rhetorica* [forthcoming].

Valesio, Paolo. *Novantiqua: Rhetorics as a Contemporary Theory*. Bloomington: Indiana University Press, 1980.

Vickers, Brian. *In Defense of Rhetoric*. Oxford: Clarendon / Oxford University Press, 1988.

Warnick, Barbara. "Judgment, Probability, and Aristotle's *Rhetoric*." *Quarterly Journal of Speech* 9 (1989): 299–311.

Weaver, Richard. "The *Phaedrus* and the Nature of Rhetoric." Patricia Bizzell and Bruce Herzberg, eds. *The Rhetorical Tradition*. New York: Bedford / St. Martin's, 1990, 1054–65.

Weinsheimer, Joel. *Gadamer's Hermeneutics: A Reading of* Truth and Method. New Haven, CT: Yale University Press, 1985.

West, Cornel. *The American Evasion of Philosophy: A Geneology of Pragmatism*. Madison: University of Wisconsin Press, 1989.

Wilkerson, Isabel. "Acquittal in Beating Raises Fears Over Race Relations." *New York Times* May 1, 1992: A23.

Williams, Jeffrey. "Packaging Theory." *College English* 56/3 (March 1994): 280–99.

Wines, Michael. "A Bush-Clinton Exchange on the Riots Turns Partisan." *New York Times* May 1, 1992: A22.

"White House Links Riots to Welfare." *New York Times* 5 May 1992: A1].

Zavarzadeh, Mas'ud and Donald Morton, eds. *Theory/Pedagogy/ Politics: Texts for Change*. Urbana: University of Illinois Press, 1990.

"Theory as Resistance." Maria-Regina Kecht, ed. *Pedagogy is Politics*. Urbana: University of Illinois Press, 1991, 25–47.

Žižek, Slavoj. *The Sublime Object of Ideology*. London: Verso, 1989.

Index